Pelican Books
Film and Reality

Roy Armes was born in Norwich in 1937 and educated at
the City of Norwich School and at the Universities of
Bristol and Exeter. He taught modern languages for eight
years, and in 1969 began a three-year spell as Research
Fellow in Film and Television Studies at Hornsey College
of Art, where he has recently been co-opted to oversee the
transformation of the Hornsey Film Unit into a 'viable
educational response to the questionable realities of the
polytechnic and electronic age'. He has lectured
occasionally at various colleges and universities and has
organized courses in film study at the University of Surrey.
He has written articles for a number of magazines,
including film reviews for *London Magazine* and book
reviews for the *Times Educational Supplement*. His own
books have been a deliberately varied exploration of
possibilities offered within the confines of film criticism:
the historical study (*French Cinema since 1946*), the
director monograph (*The Cinema of Alain Resnais*), the
pictorial survey (*French Film*) and the definition of a
specific film movement (Italian neo-realism in *Patterns of
Realism*). The present volume and his current project of
an analysis of narrative structure in the modern cinema
over the past decade (*The Ambiguous Image*) derive from
the same impulse. Roy Armes is married with three
children.

ROY ARMES

Film and Reality

An Historical Survey

PENGUIN BOOKS

Penguin Books Ltd, Harmondsworth,
Middlesex, England
Penguin Books Inc., 7110 Ambassador Road,
Baltimore, Maryland 21207, U.S.A.
Penguin Books Australia Ltd, Ringwood,
Victoria, Australia
Penguin Books Canada Ltd,
41 Steelcase Road West, Markham, Ontario, Canada
Penguin Books (N.Z.) Ltd,
182–190 Wairau Road, Auckland 10, New Zealand

First published in Pelican Books 1974
Reprinted 1975

Copyright © Roy Armes, 1974

Made and printed in Great Britain by
Cox & Wyman Ltd, London, Reading and Fakenham
Set in Intertype Lectura

Contents

INTRODUCTION 9

PART ONE FILM REALISM

1. Realism in the Cinema 17
2. Lumière or Méliès? 22
3. Flaherty and the Idea of Documentary 30
4. Vertov and Soviet Cinema 38
5. Sound Documentary 44
6. Stroheim and the Realist Fiction Film 50
7. Renoir's Poetic Realism 56
8. Rossellini and Neo-Realism 64
9. *Cinéma-Vérité* 70
10. Realist Film and Television Realism 76

PART TWO FILM ILLUSION

11. The Techniques of Spectacle 85
12. Edison and the Origins of Hollywood 90
13. Griffith and Film Drama 97
14. The Comedians 105
15. The Studio Era 115
16. Disney and Animation 125
17. The Stars 132
18. The Western as a Film Genre 141
19. Hitchcock and Authorship in Hollywood 150
20. Hollywood's Heritage and Influence 159

PART THREE FILM MODERNISM

21. Film's Space-Time Potential 167
22. Silent Experiment 173
23. Expressionism 179
24. Buñuel and Surrealism 185
25. Post-Disney Animation 191
26. New Narrative Structures 196
27. Resnais and Time 202
28. Film and the Modern Novel 209
29. Godard – The Self-Conscious Film-Maker 215
30. Anger and the Underground 222

Bibliography 229
Index 245

Introduction

The following pages trace three strands of development through the eighty or so years of the cinema's history. The aim is to put the study of film history into some kind of perspective and to allow the general reader to find his bearings more easily amid the voluminous and increasingly fragmentary mass of critical writings currently available about the cinema. Rather than take a single aesthetic standpoint, from which the whole of the cinema's output is to be assessed, this volume adopts a triple perspective. Film does not have a single unitary potential to which all of its achievements must be referred, and one of the main problems of film aesthetics stems from the way in which the cinema's more influential theorists have usually been wedded to an exclusive aesthetic approach. One thinks of Siegfried Kracauer and his concept of the 'redemption of physical reality', or André Bazin, whose advocacy of the realist film went hand in hand with a total opposition to the expressionist film style. The onesidedness deriving from this lack of academic detachment on the part of film theorists is compounded by the fact that so many of the principal statements about film's potentialities have come from the film-makers themselves. The result has been great insight, but a limitation of perspective: the statements of Vertov or Eisenstein, Rotha or Zavattini, Pasolini or Robbe-Grillet stand primarily as justifications of the author's own work and inevitably distort alien but equally valid possibilities. The time has come, however, to attempt to order these divergent points of view and to see that the cinema's achievements derive not from a single global premiss, but from a nexus of related but often conflicting potentialities. This, indeed, is as one might expect, for film-making is by no means a simple unified activity like photography. It has the same possibility of closeness to life, but possesses in addition a time dimension, new features such as movement, word and music, and very often a narrative element as well. It is inevitable therefore that film's potential should be multiple and that its essence should lie in a synthesis of many arts and activities. While setting out from possibilities shared with photography, the cinema ends up closest to a synthetic art form like opera.

For the present analysis we have chosen just three aspects of this potential for discussion, not because this classification is seen as being in any way an exhaustive list, but because a triadic model of this kind lets us see clearly the range of the cinema as an art form. We are concerned with three major cinematic approaches to reality: the uncovering of the real, the imitating of the real, and the questioning of the real. From the first of these stems the evolution of a realist aesthetic and a whole tradition of works in which the aim is quite simply to show the world as it is. The artist's prime concern is not to invent or to imagine, but to place people, objects, settings and experiences as directly as possible in front of the camera and to make the audience *see*. The second tradition – which is almost as old as the first – discards this direct link with reality and fastens instead on the film's power to offer a resemblance or imitation of life. The resemblance is used not as an end in itself but as a means of creating satisfying fictions. It is the cinema's role as the universal storyteller that gave rise to Hollywood and prompted the growth of a world-wide entertainment industry. Since the prime purpose of the cinema is seen here to be the narrative function, reality in an unmediated form is an irrelevance. Verisimilitude is more relevant than realism, but the power of the medium to sustain an illusion is more important than either. The third, and perhaps least-developed, tradition is that of using film not to convey surface reality or to sustain a make-believe but to explore an inner reality beneath the surface. This means using the dreamlike aspects of the film experience – the darkened room and the bright hypnotic images – in a way which reduces objects and people to mere ciphers, deprived of independent existence. Theoretically at least, from this point of view, the cinema is a most exciting medium for the expression of modernist ideas: creating its own space-time continuum, mixing the real and the fictional, objective narration and subjective viewpoint, and building up a multiple perspective in the manner of a cubist painting.

This triple classification is by no means arbitrary. It may be argued that it is inherent in the very nature of film as a combination of images and sounds. In his book, *Signs and Meaning in the Cinema*, Peter Wollen applies to the film image as an element in a system of signs the three categories posited by the American logician Charles Pierce as the only possible dimensions of a sign: it may be an index, an icon or a symbol. An index, in this sense, is a sign which is based on a real bond existing between the object and the sign which represents it (examples are such signs as weather cocks, sundials, footprints or, in medical terms, pulse rates). An icon, by contrast, is a sign which works by virtue of its resemblance, just as a portrait resembles its sitter, a map the terrain it covers, or a diagram the function it explains. The third category, the symbol, denotes a link which is purely conventional. The obvious example of this is verbal language, where there need be no link in reality or resemblance between say, the word – dog, *Hund*, *chien* – and the object it represents. The relevance to the cinema of these categorizations, which are to be seen as overlapping entities rather than as watertight compartments, is immediately apparent. The three categories of sign can all be found in a virtually pure state in certain types of cinematic images. The indexical mode underlies the reality-bound images of the documentary; the studio-built exteriors of a Hollywood gangster film have an iconic dimension; while in a work like Luis Buñuel's *Un Chien andalou* the whole imagery has that lack of direct connection with reality (by transcription or resemblance) that is characteristic of the symbol. Though Wollen does not go into this, the same holds true for the film sound track. At one extreme we have the indexical dimension of the *cinéma-vérité* track recorded live and unscripted, at the other the purely symbolic use of musical accompaniment, while in between lies the studio-contrived track using real elements artificially blended to create an iconic resemblance.

Wollen refers briefly to directors whose work as a whole exemplifies the three types of code: the neo-realist Roberto Rossellini (indexical), Hollywood's master of light, Joseph von Sternberg (iconic) and the greatest theorist of film editing, Sergei Eisenstein (symbolic). But in fact the categorization can be taken much farther than this, and the whole development of the cinema can be seen in terms of a realization of these basic qualities of image and sound. If this is so, then an aesthetic is needed that is flexible enough to apply the appropriate criteria to each type of film. In each of the three main sections of the present book we shall therefore be adopting a different standpoint and examining the relevance of varying critical approaches. The tradition of realism in the cinema treated in Part One derives its validity from the uniquely close link between the film image and the reality which it records. The personality of the film-maker is subordinate to what Kracauer has aptly termed his permeability to events, and the films produced in this mode can be measured by the extent to which they conform to the requirements of an indexical code. By contrast it is on the iconic level of resemblance that most of the Hollywood tradition of film-making – which forms the subject of Part Two – must be judged. In a narrative film style which demands that a film-maker should use studio sets to represent his locations, should embody his characters by means of well-known actors and deal with stories that may be plausible but are certainly not true, judgement by such a standard as fidelity to reality would be absurd. The film-maker's vision can only be realized with the help of a whole team of artificers and the real question is whether a film can be powerful while still remaining a charade or make-believe. In a similar way there are fresh requirements made on the films in Part Three, which are divorced from the claims of realism and resemblance and which set out to use the cinema to question everyday reality and normal assumptions about logic and sequence. Here what must be called into question is the force and coherence of the alternative reality which the film-maker constructs, and his own creative individuality is given far more weight (he is, that is to say, more of an artist in the traditional, pre-cinematic sense). By means of this threefold investigation it is hoped to demonstrate the wealth of the cinema as a medium of expression, a wealth which lies in its capacity to cope with the contradictory demands of reality, fiction and modernist ideals.

PART ONE

Film Realism

Realism in the Cinema

Today, when we are accustomed to the idea of television images being sent back to us live from the surface of the moon, it is difficult to imagine a world without moving pictures. Yet even the pre-history of the cinema really goes back no farther than the latter part of the nineteenth century. The discovery that the human eye can be deceived into seeing connections between quite separate images, provided that these follow each other with sufficient speed, had, it is true, been made much earlier than this. Revolving toys, such as the zoetrope, which exploited this persistence of vision had long been popular. But it was only with the improvement of photography in the 1870s after the introduction of the dry plate process that it became possible to obtain by photographic means a series of images suitable for the creation of such an illusion of movement. This is a crucial development, because if we leave aside the rather special case of the cartoon or animated film, the cinema as an art of movement is indissolubly linked to the camera as a means of obtaining the basic images. The cinema has a potential for realism because, though film projection is a process of illusion, relying on a defect of the eye (the inability to differentiate images which follow one another at a rate of sixteen or twenty-four frames a second), the camera itself does not cheat. The images it gives are those which record the successive stages of a movement as they occurred in real life. For this reason, among the scientists and engineers, showmen and cranks, businessmen and conjurors who collectively made the cinema possible in the nineteenth century, a special place of honour must be reserved for those who used cameras to record and analyse movement.

One such pioneer was Eadweard Muybridge, a professional photographer born in Kingston-upon-Thames, who became one of the nineteenth century's leading authorities on animal locomotion. It was in 1877 that he attracted attention by solving the problem of how a galloping horse places its feet on the ground. The issue had been debated for centuries but before Muybridge no one knew the answer, for the movement is too quick for the human eye to detect unaided. Muybridge himself needed years of experiment and a complicated battery of twenty-four still cameras to come up with his answer. Inspired by Muybridge's example, a French physiologist, Etienne Marey, developed his own means of recording animal and bird movement. In the 1880s he developed his 'photographic gun' which had most of the ingredients of a successful motion-picture camera. Muybridge and Marey were both concerned with analysing movement and had no thought of creating a means of mass entertainment, but through their contact with the American inventor Thomas Edison both can claim a considerable influence on the creation of the cinema.

From the very earliest days – beginning with Louis Lumière himself – the desire to use the camera to probe and record aspects of reality has been a constant preoccupation of film-makers. There is a twofold tradition – with factual documentary and fictional realism running side by side – that extends up to the present, and those whose work shows a concern with such problems of film and reality are among the very greatest of film artists. The documentary looks back for its origins to the period of the First World War and the debuts of the American-born Robert Flaherty and the Russian Dziga Vertov. The linking of realism and fiction under the influence of the nineteenth century naturalist novel occupied much of the energies of D. W. Griffith and Erich von Stroheim, while in the sound era realism became a dominant mode in Europe with the films of Jean

Renoir in the 1930s and the Italian neo-realist directors – Roberto Rossellini, Vittorio de Sica and Luchino Visconti – in the 1940s. Since then the concern with realism has been an international one: Akira Kurosawa and Yashiro Ozu in Japan and Satyajit Ray in India are names that spring immediately to mind. With new developments in the 1960s which have led to the manufacture of lightweight, portable equipment for both filming and sound-recording, we find film-makers evolving fresh relationships of images and sounds, of documentary and fiction, as are shown by such forms as *cinéma-vérité* and television reportage. Accompanying all this creative activity has been an intense theoretical concern with the problem of the relationship of the film image and reality. If early silent film theory was chiefly concerned with the dream potential of the film, the advent of sound in the late 1920s led to more and more stress being placed on the realist aspect of the cinema. The documentary film-makers and theorists in Great Britain, Paul Rotha and John Grierson at their head, stressed the educative and positively propagandist functions of the documentary film, as opposed to the alleged frivolities of Hollywood. Italian critics and film-makers – particularly de Sica's inseparable script-writer, Cesare Zavattini – laid the foundations of neo-realism in the early 1940s and drew the lessons to be learned from it in the 1950s. In France, André Bazin questioned the view inherited from the silent theorists that the essence of the cinema as an art form lies in the editing or *montage*, and showed that Renoir and Rossellini, Orson Welles and William Wyler were all part of the same realist tradition. In the USA Siegfried Kracauer attempted in his book, *Theory of Film*, to deduce a whole aesthetic of the cinema from the realist functions shared by film and photography.

It is easy to see why the cinema concerns itself with being realistic. The camera is a unique instrument for capturing the surface detail of life. It can show faces, streets, landscapes, human groups and activities as well as tiny quirks of behaviour, all with great power. Life itself is so engrossing on this level that the material can never be exhausted. Film-makers will continue to be born who want to show life as it is, just as there will no doubt always be painters who are totally absorbed in painting the human face or the rural landscape.

Yet as a way of looking at life realism in this sense does have its limitations. The surface of life is fascinating but all sorts of things which are equally important happen in secret, in our minds and imaginings. The best realist films tend to be made when there is natural drama in the happenings of the time – in Italy at the end of the Second World War, for example, or in Soviet Russia after the Revolution. If this natural drama is present, it is enough for the film-maker to record it honestly and directly. But this cannot be regarded as the sole aim of the cinema, which can fulfil other equally important functions too. Life needs to be interpreted as well as simply recorded and this means that other elements may, and indeed must, be brought into play: spectacle and irony, dream and imagination. The cinema is an entertainment that takes us out of ourselves just as much as it is a factual record of our lives; it can concern itself with our dreams as well as it can portray our social problems. Audiences certainly feel this, and they turn out in greater numbers to watch a musical or a western than to see a realistic film about workers or fishermen. The realist film-maker or documentarist continually finds himself at odds with the audience he wishes to meet, and directors who make studies of social problems in their own countries frequently achieve a greater success with audiences abroad. It is not that such audiences have a greater interest in realism. It is simply that there is an added exotic element in the sight of a Sicilian fisherman or an Indian peasant for a spectator who has not visited those countries.

Realism in the cinema is just one way of looking at life, one style among several. The discipline the film-maker imposes on himself and the social issues his films inevitably raise make it a very valuable form, but a western or a musical is just as much a part of the cinema as a whole. On the other hand, realism is perhaps the most lasting of all trends in the cinema. The problem of the realist fictional film – how to link the recording of life (which is not art) with the creation of a story (which is not real) – is one that can never be exhausted and will always provoke new ideas. Certainly, it is true to say that many a modest little film that is honest and straightforward has a better chance of survival than big spectacles made with a great deal of money and world-famous stars. Realism suits the cinema because the camera is merciless at exposing pretence and fraud. If you wish to put on film actors in seventeenth-century costumes and settings supposed to be the palaces of the king of France, then you need to be very skilful indeed. Otherwise, in a few years, when the gloss has worn off, audiences looking at your film will see not what you pretend – that this is the court of Louis XIV – but what you actually show – actors in wigs and funny costumes gesticulating in front of cardboard sets.

2

Lumière or Méliès

The cinema differs from all the older arts in the amount we know about its origins. To investigate the origins of the cinema and the twin impulses of realism and spectacle we do not need to look into antiquity or ponder the sayings of Greek philosophers. We have only to look at the work and careers of two Frenchmen, both sons of well-to-do manufacturers, who together laid the basis of the French cinema and, in a very real sense, of film as we know it today. The two men are Louis Lumière and Georges Méliès. It was Lumière who in the 1890s drew on the work of pioneer inventors and scientists to perfect his own device which he called the cinematograph. He was the man behind the first showing of projected films to a paying public on 28 December 1895 at the so-called 'Indian Room', situated below the Grand Café at No. 14 Boulevard des Capucines in Paris. Though today we look back on this date as that of the birth of the cinema, it hardly seemed that important at the time. There was no prior advertising in the press and Lumière himself did not even bother to attend the first showing. He remained behind in Lyon, attending to what at the time seemed more vital, namely the large factory producing photographic materials which he ran with his elder brother, Auguste. Louis Lumière's contribution to the engineering side of the cinema is quite small — he merely devised a way of synchronizing the shutter movement of the camera with the movement of the strip of photographic film – and if he had done no more than this, he would merit little more than a footnote in the books of film history. His real importance lies elsewhere and is twofold. In the first place, he established the cinema as an industry. His cinematograph was tough, precise and reliable and he had the business sense needed to exploit it internationally for ten years. The second reason for his importance is that from the beginning he saw the cinema as a way of recording real life in movement, so that his films constitute the very first examples of realism in the cinema.

The programme which so excited audiences in 1895 lasted about half-an-hour and comprised a dozen or so little films, all shot, developed and printed by Louis Lumière himself, who was much too shrewd to allow his invention to get into other hands before he had had time to exploit it himself. Each film lasted only a minute, the length being determined by the size of the reel of film with which the cinematograph (used as both camera and projector) could cope. By the time of the first showing in December 1895 Lumière had made about fifty tiny films and, as no records were kept, we do not know which of these were shown in that initial programme. But we can get a very clear idea of the possibilities which he saw in the device he had invented. From the beginning the keynote was the recording of everyday occurrences. The very first film he made showed workers leaving the Lumière factory in Lyon and was shot from the window of the house opposite. The workers who stream through the gates are totally unaware of the fact that they are being photographed (the first 'candid camera' shots in fact) and the film ends with the gates being shut. Many of Lumière's films showed official or public events: a congress of photographers disembarking after an excursion on the river, a prince or head of state arriving for a reception, street entertainers performing, or trams and carriages moving to and fro. Other early films showed scenes of family life: Lumière's father playing cards with friends and his brother Auguste helping his wife to feed the baby. These impressed spectators by the details which to us seem trivial – the wind moving the leaves in the trees or figures in the background of a street scene bustling about. Still other films were more spectacular – for audiences of 1895 at least. Lumière impressed those who had never seen the sea by filming boats leaving harbour and waves breaking on the shore. Even more striking were the films of trains entering a station. So powerful was the impact of such scenes that many members of the audience are said to have dived beneath the seats for safety.

Some of Lumière's films opened up new and unexpected possibilities which his successors were to explore. For instance, he filmed a very innocuous scene of workmen knocking down a wall. A not particularly exciting occurrence. But as soon as this happened to be projected in reverse, the illusion of something totally magical was given. A wall rose up from the dust and pieced itself together in a way that defied all the natural laws as we know them, a seeming miracle. Another early film showed a gardener watering plants. A naughty boy creeps up behind him, steps on the hose, and then releases his foot at just the right moment to drench the gardener. Here is the origin of all those comedy films which delighted spectators of the silent cinema – there is even a remote ancestor of the classic chase sequence, as the gardener pursues and punishes the boy. This was obviously among the most popular of the Lumière films, for it was illustrated on one of the first cinematograph posters. But Lumière himself saw little interest in the possibilities of magic and story-telling which proved so vital to the growth of the cinema as an art and an industry.

For ten years, from 1895 to 1905, the Lumière brothers exploited Louis's invention all over the world. Representatives were sent to the major cities of Europe and to some Eastern countries to arrange showings of the Lumière programmes and also to send back to Paris shots of typical scenes. In this way Lumière built up a catalogue of well over a thousand items, with subjects ranging from bull-fighters entering the arena in Spain to negro dancers entertaining the crowds in London, from coolies toiling in Saigon to processions in Rome or Stockholm. For us today, the Lumière collection of films, which he gave to the French film museum, the Cinémathèque, two years before his death in 1948, serves as a fascinating storehouse of history. It gives us the exact look of life at the turn of the century, the fashions of dress and the forms of transport. It adds to what we can learn from books or still photographs the very rhythm of life in those early days when the horse had not yet been replaced by the motorcar and when a man's job and place in society were immediately apparent from the clothes he wore.

Lumière's work has strict limitations. He was content with films lasting no more than a minute, taken with a camera rigidly fixed at some appropriate point. The camera rarely moves in films shot by Lumière or by one of his employees, and then only when it has been placed in some moving vehicle – a gondola floating down the Grand Canal in Venice or a train entering Brussels station. Otherwise the camera remains quite still and only the life around it is animated. Lumière seems never to have considered whether greater impact could be achieved by joining several shots together to make a more complicated work, and the simplicity of his films is both their strength and weakness. They are superbly photographed but fragmentary, tiny but absolutely true. But, in contrast to the peepshows that preceded them, Lumière's films gave the images their real dimension and a sense of vitality. His human figures were more than life-size, and he could capture the flow of life, crowds and busy streets, trains and rivers. In the form that Lumière gave it, the film camera could easily be carried around, and the operator could work with the same freedom as the still photographer, going out to meet life and to investigate the people and scenes around him.

We can put the Lumière style of realism into perspective if we contrast his work with that of his contemporary, Georges Méliès, who was one of those invited to the first demonstration of the cinematograph. Méliès – magician, illusionist and direc- tor of the Robert Houdin theatre – offered to buy Lumière's camera for ten thousand francs that very first night, but his offer was naturally refused. In the event, it cost him ten times that sum before he was in a position to go into business as a film-maker. His work on the stage, which had involved the use of magic lanterns and special lighting effects, put him in a

position to see quite different potentialities in the cinematograph – ones undreamed of by the sober businessman Lumière
– and he it was who first added the dimension of spectacle. He
began, like all the first film-makers, by simply imitating
Lumière, but filming real life in this way could not satisfy a
conjuror for long. The legend – fostered by Méliès himself – is
that one day while he was filming on the Place de l'Opéra in
Paris, the film jammed in his rather primitive camera. It took
him a few minutes to get the machine working again and then
he carried on filming. When he developed this film he found
that something marvellous had happened: a bus was suddenly
transformed into a hearse, and men into women, as if by magic.
Whether this is merely a legend is impossible to say. What is
certain, however, is that Méliès soon made himself familiar
with a wide variety of trick effects. In 1897 too, in the grounds
of his property at Montreuil-sous-Bois, he built the first genuine
film studio, a building some twenty feet by fifty. This was no
doubt for him the equivalent of the special stage of the Robert
Houdin theatre, where he had everything needed to help him
devise his tricks and spectacles for the public. The construction
of such a studio at a time when filming was customarily carried
out in the open air typifies Méliès's concern to create a world
that obeyed his own rules, not those of everyday life.

Méliès made films of every possible kind. In his Montreuil
studio he happily imitated real-life events – Indian mutinies,
American intervention in the Philippines, a volcanic eruption in
Martinique. There was no real attempt to cheat the public, for
the day of the on-the-spot eye-witness reporter had not yet
arrived. For Méliès, and no doubt his audience, such films –
best known of which were *The Dreyfus Affair* and *The Coronation of Edward VII* – were merely the extension of the drawings
and engravings that regularly appeared in newspapers to illus-
trate current events. Méliès also made advertising films on subjects ranging from mustard to corsets. All were gay, burlesque
little films. To sell hats, he showed live rabbits put into a machine which promptly turned out a vast quantity of new hats.
Then the procedure was reversed and the hats were put in to
produce . . . live rabbits. Today, when we are so concerned with

the morality of advertising, it is amusing to learn that mustard consumed with such relish by Méliès's characters (and their dog) was in fact chocolate cream.

Méliès's better-known short trick films use the processes of acceleration and slow motion. These effects were easy to obtain then, when the camera was cranked by hand. The camera operator just had to turn the handle more slowly or more quickly during the shooting for the opposite effect to be given during projection. He also used photographic tricks like substitution (stopping the camera, making a change and then carrying on with the shooting), superimposition (printing two or more shots one on top of the other) and dissolves (fading one scene out and bringing another into view), as well as the whole gadgetry of the theatre of illusion. Films like *The Conjuring Away of a Lady at Robert Houdin Theatre* (1896), the reproduction of a stage illusion, show his evident delight in the trickery of film. Even more striking are the films such as *The Man with the Heads* (1898), *The One-Man Orchestra* (1900) or *The Melomaniac* (1903) in which he duplicates himself or juggles with his own head. But perhaps the most famous trick of this type is *The Man with the India-Rubber Head* (1902), in which a mad scientist removes his head and amuses himself by blowing it up like a balloon. Then his assistant takes over, but he blows too hard and the film ends with an explosion. Tricks like these involve skilful manipulation of film and, in some cases, complicated machinery. But, strangely enough, Méliès never makes his camera move – to enlarge the head, he brought it towards the camera, instead of moving the camera in to it.

These films show clearly Méliès's inventiveness, but the full range of his imagination is best seen in his longer fantasies where he makes a unique personal blend of elements drawn from the Brothers Grimm, Jules Verne and pantomime. He made versions of fairy tales like Cinderella, Bluebeard, Aladdin and many others. He also achieved world fame with his films of fantastic journeys: *A Trip to the Moon* (1902), *The Voyage across the Impossible* (1904) and *The Conquest of the Pole* (1912). These films are crammed with all the creatures of his imagination – mad professors and gesticulating scientists, comic snakes and friendly monsters, prancing acrobatic devils who appear from nowhere and vanish again in a puff of smoke, and rows of plump chorus girls continually marching to and fro in unison, like Edwardian postcards brought to life. The moon is depicted as a smiling face (until the space ship lands in one eye) and the stars are pretty girls from the Châtelet theatre swinging on ropes or peering through holes in the backcloth of a painted sky.

Méliès's films have a great warmth and a humour quite without vulgarity. There is a bustling sense of life in them and the tricks and fantasies are still more striking in the hand-coloured versions which Méliès also prepared (at double the price of black and white). Though he planned his films in great detail, he told his stories without need for titles giving dialogue or explanation. For a while he maintained an enormous success but ultimately, as with all the great pioneers, the limitations of a style that had once been original, even revolutionary, became clear as the cinema progressed. The very theatrical quality that had made his films such an advance on Lumière's quickly dated, and a style that had introduced spectacle to the cinema no longer seemed spectacular. For the space which Méliès used in all his films was the tiny set in the Montreuil studio, from which he hardly budged in his later years. In front of this set – in the equivalent of the best seat in the stalls – was planted the camera, a cumbersome device, so noisy that he called it his 'coffee grinder' or 'machine gun'. Except for special effects he never varied the distance between camera and actors, just as he always built his stories in a series of complete scenes or tableaux. The creative use of the camera to take the audience into a scene and create a new sense of space was quite foreign to him.

Georges Méliès was more than just a pioneer overtaken by developments in an art he helped to create. Louis Lumière's work looks forward, not to the fiction feature film, but to the documentary. It is linked with contemporary *cinéma-vérité* studies of real happenings and, in spirit at least, with the 8 mm. home movies in which an increasing number of people record the everyday events in their lives and homes. But it is Méliès who is the first true artist of the cinema and anticipates the complex world of screen fiction. In contrast to Lumière he saw the cinema as a kind of blend of all the arts, and if he did not realize the full power of the camera and the editing process, his work nevertheless opens the way for Hollywood and the role of film as a major medium of mass entertainment. If we couple the names of Lumière and Méliès we get an idea of the enormous range of possibilities which the cinema offered even as early as 1900. It is between the two poles of the sober recording of life and the exuberant use of imaginative spectacle that virtually all film-making has found its place. The emphasis continually changes, but the duality remains and each new director has to make his own fusion of Lumière and Méliès, of real life and fantasy.

3

Flaherty and the Idea of Documentary

The term documentary is capable of many interpretations for really it covers all those films which deal with facts as opposed to the usually longer films that are works of fiction. This does not mean that documentary is limited to films with titles like *Housing in New Zealand* or *Precise Measurements for Engineers*. Indeed, nothing could be farther from drab everyday reality than the work of one of the originators of documentary, Robert Flaherty. Born in Michigan in 1884, the son of a mining engineer, Flaherty had an untroubled childhood up to the age of nine, when a slump ruined his family and sparked off a riot among the workers they employed. This drove his father to seek his fortune in the North, in Canada, and as a result between the age of twelve and fourteen Flaherty had the sort of life many boys of that age dream of. He stayed in a remote mining camp and sometimes set foot where no white man had been before. He also came into contact with the Indians who gave him presents of mocassins and Indian garb, invited him into their tepees and taught him how to hunt. He never had much formal education though at one time he did briefly and unsuccessfully attend a mining college. What he did acquire instead during these years was much that was to influence his later film work: a respect for primitive ways of life, a taste for adventure (which was increased by his reading of Fenimore Cooper and R. M. Ballantyne) and the ability to live rough. He had few qualifications for a regular career and spent several years of prospecting before he was commissioned to undertake a major expedition. Then, at the age of twenty-six, he was sent to search for iron ore on the islands off the east coast of Hudson Bay.

In the course of the next few years Flaherty made several expeditions in north-east Canada, and it was on his third trip that, at the suggestion of his employer, he took with him a film camera. He took his first shots in Baffin Land in 1913 but it was not until 1916 that he began filming in earnest. The Eskimos were more than just a subject for Flaherty. He was deeply influenced by the experience of living among these people who were daily confronted by the possibility of death, yet continued to display great cheerfulness and nobility. He always acknowledged his debt to them, admitting that no white man could survive without Eskimo help in the North. He always sought to involve them in his film-making, not just as his assistants but as co-authors as it were. It has even been suggested that his approach to film-making, which is very different from that of most feature film-makers, is in fact very like that of the Eskimo to his art. Eskimo carvers do not try to impose a shape – say that of a seal – on a piece of ivory. Their aim is to uncover or reveal the shape that is already within the material. Flaherty always tried to do something like this in his films, to allow them to grow naturally out of his experience of the people and the setting. To begin with, however, Flaherty had to face up to some disappointment. He returned from the North in 1916 with about seventy thousand feet of film, that is about seventeen-and-a-half hours' viewing at silent speed. This he began to edit slowly and patiently. Now there was one thing about early nitrate film that all who used it had to admit was a drawback – it was very inflammable. Flaherty knew this as well as anyone but one day he was careless. He dropped a cigarette on to the film he was editing and the whole seventy thousand feet went up in flames.

This sort of disaster would surely have ended the film career of most people, but not Robert Flaherty. He was not a man to get discouraged. Viewing the one print of the film he still possessed (from which it was not possible at the time to print other copies) he came to the conclusion that it was really no loss. The film would have been disjointed and boring and so he decided to remake it, this time so as to show a year in the life of an Eskimo family. It was not until 1920 that he had found a backer – the fur company of Réveillon Frères – and could go north again. He not only took two cameras, he had also decided to develop, print and project his film during the shooting, so he needed the material for this too. Filming began at Port Harrison on the Hudson Bay and Flaherty chose his actors: Nanook and three younger men together with their wives, children and dogs. For them, of course, the whole idea of a film was unbelievable. We tend to forget that we have to learn to read a picture or a film just as we have to learn to read a book. The Eskimos were at first unable to do this. Shown a photograph of themselves they used to look at it without understanding, often holding it upside down initially. Similarly, when Flaherty showed the first scenes of his film to them, they did not understand. They looked at the Nanook on the screen and the Nanook present in the audience; they looked at the screen but also at the projector, the source of the light. But when the shots of the walrus hunt began they became involved and shouted encouragement to Nanook. Flaherty saw the showing of such scenes as a vital part of the whole project, but one which caused many difficulties. To print his films he had to use daylight as his light source (because the electricity was too unreliable) and to wash it he had to have water brought in barrels from a hole chipped through six feet of ice and continually cleared of the ice that formed on the top as he worked.

Though he was concerned to record the real Eskimo life, Flaherty always staged what he filmed. Nanook and his companions had been in contact with the trading post and now no longer wore genuine Eskimo clothes. So Flaherty went to a great deal of trouble and expense finding for them 'real' clothes of the kind they had discarded. For his film interiors Flaherty could not use a normal twelve-foot diameter igloo, so Nanook spent several days building him a special larger one. Similarly, the hunting had to be carefully arranged, with the real idea being not that Nanook should catch a walrus, but that Flaherty should get an exciting piece of film. For this reason documentary as practised by Flaherty can never mean a scientific and objective recording, it is rather a sort of game. The Eskimos pretended they were living their normal lives, but in fact Flaherty's arrival totally disrupted their way of living. Because so much of their time was taken up with the film, he had to feed and support them. Perhaps it is because of this disruption that so many of the Eskimos he came into contact with suffered later. For instance, at the very time when, two years later, his face and name were becoming known throughout the world, Nanook himself died of starvation.

In 1922, when *Nanook of the North* was complete, Flaherty had great difficulty in finding a distributor for it, because it was so different from anything that had been done before. Eventually, by packing the preview audience with his friends who applauded the best parts of the film, he sold it to Pathé. Despite his trick, the film proved to be a big success, particularly in Europe and from now on Flaherty was not a prospector, but a film-maker. Jesse M. Lasky of Paramount sent him a telegram: 'I want you to go off somewhere and make me another *Nanook*. Go where you will. Do what you like. I'll foot the bills. The world's your oyster.' He went with his family to Samoa and set out to make a Polynesian *Nanook*, but the whole of life there was as different as could be from the frozen North. In Samoa there was no struggle for existence, neither land nor weather was hostile and for a while Flaherty wondered how to shape his film. He shot thousands of feet without a clear idea of how the film would turn out. In fact, nothing that he shot in the whole of the first year was used in the finished film, but in this time Flaherty did make an important photographic discovery. Up to this time films were made on what was called orthochromatic stock which gave excellent contrasts of blacks and whites and was easy to use (it had been ideal for *Nanook*) but gave little modelling of detail. Flaherty had brought with him some panchromatic stock for use in a colour camera. When this broke, Flaherty used the panchromatic film, as an experiment, to shoot black and white pictures. The result was a revelation and the beauty of the final film, *Moana* (1926), the first feature to use this film stock, was such that it helped to turn all film-makers to panchromatic within a few years. As in all his films, Flaherty sought to recreate the old ways of life and his hero had to undergo, for the sole purpose of the film, a very painful six-week tattooing ceremony which would otherwise not have taken place. The film was less successful at the box office than *Nanook*, despite an attempt by the distributors to sell it to the public as 'The Love Life of a South Sea Siren'. But the critics saw the film for what it was, and it was about *Moana* that the critic John Grierson first used the word documentary in the sense that we use it today.

After *Moana* there came a long period of frustration for Flaherty during which he shot a couple of short films, worked briefly on a Hollywood epic set in the South Seas, and tried to collaborate with the great German director, Friedrich Murnau, on a film called *Tabu*. The result was a splendid film, but it had very little to do with Flaherty and his conception of life. So it was that in 1931 Flaherty came to London to make a film called *Industrial Britain* for John Grierson and the Empire Marketing Board. This meeting is of great interest because, if it was Flaherty who had created documentary with *Nanook*, it was the British who in the 1930s turned it into a movement. But the British directors were also deeply influenced by the political mood of the period and by the Soviet cinema of the late 1920s, the revolutionary films of Eisenstein, Pudovkin and Dovzhenko. They saw their films as a progressive contribution to society and were more concerned with education than with art. Compared to them, Flaherty was a romantic, opposed to modern ideas and interested chiefly in making films about primitive cultures that were already dying. Where Grierson's documentarists worked for big organizations (like the Empire Marketing Board and the GPO) and made 'official' films about dockers and postmen, telephones and housing problems, Flaherty tried to work inside the ordinary commercial system and make personal films that brought to the screen a way of life threatened by our western civilization.

This difference is very clear in Flaherty's major film in Britain, *Man of Aran* (1934). Financed by Gaumont-British, Flaherty spent two whole years and three times his allotted budget of £10,000, to end up with a highly successful film that took £50,000 at the box office in six months. He showed that he was not interested in the harsh everyday life of the Aran islanders and their monotonous fight for food and a living. His real subject was a poem about man's struggle against the sea, and his film was built around a shark-fishing expedition and a storm that breaks on the coast. As shown in the film both of these were partly false: the fishermen did not normally go out in high seas as they do in the film (only Flaherty's offer of money and fame induced them to do this), and the last shark was caught off the islands fifty years before. For the shark-fishing episode Flaherty had to have harpoons specially made in Galloway and had to employ experts to train the islanders in the use of them. In any case, far from being dangerous as the film implies, the sun fish shark of the Aran Islands eat only plankton. Nevertheless, these scenes do convey Flaherty's own theme of man versus the sea and provide the suspense he uses in all his films to add drama to what would otherwise be a dull account of real life. What is most interesting about Flaherty's way of filming is his attitude to the camera. He used it like a living thing saying things like: 'We cannot shoot that, the camera doesn't want to.' Nowadays, when we are less concerned with the real conditions in Aran in 1934, it is easy to see that the importance of Flaherty lies in his spontaneous use of the camera. We are less shocked than were Grierson and his colleagues by the lack of social commitment, and the sheer beauty of the photography makes up for the lack of a gripping story and the poor, studio-recorded sound.

In 1935 Flaherty went to India to make a film called *Elephant Boy* but, as it was released, this merely used Flaherty's material as background for a story shot in the Denham studios of Alexander Korda. The film, needless to say, did not benefit from this mixture and was not a success, and again Flaherty was faced with a long period of unemployment and frustration. Then in 1939 he was commissioned by another important documentary producer-director, Pare Lorenz (who had himself made *The River* and *The Plow that Broke the Plains*) to make *The Land*, a documentary on the same problems of poverty and land wastage that John Steinbeck dealt with in his novel, *The Grapes of Wrath*, which was filmed around this time by John Ford. Flaherty was filled with anger at what he saw and filmed, but found it difficult to piece together a film out of his material. After another long period of inactivity Flaherty was able to make his last film in ideal circumstances, for he persuaded the Standard Oil Company to finance *Louisiana Story*, about the impact of the machine age (in the form of a company drilling for oil) on a simple rural community. Flaherty as always worked slowly and without being able to put into words exactly what he was looking for. After two years and the expenditure of a quarter of a million dollars, work on the film stopped. Aided by a beautiful musical score by Virgil Thomson, *Louisiana Story* was a prestige success. When it is contrasted with *Nanook* the director's range is at once apparent: from a factual (if acted) study of real life Flaherty has moved to a dream of childhood, in which the oil derricks are no more real than the werewolves from which the splendidly named boy hero, Alexander Napoleon Ulysses Latour, tries to protect himself with charms.

We have looked in such detail at the career of Robert Flaherty for two reasons. Firstly, because this career contains some of the major films in cinema history, and secondly, because it lights up certain of the basic issues of documentary. Now, twenty years after Flaherty's death, it is easy to see where the importance of his work lies. While the British documentary movement was alive, critics like John Grierson and Paul Rotha looked for their sort of educational propaganda in his work and were uneasy when they failed to find it. Today it is more natural for us to look at a body of films and ask ourselves how far they are the expression of a man's mind and beliefs. If we look at Flaherty in this way his work loses nothing of its importance, but is easier to put into perspective. He made documentaries the way he did because he remained at heart an explorer. Therefore he began with his material, the people and the places, and sought his story in them. Often he turned the clock back – filming tattooing in Samoa and shark-fishing off the Aran Islands long after these practices had ceased. But always, for Flaherty, the drama came out of the physical facts of the existence of his characters. In this way he is very different from most directors of fiction films who begin with a situation and then try to locate it appropriately. This difference explains why Flaherty never used a script and needed two years to complete a film, one year of which would be spent just shooting 'tests'. As a film-maker he produced a succession of beautiful and moving films. As a pioneer, he not only invented a new form of cinema, an alternative to Hollywood, he also managed, thanks to the force of his personality and powers of persuasion, to impose this on the industry and, with *Nanook*, to find a world audience for it. For both reasons the cinema is much in his debt.

4

Vertov and Soviet Cinema

Robert Flaherty's work has the spaciousness and the sense of connection between past and present which mark the primitive landscapes in which he preferred to work. The films he directed contain instinctively felt truths about the human situation, yet they are far removed from the social and political realities of their time. Flaherty's vision is so persuasive that it becomes easy to forget that the years which saw the making of *Nanook of the North* witnessed the creation of a new society and set of political ideals in Soviet Russia, as well as the passing-away of the Eskimo way of life. In the USSR all the young film-makers were caught up in a great political and cultural upheaval and, though their enthusiasm was as great as Flaherty's, it functioned only in a social context. Soviet cinema was created on 27 August 1919 when Lenin ordered the nationalization of the film industry which had shown comparatively little real creative excitement or originality in its ten years or so of existence. Five days later a film school was established, and from the first the cinema was seen as fulfilling a propagandist function. But, despite this ideological framework, Soviet film-makers worked, in the aftermath of the First World War, in much the same way as a pioneer like Flaherty: they lacked money, equipment and film stock, but were buoyed up by the sheer delight in innovation. Film could be seen by all as having a central role in the formation of the new society during the early years of the

Revolution. Not only was there the prestige conferred by Lenin's definition of the cinema as the most important of all the arts, film was also very clearly the perfect example of the fusion of art and machine which Soviet painters, writers and theorists, caught up in the spirit of the time, were seeking in the early 1920s. In the poems and manifestoes of Mayakovsky and his futurist contemporaries we find frequent equations of poet and worker, art and industry. Mayakovsky proclaims himself a factory or longs for the day when item one on the politburo's agenda will be 'Stalin's report on the output of poetry'. If such ideas seem, in retrospect, excessive when applied to the written word, they remain totally apposite to film, which combines the functions of personal expression and industrial production.

In this revolutionary context realism was only one of a number of divergent tendencies. Indeed, throughout the early years of Soviet cinema realist and formalist attributes came alternately to the fore. In the early 1920s the newsreel concerns of Dziga Vertov found a parallel in the editing experiments of Lev Kuleshov, who sought new techniques of dramatic presentation. Kuleshov is today remembered not only for films like *Mr West in the Land of the Bolsheviks* (1924) and *By the Law* (1926) but also for his earlier work at the experimental film workshop he founded. There he explored such ideas as the creation of an imaginary geography by editing varying locations together, and the creation of a synthetic woman with details derived from a number of real women. His best known experiment in dynamic editing was to cut the same expressionless close-up of the actor Mozhukhin into three separate dramatic contexts and show that it could convey perfectly to the spectator such diverse emotions as hunger, tenderness and sorrow.

The generation that followed Kuleshov and Vertov and dominated the last years of silent Soviet cinema was very concerned with the question of how to depict the new society in terms of revolutionary dramatic construction. Sergei Eisenstein, Vsevolod Pudovkin and Alexander Dovzhenko were all poets whose love of life went hand in hand with an exuberant use of all the visual possibilities of the silent screen. If works like *Battleship Potemkin* (1925), *Mother* (1926) and *Earth* (1930) pushed the documentary preoccupations of Vertov into the shade, these film-makers, too, were ignored by a succeeding generation. The silent documentary, *Turksib*, made by Victor Turin in 1929, marked a return to a more straightforward approach to reality and propaganda. In the early sound films of the 1930s it is this new and prosaic approach – closely in sympathy with the realist novel of the nineteenth century – which prevailed, while men like Eisenstein were attacked for their 'formalism'.

The cinema of Dziga Vertov, the greatest of Soviet documentarists, has no literary roots. It is an outgrowth of the newsreel camera's ability to report life as it happens. Vertov, whose real name was Denis Kaufman, wrote poems and sketches in his youth, but his great love before he turned to the cinema in 1918 was sound. He was fascinated by the possibility of sound-recording and transposing natural sounds into words and letters. His film work includes two remarkable sound films: *Enthusiasm* (1930), in which he finally fulfilled this early ambition to 'photograph' sounds, and *Three Songs of Lenin* (1934), which drew on folk tales and legends to build up a unique picture of the man whose presence dominated this whole era of Soviet life. But Vertov is best remembered for his concern with visuals – his theory of the Kino-eye. Vertov began as an editor, piecing together the short propaganda films and newsreel material sent back by the cameramen sent out on the so-called agit trains which toured the war fronts in 1918 politicizing the soldiers and the peasants. From this he turned to editing the *Kino Weekly* newsreel, producing occasional special issues. It was with the foundation of *Kino-Pravda*, designed as a film equivalent to the official party newspaper *Pravda*, that his originality began to become apparent. Here he gradually evolved new non-narrative ways of editing material together, and gathered around him a whole group of collaborators and disciples, who called themselves *Kinoki* or *'cinema-eyes'*. Vertov and his group accompanied their practical film-making with a vigorous series of pronouncements and manifestoes, all proclaiming the unique quality of the 'Kino-eye'.

Vertov saw film drama and the literary scenario as relics of the bourgeois past which had to be destroyed if the cinema was to fulfil its destiny. Whereas Flaherty could use simple narratives for his studies of the family group in a primitive society, Vertov was driven by the very nature of his material to more complex methods. He wanted to analyse the changes (such as industrialization and collectivization) wrought on all aspects of contemporary life by the revolution, and to show the essential unity of the vast territory united under the banner of socialism. His concern was to use the camera as his means of research into the visual chaos of this world and, for this to be accomplished, he felt that it had to be unfettered from the limitations of the human eye. Where, for Flaherty, the essence of the documentary lay in the contemplative power of the single camera, Vertov needed whole batteries of cameramen to overcome the limitations of space, and used the device of varying the pace of the images as a way of outstepping the confines of time. These and similar ideas Vertov proclaimed with a prophetic fervour:

... I am eye. I am a mechanical eye.

I, a machine, am showing you a world, the likes of which only I can see. I free myself from today and forever from human immobility. I am in constant movement, I approach and draw away from objects, I crawl under them, I move alongside the mouth of a running horse, I cut into a crowd at full speed, I run in front of running soldiers, I turn on my back, I rise with an aeroplane, I fall and soar together with falling and rising bodies.

This is I, apparatus, manoeuvring in the chaos of movements, recording one movement after another in the most complex combinations ...

The full realization of these ambitions took all of Vertov's energies during the 1920s. The most famous of his *Kino-Pravda*, which comprised twenty-three numbers compiled between 1922 and 1925, are those dealing with a contemporary issue about which he felt most deeply, the death of Lenin in 1924 and its aftermath. Here Vertov's skill in using archive material and piecing it together with newsreel shots is clearly apparent.

Further steps towards the idea of 'cinema truth' were taken in Vertov's later and longer films. In *Stride Soviet* (1926) he told the story of the Moscow Soviet, basing his film on the contrast of past and present. This was the first film for which Vertov composed a script, but in fact this had little effect on his methods, for the final film turned out to be quite different from what had been planned. Here Vertov was able to demonstrate the virtues of the candid-camera technique, basing much of his film on material shot with concealed cameras. His next film, *A Sixth of the World* (1926), was the best received of all his films. It traced the wealth and variety of the USSR with material shot throughout the country by ten teams of cameramen. Here Vertov moved away from the straightforward documentary to create something more aptly termed a cine-poem, mixing images and written titles into a hymn of praise of the new society. In *Eleventh* (1928), the first of three films shot in the Ukraine, Vertov examined the eleventh anniversary of the Revolution, building his film around the construction of a dam on the Dnieper. The image of Lenin superimposed over lyrical shots of water flowing through the completed dam remains the film's most memorable moment.

While these three films had all been concerned with the creation of a new Soviet society, Vertov's masterpiece, *The Man with the Movie Camera* (1929), can only be seen as a study of the power of the camera. On the eve of sound, and before beginning the aural experiments of *Enthusiasm*, Vertov applied himself to creating a last purely visual work. The real hero is not Soviet man, but the camera itself, which at one point is animated so as to move by itself and even to take a bow. Vertov shows the whole process of movie-making, and follows the cameraman (his brother and constant collaborator, Mikhail Kaufman) through the chaos and turmoil of the world. Rhythmic editing, superimposition, multiple exposure, camera movement and variation of the speed of the action are all used to great effect. In the final analysis the film becomes less a statement about the USSR than an illustration of the virtuosity of Vertov and his Kino-eye team.

In the 1930s the importance of Vertov's work tended to be obscured in the debate about realism and formalism, and certainly a work like *The Man with the Movie Camera* has moved a long way from the simple recording of everyday (but significant) reality. Yet his editing methods had some influence on Eisenstein and his sound experiments preceded those of the British documentarists. Thirty years later Vertov found his rightful position as one of the great film pioneers when his *Kino-Pravda*, translated into French, gave its name to the *cinéma-vérité* school of film reporting. As a new generation of film-makers shed the desire to make films on the Hollywood model and set out instead to discover the world with their new lightweight equipment, the lessons of Vertov became clear. His example of enthusiasm and ingenuity, commitment to Leninism as a political ideal and his passion for cinematic innovation suddenly became alive and meaningful. With this increasing interest in the use of film to do things other than simply tell stories, Vertov could be seen as Flaherty's equal and as the embodiment of ideas that have more than a 1920s relevance. Film-makers interested in the cinema as a medium of ideas and in the filmic equivalent of the propaganda slogan could learn much from the work of Vertov: his early use of titles as a vital graphic component of a film, his tireless quest to capture the complexity of contemporary society and politics and his faith in the power of the camera as a means of analysis. The link is well symbolized by the fact that the political films of Jean-Luc Godard in the late 1960s were made in collaboration with Marxist students who called themselves the Dziga Vertov group.

5

Sound Documentary

On the basis of the examples furnished by the silent documentaries of Robert Flaherty and the films of the Soviet directors, but with the added ingredient of sound, a whole documentary movement grew up in Great Britain in the 1930s. The central figure and prime organizer was a serious-minded Scot, John Grierson, who gathered around him a group of keen young film-makers, many of them university-educated. Among these were Paul Rotha, Basil Wright, Harry Watt, Edgar Anstey and Arthur Elton, aided too by the Brazilian-born Alberto Cavalcanti. Grierson himself directed only one important film, *Drifters*, in 1929, and was principally a producer and theorist. Much of the influence of the group stems from the fact that so many of its members followed his example and combined the roles of film-maker and critic. The movement was never a monolithic one and there was room for a whole range of attitudes between, on the one hand, Grierson's conception of the documentary film as the creative treatment of actuality and, on the other, Rotha's more directly propagandist concern. But it is fair to say that all the directors associated with the movement subscribed to the basic principles set down by Grierson in an article published in 1932. These were, firstly, a belief in the capacity of the cinema for getting around, for observing and selecting from life itself, rather than using an invented story acted out against an artificial background. Secondly, there was a desire to persuade ordinary people to act out their lives in real settings, and, finally, an awareness of the importance of capturing the spontaneous gesture and the natural inflection of speech.

Aside from the theory and critical writing which it produced (Rotha, for instance, was one of the first historians of world cinema), the documentary movement has two other claims to importance: it established a structure for a new kind of film-making, and, within this, produced individual works of great interest and considerable power. The organizational structure was the great creation of Grierson. The documentary film-makers scorned the products of the studios and the attitudes of conventional producers and film financiers. They had, there-fore, to find an alternative source of finance. For this they turned to government and official bodies, offering in return a service of education for the public in the workings of bureau-cracy and public affairs. Most of the more important films pro-duced were made for – and to a large extent reflected the points of view of – big business and government-sponsored organizations. Wright's *Song of Ceylon* (1934), for example, was made for the Ceylon Tea Propaganda Board, and Anstey's *Enough to Eat* (1936) for the Gas, Light and Coke Company of London. The core of the sponsorship of documentary film-making came from a succession of public bodies: the Empire Marketing Board, the GPO Film Unit and the Crown Film Unit. The subjects tended therefore to be drawn from major indus-tries and public service organizations: mining, fishing, trans-port, the postal service, and so on. The tone of the movement was set by the twenty-minute film, *Industrial Britain*, released in 1933. This was very much a joint effort. It was produced by John Grierson for the Empire Marketing Board and the original footage was shot by Robert Flaherty, the great idol of the young documentarists, who was in Britain on the visit that cul-minated in the making of *Man of Aran*. Working with Flaherty deeply influenced the group, but he did not complete the film himself. Additional footage was shot by Wright and Elton and the final version edited by Anstey under the close supervision of Grierson, who also provided much of the commentary.

The film ignores such realities as unemployment and trade unionism, and despite its title concentrates on the individual craftsman rather than the role of organized labour. The result is a very romanticized vision of the industrial process.

At the peak of the movement in the mid 1930s the documentarists showed an intense preoccupation with the technicalities of film-making, particularly the use of sound. Typical of this tendency were Cavalcanti's *Coalface* (1935) and the Wright and Watt film of 1936, *Night Mail*. In both the visuals based on actual observation were subordinated in the overall design to a highly elaborate sound track composed in a studio. There was no attempt to render the actual sound of industry or transport directly. Snatches of ordinary conversation and the sounds of engines and machines were blended with the informative commentary and then fitted into a rhythmical pattern made up of the musical score by Benjamin Britten and poems by W. H. Auden. The mixture was an exciting one, but far removed from the original documentary intention of maintaining a close contact with everyday reality. A reaction came in the form of two documentaries made at about the same time by Elton and Anstey, *Workers and Jobs* and *Housing Problems*. These turned their backs on the stylistic experiment and fundamental romanticism of *Coalface* and *Night Mail*. Instead the film-makers allowed ordinary people to communicate through the camera. The voices of workmen and housewives talking simply and directly to the audience replace the elaborate sound tracks, and the day-to-day problems come across with a spontaneity that had been lost in the more experimental works. Though much of the interview technique is crude by modern standards, the approach was an original one in the context of British cinema and brought together again the notions of documentary and realism.

The 1940s and 1950s gave new types of documentary that are also of real interest. During the Second World War Humphrey Jennings made a number of films about Britain, such as *The First Days, Listen to Britain* and the longer story film about the fire service, *Fires Were Started*. It would be difficult to imagine a more different man from Flaherty than Humphrey Jennings.

Where Flaherty wandered the world, Jennings stayed linked to one place, Cambridge, where he went to school, studied at the university and acquired his basic values. Jennings cared deeply about art and literature and was fascinated by the way in which the Industrial Revolution had changed the British way of life and by the way great scientists and thinkers have influenced our view of the world. He dabbled in other art forms, writing poetry and painting, and was interested in systems of ideas as different as Marxism and surrealism. But whether he was composing a poem or compiling his long (and never completed) study of the Industrial Revolution, he felt that it was wrong to invent either ideas or images. For his history he used original documents and for his poems the sentences, quotations and phrases that he found in his reading.

For a man like this, the cinema, which after all can be a literal medium that deals with people and objects directly, by showing them, was a natural form of expression. Making his documentaries he was dealing with reality at first hand, filming the life around him, men at work or at rest, factories or dance halls, statues and buildings, streets and trees. He had a natural sympathy for all things that are essentially British – Shakespeare, St Paul's Cathedral, the River Thames. When during the war with Germany he felt these things to be threatened, he reacted with a series of films that weave together patterns of the pictures and sounds that go to make up Britain. At the end of *Listen to Britain*, for instance, Jennings moves from the variety team of Flanagan and Allen entertaining workers in a factory canteen to Myra Hess playing Mozart in a National Gallery denuded of its pictures (away in the country for safe keeping from bombs). Then, without a break, he takes us on to the sight and sound of a tank factory, a brass band, welders at work, then to cornfields and a choir singing Rule Britannia. Jennings's great achievement – and one that has never been surpassed in its own sphere – was to make this mass of images and sounds into a kind of film symphony that showed the people of Britain what they were fighting for directly, without a word of commentary.

An idea of the enormous range of the sound-image mixture

of the cinema is obtained if we contrast Jennings with Georges Franju, who is as essentially French as Jennings is English. Both film-makers delight in the use of eye and ear, but whereas Jennings blends differing elements into a single whole (the idea of Britain), Franju bases his style on contrasts and divisions. In his first and perhaps most striking short film, *Le Sang des bêtes*, Franju shows the very ordinariness of a Paris suburb and then moves in to reveal the work of a slaughter house where in a matter of minutes a noble white horse is killed, skinned, gutted and carved up. Unlike Jennings, Franju has a basic distrust of authority and delighted in the days when he made documentaries (he is now a feature film-maker) in persuading official organizations to back films that attacked their own views. The best example of this is his film about the French War Museum, the *Hôtel des Invalides*. The film was sponsored by the military authorities but set out to attack what Franju sees as the false glory of Napoleon and the phoney glamour of war. Franju did this simply by the way in which he showed his material – there is not a word of direct preaching in the whole film. He kept his camera fixed on a very small bust of Napoleon while his elaborate praises were being sung, printed the words of a popular military song that all French schoolboys know, so as to bring home the meaning of the words, and used an image of a half-destroyed statue in such a way that it pointed up the whole horror of war. To underline his message he employed a wonderfully sensitive musical score by Maurice Jarre in place of a commentary.

We have mentioned only a few of the many ways in which documentary methods can be applied to films. What all documentarists do have in common is that they set out from the actual subject matter – be it a primitive community or a new socialist society, the sights and sounds of Britain or the French War Museum – and try to extract from this the ideas they wish to put across. In this way any documentary can be measured against something outside the film, if not the literal subject, then at least the idea that this represents. That is to say, if Flaherty chooses to make a film about man's basic struggle against the sea and sets it in the Aran Islands, it does not have to show what literally happens there in the year of filming (1934) but it does have to agree with what we learn about the struggles of primitive societies from other sources. It is fair to ask of a documentary film-maker whether he has been true to his subject and whether his film reflects the issues it raises truthfully. This is the basic difference between the documentary and the story film. Makers of fictional films may begin with similar ideas to express but they are free to shape and alter what they tell to suit the needs of the story. Of a fiction film we cannot ask whether it is true to facts and circumstances outside itself, but only whether it creates a convincing make-believe. Nowadays, for various reasons the documentary is becoming less of a form of cinema and more a genre of television. There are some very big advantages in this shift – 16 mm. film can be used and this means that the filming can be freer and more personal. But whether on the cinema or the television screen documentary is essentially the same: it serves the double purpose of informing us about the world around us and making us widen our responses to it.

6

Stroheim and the Realist Fiction Film

The extent to which the cinema is an international art is immediately clear if we consider those fiction films which try to picture life as realistically as possible. The urge to show life as it is is as old as the cinema itself, but it was not until D. W. Griffith that the cinema developed a camera style which, by breaking the scenes into shots, allowed the camera to probe into life and give an adequately complex picture of it. Already here we come to one of the contradictions of the realistic film: a single long shot of an action really happening often gives less of the real feel of the event than a series of shots from carefully chosen angles and from varying distances. The usefulness of the first method is limited to stunts which we would otherwise think were false (some of Buster Keaton's more amazing feats, for example) or events which happen only once and have some interest in their own right (a procession recorded for a newsreel, etc). The story film, on the other hand, uses the second method, that is to say, however realistic a film is intended to be, it does not simply record reality, it rebuilds it. Events have to be staged several times, so that the parts can be filmed from the appropriate angle, and the pieces, which were perhaps shot over a period of days, must be put together again, to give the illusion of one single happening.

Griffith was interested in both operations – the attempt to picture life as accurately as possibly and the fragmentation of events – but later film-makers often laid more emphasis on either one or the other. In this way it is possible to pick out two separate strands of cinema. The one – that followed by the Russian Sergei Eisenstein and many others – placed the stress on the way shots are joined together. Eisenstein soon discovered that if you put two shots together they create something new which is not just the sum of their parts. He explained this by pointing out that in Japanese writing more complicated ideas are built by putting two simple ones together: water + eye = weep; dog + mouth = bark; knife + heart = sorrow, and so on. He felt that the editing of the film (what he called *montage*) was the key stage because it allowed such a process to occur. As a simple example we might take the lions in *Battleship Potemkin*. While he was shooting the scenes of the massacre on the Odessa steps (one of the most famous sequences in film history) Eisenstein also photographed three stone lions, one lying, one sitting, one roaring. Edited together in the film they show a single lion coming to life and conveyed the idea of protest – with an emotional meaning something like 'Even the very stones cried out'. In the 1920s Eisenstein built his films around such links (and of course more complicated ones) yet he also used real settings, took as his actors amateurs whose faces looked right and made stories about the groups who created the revolution. The method is a very valid one and finds echoes in both the British documentary cinema and also in the sharp and startling editing of many exciting thrillers, but what we generally think of as realistic cinema develops in a very different way.

The most striking example of realism in the 1920s, and a work to set alongside *Battleship Potemkin* as a screen masterpiece, is Erich von Stroheim's *Greed*. Stroheim, one of the most remarkable figures in film history, is the direct heir of D. W. Griffith, having served as assistant director and bit player on both *The Birth of a Nation* and *Intolerance*. In Griffith's *Hearts of the World* and a number of lesser films in 1917 he first created for himself the role of Prussian officer – 'the man you love to hate' – which he perfected in his first three films as a director, *Blind Husbands* (1918), *The Devil's Pass Key* (1919)

and *Foolish Wives* (1920). Stroheim's debut was a most striking one. Not only did he direct these films for Universal, he also
wrote the script and dominated the screen in the role of an
unscrupulous officer attempting to seduce another man's young
and frivolous wife. Stroheim's immensely detailed characterization of the officer figure – immaculate in dress, de-
portment and gesture – was so striking that all kinds of tales,
many of them fostered by the director himself, grew up about
his Viennese background. He was said to be son of a colonel in
the dragoons and a lady-in-waiting to the Empress and himself
to have been commissioned as a cavalry officer at the age of
seventeen. In fact, he was the son of a Jewish merchant and
hat-maker and his military career (as a private!) seems to have
come to a speedy and ignominious end. The image, however,
was one that Stroheim preserved, on screen and off, for over
forty years and the fictitious 'von' became his nickname. As
early as *Foolish Wives* the pattern of his career was clearly
apparent. He had already begun to assemble his team of favoured
actors and actresses, run into trouble with censors over the
content of his work and with producers over its length. His
next film, *Merry-Go-Round* (1922), set in Vienna and with the
customary Stroheim theme of a love affair between a nobleman
and a beautiful commoner, was an even stronger anticipation
of the troubles that were to dog *Greed* the following year, in
that he was taken off the film half-way through the shooting.

The story of *Greed* (1923) itself is one worth recounting at
some length, for it highlights the problems of the realist film-
maker in the commercial cinema. An adaptation of the Frank
Norris novel *McTeague*, *Greed* was made for Sam Goldwyn's
company, but without any close studio supervision, the director acting as his own producer. Unfortunately for Stroheim, by
the time his film was finished the Goldwyn company had been
merged with others to form Metro-Goldwyn-Mayer, and he
found himself confronted with an unsympathetic production
team. One can understand the difficulties of Louis B. Mayer and
Irving Thalberg when faced with a forty-two reel film with little
or no obvious audience appeal. The outcome was inevitable –

Stroheim's masterpiece was cut down to a quarter of its length (a mere ten reels but still two-and-a-half hours of screen time), and his reputation as an extravagant and unmanageable artist was firmly established. The abridgement was accomplished by removing all but seven minutes of the two-and-a-half-hour prologue totally invented by Stroheim and tracing in detail the hero's antecedents. All the subplots used to parallel and highlight the main action were also deleted, together with all the symbolic episodes and much of the characteristic Stroheim grotesque exaggeration. What was left was the film's major narrative line – the doomed relationship of McTeague and his wife Trina – complete and in its natural sequence, but with its rhythm destroyed by numerous cuts and its delicacy spoiled by the crude titles often used to gloss over the gaps.

What is most remarkable today is the power of *Greed* even in its mutilated form. Its scope still extends from McTeague's upbringing by an alcoholic father in a remote mining town in the Californian mountains to the final confrontation between Mac and his onetime friend Marcus in the heat of Death Valley. The core of the film, as of the novel, is McTeague's rise and fall in San Francisco. At first he prospers, falls in love and marries. But already the seeds of his downfall are set. Trina wins $5,000 in a lottery, thereby arousing the jealousy of her cousin, and Mac's friend, Marcus. All continues well until Mac loses his job (he is an unqualified dentist). He then declines into drink and violence, while Trina becomes more and more obsessed with her money. Though they live in total poverty, she refuses to spend her lottery win or to offer Mac any support. Finally he murders her, takes the money and sets off on his travels. But Nemesis catches up with him in the form of Marcus, and the last sequence of the film shows him after the final confrontation: handcuffed to the dead body of the other man, lost in the vastness of the desert.

What protected Stroheim's film from total dismemberment was his method of developing his scenes not by a mass of tiny shots but in long takes with a wealth of detail crammed into each shot. The editors, therefore, when they came to shorten the film, left the major sequences largely intact, though sometimes trimmed at the beginning and end. In these sequences the mastery of Stroheim is always apparent. From Gibson Gowland and Zasu Pitts he extracted splendid performances ranging in mood from a tender excursion and first kiss (by, of all things, a sewage outlet) to the eventual murder amid the tinsel of Christmas decorations. Stroheim makes the whole image come to life. He organizes the actions of his characters in depth and, instead of intercutting contrasting events as Griffith was wont to do, he combines the two in a single expressive image, as when a funeral passes in the background, seen through the window, in the scene where Mac and Trina are married. His use of settings is remarkably modern. Refusing the easy option of studio settings, Stroheim took his actors out into the real locations, shooting the finale, for instance, in very difficult conditions in Death Valley itself. The house where Mac and Trina spend most of their married life was recreated in San Francisco from the descriptions contained in Norris's novel with total fidelity to detail. In its present pared-down form *Greed* has few immediate similarities with the rest of Stroheim's work. It lacks the decadent aristocratic atmosphere, the obsession with class barriers and the officer code, the paralleling of main action and subplot. But it does show the same ruthless dissection of human behaviour and relentless working out of the action from its given premisses. Like Frank Norris in the original novel, Stroheim shows himself to be the heir of Zola's naturalism, basing his work on the accumulation of a mass of objectively observed detail and depicting characters at the mercy of powerful and primitive emotions.

Despite the failure of *Greed*, M-G-M gave Stroheim a new directorial assignment, *The Merry Widow* (1925), the first of a trio of Stroheim films – the others are *The Wedding March* (1926–7) and *Queen Kelly* (1928) – depicting themes of romance and misalliance in a basically Ruritanian setting. In all three Stroheim was working against studio pressures, unable to make the enormously long films of which he dreamed and working with imposed themes and actors. He managed, nevertheless, to win for himself a considerable freedom in his choice of minor players, in the elaboration of scenes of degradation and grotesqueness and in the way he re-shaped basic plot structures. Indeed, in *The Merry Widow* Stroheim's invented prologue to the operetta story takes up two thirds of the screen time.

However, Stroheim's lack of real commercial success and the myth of the extravagant, untameable artist brought him under fire from producers. After the coming of sound he directed only one more film, *Walking down Broadway*, in 1932, which was not released because of a studio upheaval. Forced to work simply as a screenwriter and actor, Stroheim sought a new career in France. This led to one memorable role, that of von Rauffenstein in *La Grande Illusion* (1937), directed by Jean Renoir, who had been deeply influenced by his early work. But mostly he had to act in totally mediocre films, and, when he planned to direct another film, his project, *La Dame Blanche*, was abandoned because of the outbreak of war. The last decade of his life was the most barren artistically, with only one notable part, that of the old and forgotten film director, Max von Mayerling, in Billy Wilder's drama of Hollywood, *Sunset Boulevard* (1950), which looked back explicitly to his last Hollywood film, *Queen Kelly*. Stroheim, like Welles and Chaplin, is one of those film artists incompatible with the Hollywood system. His work and career are monumental but fragmentary and his work full of questions and contradictions. But with *Greed* he demonstrated the ability of silent cinema to equal the naturalist novel in scope and intensity.

7

Renoir's Poetic Realism

In the 1930s the man who took up and developed to its fullest the Stroheim tradition was the Frenchman Jean Renoir, the son of the great Impressionist painter. The 1930s were a very rich and decisive period in the history of the French cinema. The sound era got off to a brilliant start with René Clair's comedies – most notably *Sous les toits de Paris*, *Le Million* and *A Nous la liberté*. For two brief years, while Clair's inspiration was beginning to flag, Jean Vigo produced dazzling works – *Zéro de conduite* and *L'Atalante* – which distressed contemporary censors and distributors, but which today still retain a striking impact. When the death of Vigo in 1934 and Clair's departure for England (and ultimately Hollywood) in 1935 coincided with a production crisis of unusual severity, it seemed that the French cinema was doomed to inglorious extinction. But out of the ruins was born a new golden age of film-making and a new filmic style made up of almost equal doses of Jean Gabin gloom and Popular Front idealism. The veteran Jacques Feyder returned from the USA to give French directors a lesson in sheer professionalism with *La Kermesse héroïque*. Another experienced director, Julien Duvivier, reached heights he has never since equalled with a trio of films starring Gabin: *La Bandéra*, *La Belle Équipe* and *Pépé-le-Moko*. Feyder's young assistant, Marcel Carné, made a feature debut with *Jenny* in 1936 and, before reaching the age of thirty, he had directed a succession of works that stand comparison with those of any film-maker of a similar age: *Drôle de drame*, *Quai des brumes*, *Hôtel du Nord* and *Le Jour se lève*.

Yet amid this wealth of talent, which was decisively to affect film-making in both France and Italy for years to come, there was only one man who produced masterworks throughout the decade – Jean Renoir. Between 1930 and 1939 he made no less than fifteen films of very varying kinds, all of them profoundly linked to the mood and ambitions of the French nation. Renoir was not a hermetic artist, pursuing a course independent of the pressures and fashions of the moment. His work was almost always precisely related to its social and economic context and yet it was, at the same time, shot through with a vein of poetry. Realism and poetry – in their varying interpretations and differing combinations – are the essential elements of any analysis of Renoir's contribution to film-making in the period up to the outbreak of war, which disrupted production and drove many French film-makers, including Renoir, into exile.

The range of Renoir's poetic realism is enormous, even if only his films of the 1930s are taken into consideration. At one extreme there is the sober realism of *Toni* (1934), a film made on location, without stars and based on real-life events. *Toni* stands centrally in the realist tradition of world cinema. It recalls the silent work of Erich von Stroheim in the 1920s and anticipates many aspects of the Italian neo-realism of the 1940s, particularly Luchino Visconti's *Ossessione*, made in 1942. Like this latter work, and unlike most other neo-realist masterpieces, *Toni* is essentially a timeless film. It is not linked to any specific social conditions in the France of 1934 (the actual events on which it was based had occurred some twelve years before) and, though the hero is an Italian migrant worker, the pattern of the film would be little changed if he were, say, a French peasant. The visual style of *Toni* shows Renoir at his most restrained. The unemphatic shooting and deliberate refusal to build up scenes dramatically give it a news-reel quality which is totally in keeping with the director's neutral acceptance of the characters' emotions, needs and be-trayals. If one seeks analogies outside the cinema for a work like *Toni*, it is inevitably to French naturalism that one turns. The naturalist tradition in literature had a strong influence on Renoir. He adapted novels by Zola to make *Nana* in 1926 and *La Bête humaine* in 1938, and also filmed versions of a Maupassant story and the soberly realist Flaubert novel *Madame Bovary*. The Maupassant adaptation – Renoir's beautiful forty-five minute film, *Une Partie de campagne* (1936) – also reveals another aspect of the director's realism, namely the desire to recapture the snap-shot quality of the great Impressionist painters. As a result, the film, instead of being a sombre document on the sorrows of love, is imbued with the whole atmosphere of Auguste Renoir's art.

An even stronger counterbalance to a possible documentary impulse in Renoir is his profound love of the theatre, which was later to culminate in the reflections on the relationship of life and art contained in *The Golden Coach* made in 1952. Several of Renoir's early sound films of 1931–3 were in fact based on stage plays: *On purge Bébé, Boudu sauvé des eaux* and *Chotard et Cie*. What one might call the charade aspect is constant throughout the 1930s. As examples one might cite the puppet-play prologue of *La Chienne*, the amateur dramatics of *La Grande Illusion* and *La Règle du jeu*, as well as, perhaps: the court etiquette scenes of *La Marseillaise*. More important still, it would be possible to argue that Renoir's conception of a society rigidly structured so as to separate masters and servants, officers and men, is derived less from a Marxist analysis of the world than from the basic pattern of French classical drama. This is certainly true of *La Règle du jeu* (1939), for which Renoir prepared himself by re-reading eighteenth- and nineteenth-century stage classics and in which Lisette, for instance, is far more the theatrical soubrette than the representative of a politically unenlightened proletariat. After films like *La Bête humaine* and *Les Bas-Fonds*, both of which starred Jean Gabin, Renoir was here trying to get away from naturalism and discover a more poetic style. This he found especially in the plays of the eighteenth-century dramatist, Marivaux, whose work seemed to him to be half-way between poetry and realism.

Renoir's use of actors follows the same tendency. He is at the very opposite pole to the neo-realists who conceived a character first and then sought a person with the appropriate face and physique, regarding the latter as far more important than acting experience. Renoir always uses actors – even *Toni* contains professionals like Blavette and Delmont in the leading roles – and he builds the character around the personality of the actor who is to play it. For him, actors are the co-authors of a film and he could never conceive of scripting a film before he knew who would play the roles in it. As a result his career has been marked by a number of successful collaborations with actors. In the 1930s he worked successively with Michel Simon, with his own brother Pierre, and with Jean Gabin, the most prominent French star of the late 1930s. Even *Une Partie de campagne*, his Maupassant adaptation shot in settings painted by his father, was originally conceived not as a homage to Auguste, but as a pretext for working with the leading actress, Sylvia Bataille.

The late 1930s are also marked by Renoir's own most sustained efforts to become an actor. He appeared in *Une Partie de campagne* and *La Bête humaine* before taking the crucial role of Octave in *La Règle du jeu*. Sometimes Renoir's enthusiasm for actors and acting betrays him. His own performance is one of the weakest aspects of *La Règle du jeu*, and the evolution undergone by this film in the course of its making shows how fleeting his responses to particular actors and actresses could be and how radically they could alter the balance of a film. But at best a great actor can have a decisive effect on a film and give it a new dimension. It is this concern with actors rather than any theoretical preconception that gives Renoir's work in the 1930s its predominant photographic style: the tendency to use lengthy shots and to work with several cameras at once. The use of deep focus is systematic, as the camera continually tracks to and fro to follow the characters and to frame them, as they group and regroup, or relate themselves to the setting in which they find themselves.

The particular tension of Renoir's style comes precisely from the way in which this involvement with the actors is set against a mature detachment from the character and his problems. While he indulges his players, Renoir manipulates his characters like puppets, leading them often through the sexual equivalent of a game of musical chairs. His detachment is remarkable. He is incapable of taking sides against any class or nationality, just as he could not conceivably impose a rigid morality on his characters. These latter are caught up in conflicting and overlapping relationships that give rise to the peculiar mixture of farce and seriousness which is the typical tone of a Renoir film. They exist on a number of levels, being part symbols, part marionettes and part characters in a conventional sense, but above all they are human beings who exist in a social context but whose behaviour, however outrageous, is never prejudged. Occasionally Renoir's sense of detachment becomes almost inhuman, but in general his universal acceptance is benevolent and beneficient, allowing him to show great insight into the strange alliances and divisions present whenever a group of people interact. The Royalists and Republicans of *La Marseillaise* are separated by little more than a misunderstanding and a different relationship to the forces of history. As Renoir admits in one of his films, everyone has such good, such convincing reasons. So it was that, despite a left-wing commitment that impelled him to make *La Vie est à nous* for the Communist Party in 1936, he was still able to draw a sympathetic portrait of two ageing aristocratic reactionaries (Erich von Stroheim and Pierre Fresnay) in *La Grande Illusion*, made the very next year.

Renoir's lack of stereotyped preconceptions and responses is nowhere more apparent than in his permeability to events. As his studies of human behaviour realistically capture the ambiguities of love, so his films of the 1930s reflect only too accurately the confused mixture of idealism, patriotism and social concern that typifies the period. Though many of the films are comparatively timeless – *Madame Bovary*, for example, owes little to the specific atmosphere of 1934 – one can nevertheless trace the evolving mood of the 1930s through a succession of films directly linked to current issues. *Boudu sauvé des eaux* (1932) reflects the carefree anarchist atmosphere of the early 1930s. The figure of the tramp and the irresponsible evasion at the end recall the world of René Clair's *A Nous la liberté* made the previous year, while Michel Simon's performance in the title role anticipates some aspects of the part he plays in Jean Vigo's *L'Atalante*. With Vigo's other masterpiece, *Zéro de conduite*, Renoir's film shares a sense of anarchist poetry and a stress on the individual's need to pursue his own life regardless of social pressures. *Toni* (1934), with its story of migrant workers, shows an increasing concern with social questions. This is developed in *Le Crime de Monsieur Lange* (1935) which is very much a study of a group, with no real individual heroes. The film's true scope is better conveyed by its original title: *On the Courtyard*. It was made in collaboration with the writer Jacques Prévert, who was at this time very much engaged with the October group, a left-wing theatre group which had gone on a tour of Moscow and Leningrad the previous year. Caught up in the atmosphere of 1935, the highwater mark of the Popular Front unity of Socialists and Communists, and using many actors associated with the October group, Renoir found himself involved in political matters without having consciously engaged himself. In the following year he made *La Vie est à nous*, although not himself a member of the Communist Party.

Several of Renoir's later films bear the mark of his involvement in politics. *La Marseillaise* (1938) finally emerged as a conventionally produced film, but it was originally planned as a work to be financed by public subscription, the first experiment of a film for the people and by the people, as the advance publicity put it. In fact the finished work is marked by the same kind of ambiguity that characterizes *La Grande Illusion* (1937). Revolution-filled Paris and the prison camp at Winterborn are both depicted as places where good humour and comradeship reign and all good men are moved by high-minded patriotism and a sense of self-sacrifice. These two films are also essentially backward-looking: *La Marseillaise* deals with the revolution of 1789, not the upheavals of the 1930s, while *La Grande Illusion* treats war in the rosy terms of the 1914 cavalry officer instead of facing the new threat of rising Nazi power. *La Règle du jeu*, perhaps because it attempts less explicit comment, is in fact a far more lucid analysis of the time in which it was shot. During the months that separated Munich from the outbreak of war, Renoir felt troubled by the state of mind of a part of French society and world society. The resulting film proves how right he was to feel that one way of reflecting this situation was to tell what, on the surface, is a totally frivolous tale.

In their production methods Renoir's films of the 1930s have marked similarities to many of the freer works of the late 1950s whose directors admired his *œuvre* and listened so intently to his views on art and life. The films show an amazing openness to life. Many sequences were improvised – *Une Partie de campagne*, for instance, was shot with a minimal script. *La Règle du jeu*, for which he was producer, director, scriptwriter and actor, is a perfect example of the extent to which a film can be the product of a single man. It was shot in conditions of total freedom and virtually made up as the shooting progressed. Though he worked with the two principal scriptwriters of the French 1930s cinema – with Jacques Prévert on *Le Crime de Monsieur Lange* and with Charles Spaak on *Les Bas-Fonds* and *La Grande Illusion* – Renoir was never at the mercy of other people's ideas. He was quite capable of scripting and dialoguing a film by himself, and his work is free from the rigidity that one finds, for example, in some of the films of Marcel Carné at this time. Nevertheless, Renoir's films from *On purge bébé* to *La Règle du jeu* are within the 1930s style of realism in that all the major points are made explicit through the dialogue. This was perhaps the least liberating effect of his concern with the theatre: even *La Règle du jeu* is built on this kind of pattern and, though the script was partly improvised, the images are seldom allowed to speak for themselves.

Renoir's films of the 1930s are very much a product of their age. If in some ways, such as the use of improvisation and deep focus, they anticipate later developments, in others – such as narrative structure and reliance on dialogue – they belong to their period. One thing these films have in common is their basic realist framework. Renoir never indulges in pure fantasy, being content to view the individual in a normal social context. What is most remarkable about this realism today is what one might call its magical aspect, which stems from the quality of the observation rather than from any kind of conscious poeticizing. Renoir's films are those of a man who knows how to leave reality to tell its own story, a man who can reveal life without recourse to flat naturalism and create a sense of mystery without ever leaving the domain of the everyday.

8

Rossellini and Neo-Realism

It was only with the Second World War that realism became the dominant mode of the cinema. There are all sorts of reasons for this re-emergence of an idea known for so many years. The war forced directors to leave the closed world of the studios and make newsreels and documentaries as part of the war effort (the effect of this was most striking on Hollywood directors). In Europe studios and expensive equipment were destroyed and those who wanted to continue film-making had to use real backgrounds and a simple style. They could not choose elaborate patterns of film-making because even the film stock on which they shot their films was often old and scrappy. The results possible with these poor means were particularly apparent in Italy and it is to an Italian, Roberto Rossellini, that we shall turn for our main example of the idea of post-war realism in practice. But the Italians were by no means alone. In Japan there were men like Akira Kurosawa and Yashiro Ozu who made films about the lives of ordinary people, and a little later India produced a great film-maker in Satyajit Ray, who began with a trilogy of films about the growing up of a little boy called Apu.

The Italian post-war film movement – usually known as neo-realism – burst on the scene with a film by Rossellini called *Rome Open City* in which the director drew on his experiences of the immediate past. Italy had been dragged, reluctantly, into the war by the ambitions of the dictator Benito Mussolini, who thought that Germany was going to win and wanted to get a share of the spoils. But quickly the tide of war had turned, Germany began to lose, Rome was bombed and Sicily invaded. Mussolini lost the support of his own Fascist council, was deposed and then restored as a puppet ruler by the Germans. In the course of these events the country was plunged into complete turmoil and now there were two battles in Italy — the big one between the Germans and the allied armies and the more personal one between the partisans and the Fascist supporters of Mussolini. It was out of this confusion that neo-realism was born. The dictator had fed the people with slogans and deceitful phrases; the film-makers aimed to tell the unvarnished truth. He had had vast projects like the setting up of a new Roman Empire; they were concerned with the problems of ordinary people. He had left Italy defeated, humiliated, torn by civil war; they looked for hope in the things around them.

All of this is apparent in *Rome Open City*. The film captures the last days of the German occupation of Rome so well that when it was first shown abroad many critics thought it must have been made with hidden cameras while the Germans were still there. The battle-cry of the neo-realist film-makers was 'Take the camera out into the streets', and this is just what Rossellini did. Most films create an imaginary geography for themselves out of various different settings and places. This is a perfectly valid way of creating illusions but it was not good enough for Rossellini, who wanted the truth. He made *Rome Open City* one of the rare examples of a film which keeps exactly to the correct streets and directions of the city in which it was filmed. The director was working with people who had lived through the German Occupation and fought with the resistance movement and he made use of their adventures. The flat in which much of the early action takes place was that of the scriptwriter who had many times had to escape from the Germans over the rooftops as the film hero does. The shooting of a woman in the street by the SS had been witnessed by one of the actors, and so on. The story was a simple one, but had a real appeal to people who had just lived through similar events to those shown on the screen. In the film, a Communist resistance leader is on the run from the Germans. For a while he manages to escape them but the net tightens. When he is finally betrayed he has also unwittingly given away the identities of several other resistance men, including a Catholic priest. The scenes of the fighting and torture look real, as real as newsreels. But the film is not all grim and serious, for there are several scenes featuring little boys who fight the Germans with bombs at dusk, then run home to their parents who smack them for staying out so late, not suspecting the real reasons for this.

After concentrating in this film on a single group of characters, Rossellini next turned to a wider subject and, in a film called *Paisà* (the Americans' slang expression for the Italians), he followed the course of the allied invasion from Sicily and Naples, through Rome, Florence and the Apennines to the Po valley in the North. He made his film out of six separate episodes, each built on the contrast of people from different backgrounds thrown together by the war, the Americans and the Italians. In one episode a Negro military policeman comes face to face with a Neapolitan urchin who steals his boots and cheats him. But his indignation disappears when he discovers that the boy is a war orphan living in squalor in caves outside Naples. In another episode, set in the Apennine mountains, a group of Catholic monks entertain three army chaplains. All goes well until they find out that one of the chaplains is a Jew and another a Protestant. Then they are filled with horror and try to convert them to the 'true' faith. Though the incidents which provide the six stories are vivid ones, often showing death and suffering, Rossellini's film was for him, and for his fellow workers on it, a rediscovery of Italy. In making it they travelled from one end of the country to the other and Rossellini showed himself more interested in the ordinary little actions of life than in big heroic ones. The invasion of Sicily, for instance, was one of the biggest military operations of the war and a major step in the defeat of Hitler, but the director shows only an explosion or two and a burning house, using these as a background for a story about a dozen GIs and their

Italian guide. This is all he needs to make a statement about the horrors of war.

In 1947 Rossellini completed his trilogy of films about war with *Germania anno zero*, about the state of Germany at the end of the war when life had to start again from nothing. It is the story of a twelve-year-old boy, Edmund, who has been brought up in Nazi schools and taught to believe lies about the master race and the need to be merciless to the weak. He kills his ailing father to put him out of his misery, then realizes what he has done. The finest section of the film follows his wandering through the ruins of Berlin. We see from his ordinary actions the way he is still partly a child, partly an adult with a crime on his conscience. In a ruined house he plays at suicide with a gun-shaped stone, then plunges to his death by leaping from a window. Rossellini shows what meaning can be got from a boy kicking a stone or walking on the cracks in the pavement, and how simply showing these things can reveal a lot more than dialogue or explanations in words. In his later career Rossellini made all kinds of films: an affectionate portrait of St Francis, some studies of tormented women starring his wife Ingrid Bergman, films about Italian history and Louis XIV of France. But all his best work has a remarkable directness: it puts us face to face with the situations and people concerned.

Rossellini is not the only realist film-maker in Italy in the 1940s but he is the one who is closest to a direct, documentary-style rendering of life. He never used a script, avoided studios wherever possible and, when he needed actors for the background parts, he just set up his camera in the road, waited for a crowd to gather and then chose his players from among the bystanders. Many of the ideas of Rossellini were shared by his fellow directors. They all tended to make films out of incidents drawn from life, items recorded briefly in the newspapers or happenings too small to merit even a mention. In this way, Vittorio de Sica made a film about what happens to a bill-poster when he loses his bicycle (*Bicycle Thieves*); Luchino Visconti told the story of a fisherman who tried to set up on his own to avoid being cheated by the wholesalers who buy his catch (*La terra trema*), and Giuseppe de Santis filmed a version of a real-life incident in which a staircase collapsed under the weight of two hundred girls who had all applied for the same job (*Rome Eleven O'Clock*). There were also films to be made about the more violent happenings in the years after the war: the story of a collective farm robbed of its money (de Santis's *Tragic Pursuit*) or a man driven to crime when he returns from the war to find his family dead and his home destroyed (Alberto Lattuada's *The Bandit*).

But always they were concerned with the way people fit together in society – a man with his family, his job, his friends. The problems were often just the lack of money with which to live decently. Generally speaking the film-makers themselves were not working-class (Visconti indeed is an aristocrat) but they made their films on small budgets with little money to pay for stars or studio settings. The stories were usually simple ones with no flashbacks in time and no spectacular scenes. The lighting was equally simple and, because they often used people who had never acted before, the directors used medium and long shots showing the characters going about their work or mixing with other people, not close-ups to probe their faces. This is not to say that neo-realism in Italy did not give us memorable portraits. Few who have seen the films will forget the dignified old-age pensioner whose only friend is his dog in de Sica's *Umberto D*, the two young people who want to get married in Renato Castellani's *Two Pennyworth of Hope* or the forceful woman of the people, played by Anna Magnani, in Luigi Zampa's *Angelina MP*. The Italian directors as a group were much more concerned with individuals than with social problems in the abstract, and in their best films they did not adopt any sort of party political line. *Rome Open City* set the pattern when it showed a Communist party worker and a Catholic priest as being equally sympathetic characters, each with a very worthwhile contribution to make. But what all the best neo-realist films did do was to issue a challenge. Most of them did not have a real ending. In a sense we are made to feel that life is going on and that the situations in which the characters have found themselves are going to be repeated. Unless, that is, we the audience do something about it. Several of the film-makers of the period made films about the South, one of the most wretched parts of Europe, backward and poverty-stricken. But the real value of films like those of Pietro Germi about Sicily, for instance, is not that they opened the way for other films of the same kind, but that they made people throughout Italy aware of the problems. As a sort of superior journalism, they helped to bring about the new laws and reconstruction programmes designed to help the people of the South which were passed by the Italian parliament in the 1950s.

The movement known as Italian neo-realism lasted only a half-dozen years or so, and all its best achievements lie between *Rome Open City* in 1945 and *Umberto D* in 1951. At first sight this seems a very short time, but in fact none of the movements in film history that we remember lasted much longer. This is true of the Swedish films set in natural surroundings that enchanted world audiences before the First World War, the German Expressionist films (all shadows and monsters and dark secrets) of 1920–27 and the Soviet revolutionary cinema of 1925–30 which showed the triumphant building of a new society in Russia. In literature movements may last a whole century, but with the cinema the pace is much quicker. Yet it is certainly true that within its brief time-spell the neo-realist cinema in Italy did pose all the key questions of a realist fictional cinema.

9

Cinéma-Vérité

Virtually all realist film-making during the first thirty years of sound – in both fiction and documentary – involved a reconstructing or restaging of reality. Film-makers studied their subjects, sometimes researching them in depth, but then organized the material themselves for the actual filming. Neo-realism in Italy used non-professional actors, but they always portrayed characters created by the director and his writers. Lamberto Maggiorani, for example, was a worker from the Breda factory, and his face and gestures – so different from those of a professional actor – add much to the power of Vittorio de Sica's *Bicycle Thieves*. But this film does not tell his story – he plays a fictional character, a bill-poster called Antonio, and acts out situations which had already been devised before he first met de Sica. Some of the leading figures of the neo-realist movement, especially the scriptwriter Cesare Zavattini, wanted to move beyond this kind of realism and have non-professionals portray their own stories. In one film called *Love in the City*, Zavattini managed to do this, but this development was never followed up in Italy. It was not until the 1960s that realist film-makers gave real thought to the possibilities of looking directly at unstaged reality, at situations, that is to say, which unfolded as the filming proceeded.

The roots of this new approach are to be found not in Italy but in the United States, in France and in Canada, and to find equivalents for it one has to go back to the pioneer work of Dziga Vertov in Soviet Russia. It is not by chance, therefore, that this form of cinema became known as *cinéma-vérité*, a literal translation of Vertov's watchword, *Kino-Pravda* (Cinema-truth). There were some other links with the past, too, but these take the form of a reaction against earlier documentary film-making methods. Richard Leacock, for example, a key figure in *cinéma-vérité* in the United States, had been deeply influenced by his work as cameraman on Robert Flaherty's last film, *Louisiana Story*, in 1948. But his own work is largely a refutation of the approach of Flaherty, who typifies the attitudes and methods of the older film documentarists in that he always worked in 35 mm., restaged for the camera those scenes he wished to record, and in general placed the emphasis squarely on the visuals, with the subsequently compiled sound track playing only a subordinate part. The importance of Leacock and his collaborators is that they questioned each of these premises and in so doing gave new definitions to concepts like realism and spectacle and a new role to the participants in the particular drama which they had set out to record with their cameras. In part they could do this because they had found a new outlet for their work, the television screen.

Toby, Leacock's first film for television, made in 1955 when he was thirty-four, was about a travelling circus in the American Mid-West and was filmed with methods not all that different from those of Flaherty. Though not totally successful, it aroused the interest of Robert Drew, a journalist from *Life* magazine who was currently doing research into new methods of reporting under the sponsorship of Time Inc. With Drew as his producer, Leacock was able to shed the desire to make 'artistic' films and see himself rather as a new kind of journalist. To Drew television reporting seemed basically a word story illustrated with pictures and he was very much in agreement with Leacock about the need to develop new lightweight equipment for film-making. Through his association with Time Inc., Drew was able to help finance Leacock's experiments in devising equipment that would allow the film-maker to move

freely without lights, tripods, wires and so on. As a group of
enthusiasts – including Morris Engel, Don Pennebaker and the
Maysles brothers – gradually formed, Drew's ambition of fifty-
two one-hour television films a year seemed increasingly feas-
ible.

Fundamental to the whole notion of *cinéma-vérité* was
the rejection of traditional but cumbersome 35mm. format in
favour of 16 mm. (which was already widely used by underground film-makers). This implied a certain loss of picture
quality, but this was more than compensated for by the reduced cost and the vastly improved prospects of developing a
really light-weight camera that could be handled by a single
cameraman. An equal priority for Leacock was the creation
of portable and manoeuvrable sound recording equipment
capable of providing a synchronous sound track. In Leacock's
view, the whole power of the spontaneously captured images
would be lost if dialogue had to be dubbed on afterwards (as
was the custom in Italy, even during the neo-realist period).
When the kind of equipment he envisaged was at hand, the
two-man film team – one holding the camera and the other
working the tape recorder – became a reality. There was now
no need to re-stage events for the camera – the team could
follow their subject from room to room, up stairs and through
doorways, even into his car, capturing sound and images simultaneously. The film-maker was thus placed in a potentially very
fruitful but also quite delicate situation. He relinquished his
role as director of the action, for if he tried to influence events,
he would obtain only false reactions and responses, reflecting
his own presence and not the natural inclinations of his subject.
If, on the other hand, he tried to be invisible – using a concealed
camera, for instance – he was likely to become, and be regarded
as, an intruder and be excluded from the crucial moments of
the situation he was recording.

Leacock's refusal to create artificial drama with acting and
scripts does imply a certain limitation of subject matter for the
cinéma-vérité film, in that situations containing a great
deal of natural drama are needed. Thus Leacock's films tend to
be about real conflict or struggle of some kind, and situations

which do not have their own natural drama are ignored. The first successful film of the Drew-Leacock team, *Primary*, is typical. Made with two frequent collaborators of Leacock, Al Maysles and Don Pennebaker, it recorded the election conflict of John Kennedy and Hubert Humphrey in Wisconsin in 1960, capturing such moments as the candidates picking up a telephone to learn the result. The team followed this with films about a racing driver (*Eddie Sachs at Minneapolis*), about the actress Jane Fonda opening in a play that turned out to be a flop (*Jane*), and about the efforts of a young man to fight his urge to leave a rehabilitation centre for drug addicts (*David*). In addition to the need for such eventful subject matter, filmmaking for Leacock also involved a special relationship with his subject and a new moral responsibility. When the first was lacking, as when, with Greg Shuker, he tried to make a film about Nehru, then the project in its original form simply had to be abandoned. During the shooting stage of his films Leacock had no real problems about the morality of what he was doing, since the complications of following the unpredictable movements of a subject engaged in activities which were not preplanned were sufficient to absorb the film-maker totally. But during the editing the need to produce from the mass of material shot a coherent, saleable film did set up certain conflicts. Occasionally Leacock was guilty of cheating, as in one of his most absorbing films, *The Chair*. This story is about the last appeal of a man condemned to the electric chair for murder and has a great simplicity and apparently natural drama. But much of the latter – the question: Will he or won't he be reprieved? – was contrived during the putting-together of the film after the verdict was known. Not only were a number of interesting sequences scrapped because they did not relate directly with this theme, Leacock's team even went out and shot missing scenes to help the film to fit this chosen interpretation of events a month after the court's decision was known.

As a method of working, Leacock's *cinéma-vérité* involves the rejection of the whole technical apparatus and hierarchy of the normal commercial cinema. There can be no assistants engaged on the production, since their presence would destroy the sense of intimacy still possible for the two-man team of cameraman and recordist. There can be no question of the film-makers simply handing over the material to an editor to piece together along with an indication of what they had set out to achieve, because the real value of the method is that it throws up events and incidents which could not have been foreseen but which of course totally colour the final result. As Leacock himself has admitted, in this kind of cinema every time you cut a section and put the remainder together, you are in fact telling a lie. For the film to be a true reflection of the situation recorded the film-maker must do his own editing. If one of the limitations of this approach is that, when the film-makers miss an interesting moment, there is no way (apart from cheating) in which they can go back and capture it, one of the style's great virtues is that the real subject of the film may not become known until the filming is over and the rushes can be viewed. *Nehru*, for example, turned out to be not a film about how the Indian premier won an election, but rather a study of the relationship of the film-maker and his subject.

Though Leacock's film-making is one of the more fascinating examples of *cinéma-vérité*, it is perhaps wrong to place too much weight on him as an individual figure. All his most important works have been made in collaboration, and in his more recent films – particularly the series of pop music films such as *Don't Look Back* and *Monterey Pop* made with Don Pennebaker – he has been content to act simply as a cameraman and to leave the overall creative responsibility to his partner. Moreover, it would be wrong to see his work outside the international context. In France, for instance, the early 1960s saw a great deal of similarly fascinating *cinéma-vérité* experiment. The key figure here was Jean Rouch, an ethnographer whose earliest films were simple records of tribal customs in Africa. Lacking any training in film techniques and devoid of all aesthetic concern, Rouch was free to concentrate on the impact of filming his subjects. From the first, his feature-length films show a desire to involve the characters in the making of the film. *Moi un noir* (1958), a study of an African stevedore, used the subject's reaction to Rouch's images as its commentary. *Chronicle of a Summer*, made with Edgar Morin a few years later, applied the sociologist's traditional mode of inquiry to the Parisian scene and was built around a series of interviews and confrontations. Thus, in contrast to Leacock, Rouch never tries to pretend that the camera is a mere observer. He sees it as conditioning the responses of the people filmed, and in films like *La Pyramide humaine*, set in a multi-racial African high school, and *La Punition*, shot on the streets of Paris, he shows an increasing interest in recording the results to be achieved from filming an improvised sequence which sets amateur players in situations which are fictional, but close to the circumstances of their own lives. In this way the *cinéma-vérité* film-maker's usual and dubious claims to an 'objective' statement are forgotten, but new forms of film drama are made possible.

Cinéma-vérité as envisaged by Leacock and Rouch has a restricted aim in that it can never conceivably do more than supplement normal cinema. It is not a total revolution in method applicable to all film-making. But it does serve to widen the range of reality open to the camera, by allowing it to record not the film-maker's assumptions as to what might have happened, but events and situations as they do actually take place.

10

Realist Film and
Television Realism

One of the central preoccupations of twentieth-century art has been to redefine the boundaries of the actual and the illusory. There are numerous examples of this that could be cited, from the cubists' first use of collage techniques right up to the pop artists' employment of the given idiom of the commercial, the strip cartoon and the advertising display. In this movement towards the real the cinema's role has most frequently been a somewhat paradoxical one. As a medium using photographic reproductions of reality in movement as its basic raw material, the cinema has undoubtedly helped to foster this realistic tendency of modern art. But film realists have in general turned their backs on the full implications of this and remained wedded to a basically nineteenth-century conception of realism. This backward-looking attitude is reflected in the approach of such film-makers to technical advances like colour, sound, wide screen, stereophonic sound and three-dimensional images. The realistic possibilities of these have largely been ignored and a realist film has been traditionally conceived as a technically restrained work in black and white with a post-synchronized dialogue and an emotive musical score. It took the advent of television to alter a conception of realism that held sway in the cinema from Lumière till the 1950s.

At the time when film-makers first faced up to the impact of television such an effect hardly seemed likely. Producers put their faith in the production values which film-makers had always seen as the prerogative of Hollywood and which television could then not equal. To a certain extent this polarization of film and television has persisted up to the present. Just as the invention of photography in the nineteenth century, by depriving the painter of sole claim to his traditional representational role, allowed – perhaps even compelled – him to turn to abstraction, so too television's fundamental naturalism has served to free the film image for new expressive functions. But the counter-current towards a synthesis of film and television has been equally strong. Part of the impetus behind this fusion has been economic, for, ironically enough, only a decade or so passed before the film companies struggling to maintain their solvency were endeavouring to sell their earlier 'ante-television' films to the television organizations. Equally, the increased use of colour in film-making in the 1970s stems less from audience demand or the requirements of film directors than from the imperatives dictated by the spread of colour television. The fact that, for television, 16 mm. film stock provides quite adequate images and even 8 mm. equipment can be used for some kinds of news reporting, has caused the validity of the traditional but costly 35 mm. cinema format to be increasingly questioned.

Stylistically too the impact of television has been considerable. The first real *rapprochement* came in the early 1960s with the *cinéma-vérité* movement, led by men like Rouch and Leacock, which was considered in the previous chapter. But more recently film-makers trained in the television studios have renewed the assault on traditional film assumptions. In particular, those directors who have sought to combine the naturalistic potential of the television form with the greater flexibility that film-making methods afford have modified our view of what a realist film is. Among those who have contributed most to this change, Peter Watkins and Kenneth Loach deserve particular mention. They were part of a group which came to the fore in British television in the mid 1960s. Watkins developed his style in two television films made at the BBC in 1964–5. The first of these, *Culloden*, was a

reconstruction of the 1746 battle between the English and the
Scots which finally destroyed Bonnie Prince Charlie's claim to
the throne. Unlike the traditional historical film it treated the
battle as if it were a real event at which the camera crews and
reporters happened to be present. Watkins used a newsreel style
– handheld cameras, jagged editing, uneven tracking shots –
calculated to play on the audience's associations with normal
news programmes. As a result the fact that this is a two-
hundred-year-old battle is forgotten and Culloden is experienced as a contemporary happening. The apparently casual
style is in fact a deliberately contrived one, for this, like all
Watkins's films, was fully pre-scripted, for all its avoidance of
any form of professionalism.

Most striking of all is Watkins's frequent insertion of interviews with the protagonists – princes and officers, soldiers on
both sides and even a military observer – all questioned about
their hopes, fears and ambitions. These interviews, staged to
look as authentic as possible with the faces framed so as to
make us forget the eighteenth-century dress, confront the
spectator with a direct experience of the battle and its aftermath. In this way the horror of Culloden comes over particularly forcibly. To give a wider context a narrator's voice is
used to pick out the relevant facts and present the social and
economic background to the conflict. Watkins's subsequent
work develops this same style in new and more forceful ways,
treating it to futuristic instead of historical themes. *The War
Game*, made in 1965, caused the director to break with the
BBC, which refused to show this film on the grounds of its
allegedly excessive violence. It is, however, hard to see how the
subject Watkins was commissioned to treat – a nuclear attack
on Kent in the context of a worsening world political crisis –
could have benefited from a cosier or more comforting approach. The mixture of a future nightmare subject – literally
unimaginable carnage and destruction – with a resolutely contemporary, everyday television reportage style is a very potent
one.

Watkins later went on to apply the same techniques in the
cinema, especially in *Punishment Park*, made in 1970, which

was a study of the violent backlash of ordinary middle-of-the-road American citizens against hippies and social deviants in a society threatened with war from without. Watkins's carefully documented imaginings are all too convincing and the power of the staged, but apparently authentic, interviews points out a whole new dramatic aspect of the film-maker's response to reality. Through all his work Watkins's vision of the horrors in store for us unless we change the society in which we live is put across with apocalyptic force.

An equally strong but very different challenge to traditional film values is provided by the work of Watkins's contemporary at the BBC, Kenneth Loach. Loach's style was formed in the series of Wednesday plays he directed with Tony Garnett as a producer in the mid 1960s. The scripts he used – Nell Dunn's *Up the Junction*, Jeremy Sandford's *Cathy Come Home* and David Mercer's *In Two Minds*, for example – were all fictional, but based on first-hand research and documentation. In each case the direction aimed at making the play look as totally authentic as possible. In part this was the result of Loach's rejection of the studio production method in favour of low budget location shooting with unknown players. But the television format itself was also a great influence. The particular qualities of the television image and the habitual viewing pattern of the audience both tend to foster a blurring of the distinctions between fact and fiction. News broadcasts and dramas, sports reports and variety shows all form a part of the same undistinguished mosaic, presented on the same level of reality, uniformly structured as entertainment and trimmed to fit pre-arranged time slots. Unlike film-making, where weeks, or even months, will be spent on editing after the shooting has been completed, television has the potential of showing life in its real time, as it actually happens. Television direction itself reflects this possibility. The director sits in front of a number of monitors or television sets making an instant choice of images and determining the cutting between one image and another during the actual performance. For these reasons perhaps television dramas which have a live 'feel' to them are among the most successful, and the standard dramatic structure most favoured is one which allows an involvement in an unfolding process. Trials and inquiries of all forms can hardly fail to grip when shown on television. The lack of definition in the images also means that television is a close-up medium. A shot of a dozen faces which would be perfectly clear on a cinema screen is simply a blur on television. The ideal television performance takes this into account and stresses such qualities as intimacy, spontaneity, casualness and underplaying. As a result the relationship between actor and audience is different. Whereas film stars have frequently carried over the same looks, qualities and gestures from one film to another and yet maintained their own personality distinct from the role, television performers are swallowed up by their parts. The audience sees not actors playing roles, but real people acting out their lives, so that the player becomes inseparable from the part he plays.

Kenneth Loach, whose work carries on into the 1970s with both television plays – *The Rank and File* – and films – *Kes* and *Family Life* – bases the whole of his stylistic approach on a mixture of fiction and documentary with these television characteristics. *Cathy Come Home*, his most celebrated work, shows the enormous power of such a style and the huge audience it can reach and involve in its subject. Seen by about half the entire population of the country in its initial screenings, it helped foster a new national awareness of the problems of the homeless by simply portraying the gradual destruction of a family through its inability to obtain adequate housing. The struggles of the young couple to cope with parenthood, unemployment and a uniformly hostile bureaucracy are handled with complete naturalness, acted scenes and pre-scripted dialogue blending indissolubly with snatches of authentic speech and candid-camera shots.

Yet this new form of screen naturalism poses the same basic issues which occur throughout the whole development of realist film-making. Loach, like so many documentarists and neo-realists before him, wants both to show and to inform. Film can reflect the surface totally, particularly when handled in Loach's manner. Capturing seemingly authentic faces, words and gestures, it can make us forget the existence of the script and the camera, and experience the narrated story as a slice of real life. But this very naturalism is at odds with any attempt to induce a change in audience views. Loach has very definite attitudes about the need to change the social system, to nationalize industries (including the film industry) and to attack bureaucratic indifference. This is clear from all his film and television work and much of its power comes from his evident total sincerity. Yet the naturalistic style he has perfected does not convince as a mode of arguing the issues of equality or social priority. With *Cathy Come Home* he reached a very large audience and created a great stir, but, as Garnett has pointed out, two years later when the play was reshown the problem of the homeless had actually increased. A means of combining fiction and documentary which will actually foster change instead of merely reflecting what injustices exist has still to be devised.

PART TWO

Film Illusion

11

The Techniques of Spectacle

The linking of film and fiction to provide entertainment for an audience is almost as old as the cinema itself. As we have seen, Méliès was rivalling the theatre with his little comedies before 1900. Drama can be defined in many ways, but the film drama which reached its climax in the Hollywood studios during the 1930s and 1940s is most aptly characterized in Alfred Hitchcock's definition of it as 'life with the dull bits cut out'. This implies a totally different attitude to life from that shown by realist film-makers. In Hollywood life is not observed, but pillaged as source material. The film-maker does not attempt to capture the feel, texture and rhythm of reality, but instead creates a facsimile, an independent entity which will give the illusion of being true while in fact obeying the laws of audience involvement. In place of a reproduction of life, we have life turned into a spectacle, that is to say, made visual, public, dramatic. Whereas the realist cinema involves a rejection or at best a simplification of technical possibilities, the Hollywood film drama is tied up with the industrial and technological progress of the cinema. Despite the haphazard and in many ways unsatisfactory manner in which this latter occurs, it is genuine progress, for, as it becomes more complicated, the cinema achieves one of its ideal aims, evolving into a spectacular form of entertainment uniting action and size of image, sound and music, depth and colour. It is only an historical accident that

Lumière's cinematograph was black and white, silent and two dimensional – no one would have aimed at creating a means of reproducing reality that had these limitations. Even within these constrictions the cinema could achieve great dramatic effect, as the history of the silent cinema shows. But from the very earliest days film-makers did experiment by adding colour and sound to their films and using new techniques of photography and editing to give an illusion of depth and space. One of the major contributions of Hollywood to the development of the cinema is that it gave these isolated experiments viable commercial form.

The cinema as spectacle is by its nature a highly technical product. If you want to write a book, all you need is pen and paper. Even a typewriter is not absolutely essential to begin with. But this simplicity does not mean that the book will in any way be limited in its appeal. Poems jotted down in pencil on the back of an old envelope can become recognized as masterpieces of literature. This is not true of the cinema in its normal commercial form. Nowadays a beginner can pick up an 8 mm. camera that automatically focuses and exposes his film and is almost as simple and foolproof as a pen. But the film produced can never be blown up and shown in an ordinary cinema. Even 16 mm. filming which is considerably more expensive and needs a whole new range of skills – focusing, taking light-readings to get the correct exposure, editing the images and synchronizing a sound track – is still acceptable in the cinema only in special circumstances – as a personal experiment, as a record or report, in certain kinds of *cinéma-vérité* filming. For all normal story films the standard size has always been 35 mm., and even if the fifty or sixty people who are normally present whenever a scene is shot are not all vitally necessary all the time, film-making at this level remains an expensive medium requiring a great many highly skilled craftsmen. The 16 mm. format is adequate for television transmission, but the cinema needs a large clear screen image and with the present state of mechanical and engineering skill this kind of image remains very costly to obtain.

In the cinema it is often difficult to see why changes occur at a particular moment unless we look outside the area of film-making itself. Film history is certainly not a steady march of ideas, with improvements being hailed and applied as soon as they are practical. Film-making has always been a risky business and the people who put up the money have to be gamblers of some sort. No-one knows what makes a film a hit that everyone will want to see. Imitating last year's hits is one sure way to disaster, but so for that matter is making a film that is even slightly in advance of public taste. Film-makers can only use their instinct, their feeling for what is going to work, and of course they make mistakes. In view of these problems, when things are going smoothly, producers try to keep everything as it is, and inventors with new devices get no hearing at all. But when things go wrong, the whole situation changes, for producers are the kind of people who will risk everything rather than admit defeat. The Warner Brothers film company was faced with bankruptcy, so it plunged into experiments with sound in 1926 . . . and won. The whole industry was hurt by the success of television in the early 1950s and again looked around for new gimmicks. Those who put their money into wide-screen processes backed a winner, those who invested in films with three-dimensional effects made a lot of money at first, but then lost out completely. Though millions of pounds are made annually by some films, the industry as a whole has always been precarious. It needs the banks and big business to invest money in its enterprises and is therefore at the mercy of forces from the world of high finance. The attitude of the giant electrical companies was very important in the change-over from silence to sound in the late 1920s. More recently the effect of television companies has been equally decisive in the spread of colour. Just as many film-makers in the 1920s would have preferred to continue making silent films, so too nowadays many directors regret the unstoppable move towards colour.

In the cinema, then, new technical ideas are not developed because the artists engaged in film-making demand them. For such people telling new kinds of stories in such a way as to use the full existing possibilities is generally a demanding enough occupation. New techniques are pressed upon the cinema by outside forces: things are going badly, so the public has to be given a novelty. Inevitably, the newness soon ceases to attract audiences and attendance figures go back to what they were before. The sound film – after the first excitement – was no more popular than the silent film. The reasons why some changes, like sound and wide screen, are permanent also have nothing to do with their artistic impact. The main reason is an economic one. Exhibitors and cinema-owners who have to spend a great deal of money getting their cinemas wired for sound or putting in a big screen do so on the understanding that there will be a permanent supply of suitable films. If this is not forthcoming they can put pressure on producers. There is, however, no pressure attached to inventions like technicolor that do not need new equipment. Exhibitors are happy to take films in colour or in black and white – as long as the latter can still draw crowds. On the other hand, inventions which make even small demands on the audience and in this way irritate them (for we demand to be totally absorbed without effort on our part when we go to the cinema for our diet of illusion), such inventions – 3-D with its special glasses is a good example – exhibitors reject. Or at least until the next crisis comes along.

By the normal rhythms of technical development in the cinema we are now due for a new idea or two. The cinema seems to change roughly every ten years or so. The 1910s brought feature-length films, the 1920s sound, the 1930s colour, the 1950s wide screens. Though the 1940s brought no new technical devices (they were perhaps held back by the war) new methods of realistic film-making were developed. The 1960s too were dull technically, for the studios were crumbling and running deeper and deeper into debt, with no money for technical novelties. But again these years were a period of intense change in the types of films made, as the needs of the new film audiences were explored. Yet there is still plenty of scope for new ideas that will lead the cinema on to new fields of experience. The problems of 3-D still have to be solved commercially. There is the idea of the dynamic frame, which expands and contracts according to the type of shot being shown. There is the possibility of projecting films all round on circular screens (an idea that has been used once or twice since it was first tried in 1896). For a brief moment one or two people thought we might like to smell films as well as see and hear them and systems with glorious names like Aromarama and Smellovision were devised – but the future possibilities of this idea seem limited. What is more likely is that the cinema, like the theatre, will begin to break down the distinction between film and audience, and film will be increasingly used in 'mixed media' shows where it is combined with live action. This could have a great effect on the film art.

What is most striking, however, when we look at the cinema from this kind of perspective is the extent to which it belongs to the nineteenth century. The whole technical apparatus of the cinema – celluloid, special lighting, enormous technical crews involved in the shooting – is quite outdated in an electronic age. What television transmission failed to do, namely break down the idea that films are essentially something to be viewed in public cinemas, may well be accomplished by video tape when this becomes fully available. The time is not too far distant when people will be able to play video tapes of films in their own homes as easily as they now play gramophone records or sound tapes. When this happens, all kinds of changes are likely. There will be no reason, for example, why films should not last for many hours and be 'read' over a number of days as novels are. The whole idea of spectacle may give way to new types of film experience that use other potentialities of sound and image. Meanwhile, we are well placed in time to trace the progress from the 1890s to the present of film as it has been used to create a dream world for masses and intelligentsia alike. The rise and fall of Hollywood is an epic story worthy of Cecil B. De Mille himself.

12

Edison and the Origins
of Hollywood

If the European tradition of realism in the cinema looks back to Lumière and seems a logical development of some of the potentialities that can be seen in his work, so the Hollywood tradition stems equally clearly from the work carried on at the West Orange laboratory of Thomas Alva Edison in New Jersey. All the pioneers of the cinema, in Europe and in the United States, owed a great debt to the work at West Orange, although this was aimed specifically at what proved to be a blind alleyway: the development of the kinetoscope or peepshow. Indeed it is curious that the very same fusion – in the name of entertainment – of nineteenth century scientific knowledge, technical skill and commercial enterprise that gave rise to the cinema should also, just a year or so before, have fostered this lame duck. Edison and his technicians were professional inventors with all the resources needed to give the world a succession of mechanical and scientific wonders, and moving pictures were a natural complement to Edison's newly invented phonograph. By 1890, when work commenced in earnest at West Orange, virtually all the basic problems had been resolved, in theory at least, and the task of converting a mass of research material into a working device that could be manufactured and sold in commercially profitable numbers was precisely the kind of task for which Edison's laboratory was equipped. Records show that though work on moving pictures

was carried on merely as a sideline, the creation of the kinetoscope presented no insuperable problems. Unfortunately for
Edison, the existence of the phonograph (which was exploited
as a coin-in-the-slot machine) led him into a dead end. Instead
of thinking in terms of projection, Edison asked for, and got, a
peepshow that could be seen by only one person at a time.

In the course of later lawsuits many of the facts about the
kinetoscope were obscured, dates were falsified and a number
of very fanciful claims made. But, thanks to recent research,
particularly by the film historian Gordon Hendricks, it is now
possible to establish some sort of a timetable.* Edison's own
role in the work on moving pictures was purely that of a
businessman and all the real invention was done by one of his
employees, a young engineer from Great Britain called William
Dickson, who later left the Edison group to help found the rival
Biograph company. It seems to have been in 1888 that Edison
first got the idea of a visual accompaniment to his phonograph,
and the work he set in motion drew freely on the results of
other earlier pioneers. In 1888 Muybridge lectured at Orange,
New Jersey, and there seems to have been some contact between him and the Edison people. In 1889 Edison went to
Europe and in Paris met Étienne Marey, who demonstrated
his equipment to him. By 1891 a prototype of the kinetoscope
could be privately exhibited, but a further two years passed
before all the problems were resolved. By early 1893 Edison
and Dickson had built the definitive model of the kinetoscope
viewer, as well as the kinetograph camera (which filmed virtually all Edison's own motion pictures, working at a speed of
forty images a second) and the celebrated black maria, the first
photographic studio built specifically for motion pictures. Even
then the construction of the kinetoscopes, of which over a
thousand were eventually made, proceeded slowly, and it was
not until 14 April 1894 that the first kinetoscope parlour
opened on Broadway.

* Gordon Hendricks is author of *The Edison Motion Picture Myth* (Uni-
versity of California Press, Berkeley and Los Angeles, 1961) and *The
Kinetoscope: America's First Commercially Successful Motion Picture
Exhibitor* (The Beginnings of the American Film, New York, 1966).

The kinetoscope, which was basically a box about four feet high equipped with an eyepiece through which a person who had inserted his coin could see a fifty-foot loop of tiny moving pictures, enjoyed an immediate but short-lived vogue. At first the public was eager to see the new Edison marvel and parlours were set up in major cities all over the United States. Many kinetoscopes were exported to Europe, where they not only found an enthusiastic public but also came into the hands of men like Lumière and Paul who were interested in the problems of projected moving pictures. It was the latter which proved to be the lasting innovation, but though his kinetoscope undoubtedly opened the way, Edison never seems to have considered the possibility or desirability of projected films, until, that is, others had already shown them to be profitable. If, therefore, it is to Edison's fellow industrialist, the Frenchman Louis Lumière, that the honour of being the first man to arrange a showing of projected motion pictures to a paying audience belongs, this is not to deny Edison and his fellow workers a crucial role in the invention of the cinema. Indeed, his kinetoscope films are a much more striking anticipation of what the cinema was to become in Hollywood than are Lumière's outdoor scenes. In essence the kinetoscope, despite its small scale, was a form of spectacle and set out to offer the public traditional entertainment in a new form. Edison's little films featured not the wonders of the natural world but music hall acts, dancing girls, performing animals or boxing matches. The bulky kinetograph camera could not be taken out into the world in search of such attractions; instead noted performers were summoned to the laboratory and their acts created or feats restaged within the confines of the black walls of the tiny Edison studio (in fact little more than a hut). If the kinetoscope was subsequently superseded by the cinema the reasons lie less in the nature of the entertainment provided than in the quality of the image, for the content of Edison's films and the idea of recreating events specifically for the camera lead naturally to the system we know as Hollywood. The whole history of the rise and fall of the kinetoscope in the 1890s is a striking demonstration of the way that the film conceived as entertainment becomes subject to, and in part a product of, commercial and economic pressures, thereby ceasing to be simply the outgrowth of the camera as a recording device or the projected image as a reflection of the world.

By 1896 the kinetoscope, already outpaced by a rival peepshow, the mutoscope, in its own field, was proving unable to compete with projected films. As a result, on 23 April of that year came the first projection of kinetoscope films on to a screen in New York. Though Edison himself had had little or no faith in the movies while concerned with their invention, he now showed himself a keen businessman in their exploitation, setting up his own company to produce films and harrying his rivals by clever use of his motion-picture patents. For Edison, like the pioneers in other countries, soon found himself surrounded by rivals making better use than he could of his own discoveries. Among the first of these rivals was the German-born Sigmund 'Pop' Lubin, an unscrupulous plagiarist of the works of Edison, Lumière and Méliès, whose company became one of the most important early makers of films and whose skill as a publicist did much to establish the cinema as a popular form of entertainment. Soon other companies came into being: Vitagraph, founded by J. Stuart Blackman and Albert E. Smith and numbering Florence Turner and the comedian John Bunny among its players; Kalem, named after the initials of its founders (George Kleine, Samuel Long and Frank Marion), which possessed no studios and produced films in Ireland and the Middle East as well as in the United States; and Essanay, famous for its Bronco Billy Anderson westerns and some of the early Chaplin comedies.

In 1908 all these companies, together with Selig, Biograph (later to achieve fame thanks to the work of Griffith) and the French firms of Pathé, Méliès and Gaumont, combined to form the Motion Picture Patents Company – usually known simply as the Trust – and attempted to obtain a monopoly of the cinema. By charging each exhibitor a licence fee of two dollars a week, the Trust was assured of an income of a million dollars a year, in addition to the profits from its films. The Trust seemed to hold all the trump cards – Edison's patents, the biggest production companies, most of the film theatres. Yet it was the independent producers and distributors omitted from the Trust who eventually won through, perhaps because they included in their number men of the calibre of William Fox and Carl Laemmle, both of whom founded companies that continued to survive for the next fifty years or more.

It was partly as a result of the bitterly fought patents war that production moved from New York to California, which not only offered the independents more sunshine but was also conveniently near to the Mexican border. With these advantages to back up their own skill the independents triumphed, though at the cost of severing the finance, which remained rooted in New York, from the production, which moved to the South. Hollywood itself was discovered, quite by chance, in the course of such a move. In 1913 Cecil B. De Mille, later to be renowned for his biblical epics, sent back an historic telegram to the company that had dispatched him to shoot a western called *The Squaw Man* in Flagstaff, Arizona. De Mille wired, 'Flagstaff no good for our purpose. Have proceeded to California. Want authority to rent barn in place called Hollywood for seventy-five dollars a month.' The company agreed, advising him, however, not to make a long commitment. Despite their caution, Hollywood was born.

This then was the world of the pre-1914 American cinema, a teeming world of talent and bluff, artistry and money-grabbing, with ruthless producers struggling against strong French competition for the control of their home market (an object finally achieved during the 1914–18 war) and shrewd-minded exhibitors building up chains of nickelodeons, as the first purpose-built cinemas were called. The American films of the early 1900s were directly linked to the lives of the audiences. If there was fantasy or escapism it was of a kind that related explicitly to the hopes and ideals of the working classes and the immigrant population that made up most of the paying customers. These films are the seed from which much later cinema has sprung, though today their similarity with the Hollywood films of the great years of the 1930s and 1940s is obscured by their surface oddity. They were, of course, silent in the sense that words came only in the form of written titles, but always they had the accompaniment of music, at least a piano, even in the smallest cinemas, and sometimes, in the very grandest, a full-scale orchestra. The films were often incredibly crude to look at, making much use of painted backcloths and with interior scenes rather obviously shot in sets open to the sunlight. Projection was usually poor and until 1912 a film was hardly ever more than one reel, or about ten minutes, long, and had needed perhaps only a day's shooting. But already in these days the importance of the narrative was apparent. Mostly the film had a simple moral lesson – it showed the triumph of good over evil or warned against the evils of drink or of the big city – though at this stage without any complexities or shades of meaning. In the very early years of the century a whole set of rules for film-making had been established: actors had to arrive and depart as in a stage play and they had to overact to make up for the lack of words. They also had to be photographed full length. 'Who is going to pay for half an actor when he can get a whole one somewhere else?' angry producers asked directors who wanted to bring the camera closer. Such a system threatened to strangle the development of the cinema as a form in its own right, but gradually film-makers won themselves the freedom to use the medium more creatively, partly by pointing to the success of imported films which were often longer and more sophisticated and partly by demonstrating that their ideas would please audiences.

Among those who did most for the American cinema in these very early years was Edwin S. Porter. He provides a link between Edison, who established the American industry, and Griffith, who made the cinema an art. Porter was in charge of production at the Edison studio from 1900 until 1909 and there is a pleasing rightness in the fact that it was to him that Griffith turned when he entered the film industry. For Porter, more than any other director, laid the foundations of the kind of narrative cinema in which Griffith was to excel. Like so many of the early figures in film history, Porter was not by any stretch of the imagination an artist. He was a former mechanic and cameraman who, without trying to be experimental, had hit on new ways of telling stories. He took Méliès's pattern of a series of tableaux a stage further by making the scenes follow each other with more logic. In *The Life of an American Fireman* (1903) he mixed shots of real fire engines with invented and acted scenes. Put together in the order which Porter chose, the two elements were fused to create a new, specifically filmic sort of story and a novel excitement in the audience. In films like this and *The Great Train Robbery* (1904) Porter developed his ideas in a way that pointed to the future, but such films are of interest today only as landmarks in the history of the cinema. Unlike Méliès's films, which were naïve but not crude, they are too primitive to have the power of exciting us as works of art today. The elements of film storytelling are there, but they have not been put together with any sense of rhythm or real pattern. The fourteen scenes of *The Great Train Robbery*, for instance, are each filmed in a single shot and the shots just follow one after the other without real excitement. The construction is so loose that the close-up of the bandit shooting straight at the camera was supplied with a note to the effect that it could be used at the beginning or the end, simply for effect. For all its limitations, however, Porter's work does prepare the way for the man who ranks as probably the greatest innovator in the history of the cinema, David Wark Griffith.

13

Griffith and Film Drama

When D. W. Griffith entered the film industry in 1907 he was already over thirty years of age, an ambitious man who had so far failed to make any mark on the world in a life full of poverty and disappointment. He grew up in the South, son of a Confederate colonel known, because of the quality of his voice, as Roaring Jake. The father's best-known exploit was to have led a cavalry charge during the Civil War while riding in a buggy (he was wounded at the time). After the war he had also achieved some local fame with his readings from Shakespeare, but he failed to make money in any of his enterprises and the family was deeply in debt when he died. His son David had an ambition to be a great writer, an American Shakespeare, but his writings had little success with publishers and the one play he did sell, *A Fool and a Girl*, for which he received $1,000, flopped when it was produced in 1907. Meanwhile Griffith worked as an actor, learning the techniques of the stage in the course of ten years but achieving very little success. Again and again the company with which he was touring at the time collapsed and he found himself stranded and forced to do odd jobs to pay for his fare home. But he persevered. In 1907 he found a new outlet for his talents when he tried to sell a story (a one-reel version of *Tosca*) to Edwin S. Porter at the Edison company. His script was rejected, but he was offered the lead in Porter's next film, *Rescued from an Eagle's Nest*.

For someone like Griffith, a man with vast ambitions as a stage actor and theatrical writer, working in films was a matter for shame and secrecy, and for the first three years of his new career he signed himself 'Laurence' Griffith. In many ways the attitude of actors like Griffith was very strange. Great figures of the stage, such as Sarah Bernhardt, had appeared in films in Europe without harming their reputations, and for an unsuccessful stage actor the pay that the film companies offered was good. But ordinary stage actors still considered it degrading and welcomed the fact that they were anonymous, known as faces but not by name. There was at this time no status for the actor in the studios. An actor would play the lead in one film and be merely an extra in the background of the next. If she was playing Juliet an actress would be expected to help with the costumes, while Romeo was building the balcony. Yet within a few years this whole position was to change, as the career of Mary Pickford shows. This was a trend in which Griffith himself did not participate. He never bid to retain the services of the many budding stars he discovered (Pickford, the Gish sisters, Mae Marsh, etc.) and even his great epics were sold without the benefit of star appeal.

Griffith turned somewhat reluctantly to directing for the Biograph company in the summer of 1908. But having once begun, he poured out films at the rate of two a week without a break throughout the year, and in the five years up to 1913 he experimented with all the basic techniques that comprise the art of making films. In this time it is fair to say that he invented virtually nothing (despite his later claims to the contrary). Earlier pioneers, we now know, had proved incredibly inventive in their use of new techniques with which to give a touch of novelty to their films (like Porter with his close-up of the bandit shooting). What is important about Griffith is that he used such techniques in a genuinely dramatic way, so that in his hands the cinema became a vivid and powerful way of telling stories and captivating audiences. He had a basic awareness that the unit of film-making is not (as in the theatre) the scene, but the individual shot. He saw that a scene must be broken down into shots if it is to have its full effect. He made exciting use of his camera and found new ways of editing shots together to make a sequence. For example, the chase had been a standard pattern of film construction from very early days, and Porter had experimented with linking two stories in films like *The Kleptomaniac* (1905), but the drama which Griffith extracted from his last-minute rescues, with cross-cutting from the woman or child in peril to the advancing hero and back again, was quite unique.

Almost four hundred of Griffith's films of his 'apprentice' years (1908–13) have been reconstructed from the paper prints which were deposited in the United States Library of Congress as a proof of copyright, and many of these are films which had been unavailable to critics for many years. At the moment our knowledge of Griffith is based on a comparatively few films, to which writers and critics refer again and again, and we shall probably have to make some adjustments when these newly discovered films have been analysed. But even now we can see the broad outlines of Griffith's advances. He made one-reel films of just about every conceivable kind: adaptations from the classics, historical (even prehistorical) dramas, comedies, war films, contemporary social dramas, biblical epics. He experimented with expressive theatrical lighting in films like *The Drunkard's Reformation* (1909) and *Pippa Passes* (1909), and used linking shots and editing technique to replace the 'thought balloons' of Porter. He cross-cut to build up suspense in *The Lonely Villa* (1909) and *The Lonedale Operator* (1911) and used extreme long shots to create atmosphere in *Ramona* (1910).

With the aid of his cameramen, Billy Bitzer and Arthur Marvin, Griffith helped build up the fortunes of the Biograph company, but his employers constantly tried to hold him back. They wanted him to keep to the one-reel format in which he had been so successful, while he wanted to make longer and more elaborate films. Early in 1911 he made his first double-reel film, but Biograph released it as two separate films, *His Trust* and *His Trust Fulfilled,* and there were more problems with his producers over his second two-reel effort, *Enoch Arden,* based on Tennyson's poem. Despite the fact that long films were now being imported from Europe and successfully shown in the United States, particularly the Italian epic, *Quo Vadis,* the directors of Biograph were horrified when, in 1913, Griffith produced a four-reel biblical epic, *Judith of Bethulia*. The company refused to show this, Griffith's most ambitious film to date, until a year later, with the result that there was a quarrel and Griffith departed.

Though Griffith claimed that he never saw the long Italian films about Roman history, like *Quo Vadis* and *Cabiria*, which took the United States by storm, there can be little doubt that their existence prompted him to greater efforts. As soon as he could, he plunged with all his amazing energy into the making of a massive epic of the Civil War and its aftermath, which he first called *The Clansmen* but which was later renamed *The Birth of a Nation*. The source was a novel by Thomas Dixon, combined with Griffith's own memories of the South. Though Griffith toned down many of the worst passages in Dixon's book, the film still aroused widespread criticism because of its racialist attitude. The Negroes (all played, incidentally, by white men) were shown to be good if they were devoted and loyal servants, but totally villainous when free. The final sequence, in which the hooded Ku Klux Klan rides across country to put the blacks back in their place, is hardly one that appeals to any sensitive person today. But as shot and edited by Griffith, it was capable of arousing enormous excitement. This is a reminder of the extent to which our response to films is purely an emotional one. Because of the power of the images, we can in fact become involved with things which intellectually we reject. Apart from the ending – in its condemnation of the brutalities of war that tears a nation apart and divides families, for example – *The Birth of a Nation* is less controversial and more deeply moving. The scandal the film aroused in no way hindered its commercial success. The longest (twelve reels) and the costliest ($100,000) American film to date, it was also one of the most profitable. Within a few years it had taken the unprecedented sum of eighteen million dollars at the box office and it must still, almost sixty years later, figure in any list of the most successful pictures of all time. With it Griffith gave

Hollywood a new dimension and showed the enormous audience on which a really outstanding film could call.

Perhaps as remarkable a thing for us today as the film itself (for what we see at film societies is only a worn and faded skeleton of a great work) is the way it was made. Griffith heralded the new age of film-making, but some of his methods, even in his longest films, remained those of the early days. He not only raised the money and directed the film, he also shot it without a script, shaping the film by instinct after just six weeks of rehearsal with his cast. Hollywood did not yet exist as a relentless machine for turning out carefully tailored films, and actors were still expected in 1915 to find many of their own costumes and props and to do their own make-up. They would arrive on the set without having been given much advice on how to play the scene. Often the same actor would play several parts, and Joseph Henabery, who appeared as Lincoln in *The Birth of a Nation*, has recorded that he also played thirteen other bit parts, including both a fleeing Negro and one of the pursuing band of whites. Since Griffith preferred to work with young and inexperienced actors and actresses, the result, when he was making a two-hour epic, should logically have been disastrous. But Griffith was much more than a technician. He had a gift for building characters about whom the audience would really care, and everyone who saw his film in 1915 was caught up in its portrayal of love and hate, joy and misery.

Griffith poured all his earnings from *The Birth of a Nation* in an even vaster enterprise, the mammoth *Intolerance* (1916), which was almost as striking a flop as the earlier film had been a success. The director had started out to make a contemporary film about the evil effects of heartless employers and hypocritical moral reformers called *The Mother and the Law*, but then he felt that this was too slight a work with which to follow *The Birth of a Nation*. So he added to it three other stories: the fall of Babylon to the invading Persians because of the treachery of the priests, the massacre of the Huguenots in Paris on St Bartholomew's Day 1572 by the ruling Catholics, and the crucifixion of Christ. Griffith's aim was to build up a vast fresco of intolerance through the ages.

Therefore he did not place the four stories one after the other as they would be in a conventional four-part film; he welded them together to make one timeless epic. Griffith constantly cut from one story to another and gradually built up to what must be the greatest climax any film has ever aimed at. Babylon falls, the Huguenots are all killed, Christ is crucified ... but the young worker wrongly accused and condemned for murder is saved from execution at the very last moment. Griffith aimed to construct the film so that the four streams were wedded to create 'one mighty river of expressed emotion'. But his audiences merely found it confusing and stayed away. As a result Griffith, whose vision had so far outstepped his audience, was given a burden of debt from which he never totally freed himself.

Though the results of these two films were so different, together they changed the whole nature and status of the film industry. The enormous profits of *The Birth of a Nation*, the gigantic sets of Babylon which he built for *Intolerance*, the world-wide fame which he showed a film-maker could obtain, these were things which could not be ignored. When he had begun film-making in 1908 it had been with a sense of shame. Now when he came to England for the opening of *Intolerance* just nine years later, he was received by the Royal Family, treated as a celebrity wherever he went and given *carte blanche* by the British government to make a film about the War with Germany (*Hearts of the World*). Griffith was now forty-two and at the climax of his career. His two great epics had an untold influence on film-making both in America and in other countries, but new directors built on his achievements in ways that he himself could not. If we look at the history of the cinema in the 1920s it becomes clear that two of the major trends derive from Griffith, both the search for greater realism and the exploration of the creative possibilities of editing. But Griffith himself was gradually overtaken by the times and the creative originality went out of his work. He continued making films until the beginning of the sound era (when he made a notable biography, *Abraham Lincoln*), and indeed made some remarkable films with his young discovery, Lillian Gish. But there was a difference of emphasis now. The works up to

Intolerance invite us to examine the revolutionary new techniques used, the style of lighting, the placing of the camera, the linking of shots. The Lilian Gish films like *Broken Blossoms* (1919) *Way Down East* (1920) and *Orphans of the Storm* (1922), on the other hand, show more clearly the roots of Griffith's morality and the debt he owes to nineteenth-century novels and melodramas.

New forms of expression do not grow up simply because someone invents a new technique. The technique has to be brought to life. Nor is a new form ever totally revolutionary. In most cases it takes over the content of its predecessor. In this way silent film comedy grows out of the music hall and, as every viewer is aware, television adopts film methods, fills much of its time with old movies and so on. But at some point the two elements have to be brought together to create something quite new: the old content totally transformed in the new form. This is precisely what D. W. Griffith did for the cinema, and a comparison with television is interesting because it is arguable that television has not yet found its Griffith.

In many ways the influence of the nineteenth century was a liberating one for Griffith, in that it gave him something against which to measure himself. In his apprentice years he did not try to make films that were just a bit better than those of his rivals; he struggled to capture the dramatic drive he found in the melodramas of his youth and in the novels of Charles Dickens. To the extent that he remained faithful to these ideals he is remote from us. There is in Griffith's work a genuine concern for the poor and underprivileged and for children whose lives are ruined by unfeeling adults and a cruel world of injustice. But there is also a great sentimentality, and the cinema is a ruthless exposer of pretensions. The heroine of *Intolerance* for instance, is called in the titles 'The Little Dear One'. Griffith's favourite heroines – Mary Pickford, Lillian Gish, Mae Marsh – were all typical Victorian figures, pale, blonde teenagers, obviously very vulnerable to the violence and evil around them. Griffith's genius is such that he can rise above his limitations. It seems unlikely, in the 1970s, that we can regard seriously any film based on a story called 'The Chink and the

Child' and telling of a poor little girl, worshipped by a shy Oriental and beaten to death by her drunken father, a boxer called Battling Burroughs. But the miracle of Griffith is that he makes something timeless out of these elements, so that *Broken Blossoms* can still move us deeply.

We have traced the career of D. W. Griffith in such detail because it spans the cinema's leap from being a mere amusement to becoming a powerful art form. Griffith was ten years old when the cinema was born and thirty-two years of age before failure elsewhere drove him to seek work in the studios. But in the next ten years he transformed the whole notion of what film was capable of achieving. If we ask ourselves why Griffith should have been the man to accomplish this change, it is easy to see that the answer must lie within his character, in the certainty with which he kept to his ideals. At the outbreak of the First World War the American cinema had new markets within its reach and was ready to be transformed from a back street entertainment to a world-dominating industry. It had at its disposal all the resources from which a new language of film could be made, for it would be hard to think of a single technical device that was not known and used before 1912. But within the industry itself there was no genuine impulse for change. The men who controlled it were very conservative: they gave the public what it had always wanted and made vast sums of money doing so. Therefore they saw no need for change. It needed a Griffith who drew his standards from outside the industry to conceive of the revolution from ten-minute films to *The Birth of a Nation*. Griffith had to believe in himself as a Shakespearean genius to be able to give the cinema an awareness of itself as a powerful medium of storytelling and an expressive art form.

The Comedians

Of all the various forms and genres of the cinema comedy can fairly claim to be one of the oldest. While both the gangster film and the musical came into being only with the coming of sound, film comedy, like the film serial, developed in France in the early 1900s before being brought to its highest point in Hollywood after 1914. There were a great many comics in the the French cinema before the First World War, but only one recognized master, Max Linder. The basic forms of comedy most obviously suited to the screen – chases, comic fights, anything in fact requiring fast-moving action – were all exploited before his arrival on the scene, but it was Linder who gave the form a new depth. In the four hundred or so films he made for Pathé before 1914, he created a character of some subtlety: the elegant figure of Max, immaculately dressed, with a flower in his buttonhole and a pretty girl on his arm. The performances of Max Linder also give a clue to one of the essentials of the truly individual comic: the ability to underplay, to achieve his effects without undue exaggeration.

When comedy moved to Hollywood, however, it was not until the 1920s that comparable individual comedians emerged. Meanwhile, between 1912 and 1917, the centre of comedy was the so-called 'fun factory', the Keystone studio of Mack Sennett. Keystone provides a striking anticipation of the studio system as it was to flourish throughout Hollywood in the 1930s. Here we see many of the principles of mass production applied to what seems on the surface the most personal of forms of expression, humour. Sennett, like so many of the key figures of the American silent cinema, learned his trade from D. W. Griffith, having entered the Biograph company in 1908, a year later than the master of screen drama. Originally an ironworker, Sennett had thrown up his job to seek fame and fortune on the stage, but, despite considerable experience in the music hall, he had achieved little success by the age of twenty-eight when he turned to films. At this time the cinema was developing rapidly in the United States and there was plenty of scope for an ambitious man to make his mark. Within three years Sennett had worked his way up from tiny background roles to leading parts in films directed by himself. Then in 1912 came his big chance – financial backing, his own studio and a free hand to make the kind of films he wanted. Sennett's years on the stage had made him well able to fulfil the only condition attached to all this: that he make films that would appeal to the simple, unsophisticated tastes of the millions of spectators who flocked to the cinema every day.

Sennett was in many ways akin to the characters in his films. Though many people claim to get their best ideas in the bath, Sennett was probably the only successful businessman ever to install a bath in his office and spend a part of every working day sitting in it. He was a dominating personality. When too many films were being shot in his studio for him to supervise them all personally, he built a tower in the middle of the studio lot, installed his office at the top and looked down on his workers toiling below. Such quirks of behaviour were quite common (as we shall see later) among Hollywood studio chiefs, but Sennett's brand of comedy was quite his own. He imposed his own style on all the Keystone films, rigidly making the players fit the appointed roles instead of building new comic routines out of the individual talents of his actors. As a result the most talented of the comics he discovered soon left the Keystone studio. Chaplin, who made his debut with Sennett, left after one year, and neither Harold Lloyd nor Harry Langdon made any impact during their Keystone period.

The keynote of Mack Sennett's films was the team. His comedies were written by groups of gagmen and directed by semi-anonymous technicians. For their effects they relied on the collective talents of a crowd of comics: Ford Sterling (the police chief), Roscoe Arbuckle (the fat boy), ex-artist's model Mabel Normand and cross-eyed Ben Turpin, supported by the famous Keystone Kops and, from 1915, Mack Sennett's bathing beauties. The gags were simple but effective. A hundred Kops would pile out of one tiny taxi (easily achieved by stopping the camera to allow them to get back in again, then refilming, over and over again). Chases over rooftops, through rivers, on the edges of cliffs, and so on, were all part of the day's work. For thrills the express train would thunder to a stop an inch away from the heroine, tied helpless to the rails (achieved by filming the train backing away and then projecting the sequence in reverse). If one policeman falling over was funny, Mack Sennett thought (and his audience agreed) that a dozen falling over simultaneously was hilarious. Whenever the pace was flagging, someone would kick someone else's bottom or throw a custard pie. This latter was in fact a delicate art. The pies, filled with paste (which photographed better than real custard) had to be pushed through the air rather than thrown, and the maximum distance for accuracy was reckoned to be six to eight feet. Arbuckle, who could hit a target with either hand at ten feet, was recognized as a master.

There was nothing subtle about Sennett's Keystone films. The actors had no time to build up real characters, and they were bundled from one situation to another with phenomenal speed. This tempo was an essential part of Sennett's comedy style. Since cameras were operated by hand in those days, it was simple to vary the speed of shooting. The near-miss car crashes could be filmed at eight frames a second and when they were projected at the standard silent speed of around sixteen frames a second everything would happen twice as fast. Sennett also reckoned to take out every third or fourth frame from his films so as to speed things up. His films therefore were made to have the jerkiness we tend to associate with all silent comedy, whereas the later comedies of the 1920s appear jerky only because they are speeded up by being wrongly projected at the sound speed of twenty-four frames per second.

For Sennett, stories were unimportant, a mere prop on which to hang an action, and, generally speaking, his best works are short ten- or twenty-minute films in which a succession of gags could be kept up at breakneck speed. He did, however, make the first full-length American comedy, *Tillie's Punctured Romance* (1914) which helped set Charlie Chaplin on the road to stardom. Comedy probably played as important a part as the drama initiated by Griffith in making American films popular throughout the world, and it was with Sennett that comedy became big business. His films of 1913, for instance, took about two million dollars at the box office. With the arrival of Chaplin the stars themselves began to make untold fortunes. In 1914, when Chaplin started at Keystone he was paid $150 a week, at Mutual in 1916–17 he was making $670,000 a year, and when he signed to make eight two-reel comedies at First National a year later he was paid $1,200,000 plus bonuses. Other stars were earning similar amounts and soon Hollywood had built up its reputation as a fabulous land of dream fulfilment.

Chaplin was only one of four great comedians who flourished in the 1920s, and though he overshadowed all his rivals at the time, audiences are now rediscovering the others. At the very end of his lifetime, after thirty years of neglect, Buster Keaton was acclaimed as the great comedian he was, and the reputations of Harold Lloyd, famed for his thrill comedies that had him climbing up the face of buildings and hanging from ledges high above the traffic, and the baby-faced Harry Langdon have also grown recently. Looking back today, we can only marvel at this wealth of talent, for each of the four had a personal approach to comedy and created a totally individual comic personality. The kind of range that silent comedy had can be seen by comparing the work of the two best known comedians, Chaplin and Keaton.

In the 1920s and 1930s there was no comic who aroused greater acclaim than Charlie Chaplin. Within a few short years of leaving Keystone he had made himself a millionaire, was

mobbed by crowds everywhere he went and praised and welcomed by artists and intellectuals in every country. Inevitably a
reaction to this popstar-style celebrity set in, becoming particularly apparent in the 1960s when Keaton's films were
rediscovered and widely shown, while Chaplin's remained virtually unavailable. But for all this, Chaplin's achievements in
comedy are to be compared with those of Griffith in drama.
Like almost all the great comics he learned his art in the music
hall, in direct contact with an audience. Perhaps it is only here
that a comic can acquire his most vital gift, the art of precisely
timing his gags. Though superbly professional in his approach,
Chaplin was no dry technician. He drew on a mass of memories
of a childhood lived in a Victorian London that now seems to
belong, not to another age, but to another planet. His London
was a Dickensian world of slums and poverty, from which he
struggled to free himself. His autobiography shows us how
much his success – the wealth he earned and the celebrities he
met – meant to him, but he never lost his instinctive sympathy
for the poor and underprivileged.

Chaplin's individuality was apparent from the first. Though
he made thirty-five comedies for Keystone, he never fitted into
the Sennett pattern. He disliked the whole idea of the chase
(which was Sennett's stock plot formula) and wanted to develop a character in depth instead of just piling up gags. In
essence, from his second film, made in 1914, to *Modern Times*
(made in 1936), he did just this, creating and exploiting the one
character, Charlie, whom he made into a universal figure. The
props were simple: baggy pants, big shoes, a cane and a derby
hat. Because he was younger than Sennett's other comedians,
he added to these a small moustache. To start with, as he tells
us in his autobiography, he had no idea of the character. But
the moment he dressed like this, the clothes and the make-up
made him feel the person he was and by the time he walked out
on to the set, the character was fully born and gags and comic
ideas were racing through his mind. The great quality of this
make-up was that it allowed Chaplin to play any role: tramp or
gentleman, poet or adventurer, scientist or duke. He could be
sympathetic and downtrodden or quite mean and aggressive,

without breaking the spell of continuity. Above all, Charlie was a figure who could be recognized and appreciated anywhere in the world. It is not surprising therefore that Chaplin was one of the bitterest opponents of talkies. He held out as long as he could against them and both *City Lights* (1931) and *Modern Times* (1936) were virtually silent films with music, but eventually Chaplin, like everyone else, had to concede the victory of sound.

What is best remembered of Chaplin today, apart from the unforgettable silhouette and the awkward gait, are the set-pieces of comic mime. He showed what a comic of genius can do with the simplest of props, a mop and a bucket, a staircase or a fallen wallet. There are classic scenes which once seen will never be forgotten, like that in *The Gold Rush* (1925) where he is reduced to eating his boots, sucking the nails like fishbones and chewing the laces like spaghetti, or his brilliant Hitler mime in *The Great Dictator* (1940) where he plays balloon with a toy globe until it shatters. And to hold all of his films together there is his own personal involvement, the force with which he presents his view of life, with all its laughter and tears. It is the sentimental side of Chaplin that has perhaps dated most. When he guys Hitler and Mussolini in *The Great Dictator* he is brilliant but when he appears in his second role as a little Jewish barber and preaches to his audience, the result is merely embarrassing. Technically too Chaplin remains a film-maker of another age. He learned his technique in 1914 and even his latest films, *A King in New York* (1957) and *A Countess from Hong Kong* (1966), show that he has not developed this very much in the ensuing years. He remains a performer rather than a director, a mime not a storyteller, but the neglect from which his work has in the past suffered will surely be overcome as his films (which he owns all the rights to himself) are gradually made available to audiences once more. Few people have made a greater contribution to the universal popularity of the film art.

It would be hard to find a greater contrast to Chaplin than Buster Keaton, who is now rightly seen as an equally great screen comedian. Though he never worked for Mack Sennett,

Keaton too learned his trade by acting on the stage (from the age of five onwards) and then making short films at the rate of about one a month, perfecting his technique and working out his ideas of character. If Chaplin was a clown who mixed humour and pathos, Keaton was an actor always playing different roles in his various films. But all his parts have certain things in common. The Buster Keaton figure is an apparent dreamer or misfit who is placed in an awkward situation. Without cheating, stealing or being nasty, he manages to overcome his problems and win his girl, through a dogged energy that leads him to achieve the most astonishing feats. Keaton was a master of the chase scene. In *Go West* (1925) he dons a red devil's outfit and is chased through the streets by a herd of cattle and dozens of policemen. In *Seven Chances* (1925) it is a crowd of hundreds of women, all eager to marry him for his money, who chase him out of town and into the path of a landslide. He is always on the fringe of a disaster of this kind, caught up (without knowing it) in a cyclone in *Steamboat Bill Jr* (1928) or the Civil War in *The General* (1926).

Buster Keaton had a particular gift for seeing the comic possibilities of machines and vehicles. One of his best-known shorts is called simply *The Boat*. Keaton here builds a boat in his cellar, knocks down his house trying to get it out and runs his car over the quayside when he tows it to the water. Undaunted he launches his boat, which promptly sinks. One of Keaton's best feature films, *The Navigator* (1924), was born when one of his collaborators found that they could buy an old ocean liner for just $23,000 (and sell it again for about the same amount when they had done with it). Keaton put only two people, the rich but helpless hero and his haughty girl-friend on board, and made nearly a whole film out of their problems of adjustment in a space designed for hundreds of passengers. The solutions they adopt gave Keaton the chance to show his own mechanical ingenuity. In a similar way, *The General* is built around a railway engine which the hero loves as much as he loves his sweetheart. The film, set in the South during the Civil War, unfolds with a neat and logical story line, based as usual around the idea of a chase. The Northerners steal the hero's train with his girlfriend still on board, and he sets out in pursuit by every available means – railway trolley, penny-farthing bicycle, and a stolen engine. Having recovered the train and the girl, the hero is promptly chased back South again by the enemy, and the humour derives from the double pattern: firstly his attempts to get around the obstacles the thieves put in his way and then his successful thwarting of their efforts to catch up with him.

During the whole of his film career, which was just about over by the time he was thirty-three years old, Keaton had two ideas in mind: to make his audience laugh, and to do so without being ridiculous. For this reason he always made his films look as real as possible. He shot in the open air, on location, gave his characters authentic costumes and made almost no use of models or dummies. When, in *The General*, the enemy train tries to cross a burning bridge and plunges into the river, it was a real bridge and a real train that Keaton used (making this one of the most expensive gags in history). Keaton's visual style has a great beauty which he arrived at quite instinctively, and, when there are purely fantastic gags, these are always in a dream setting (as in *Sherlock Junior*, 1924). Elsewhere, what is most staggering about Keaton is that he actually performed the fantastic feats his heroes have to achieve. Because of his expression he earned himself the reputation of being the man who never smiled, but this was not a reflection of any deepseated melancholy. As he himself explained, he did not smile because he was concentrating on what he was doing. In one of his shorts this meant crossing a deep ravine on two planks resting on thin parallel wires, making his way by continually placing one plank in front of the other (he does this to escape from pursuing Red Indians, only to come face to face with others on the far side). In *Sherlock Junior* he rides on the handlebars of a motorcycle, apparently quite unaware that the driver has fallen off. His journey takes him through the traffic of the town and finally over a partially built bridge which has a gap in the middle and lacks a final section to bring the road down to earth again. By a miracle of timing, Keaton crosses it at the moment when two pantechnicons are crossing beneath the

gap and his weight causes the final section to collapse, bringing
him down to the ground as he drives along it.

Keaton had the physical resources of a brilliant athlete and
was quite without fear. The risks he was prepared to take in
order to get a laugh were unbelievable. In *Steamboat Bill
Jr*, during the cyclone sequence, he stands in the roadway and a
house front falls on top of him. We expect him to be crushed,
but the attic window is open and as he stands still, his head and
body pass through the hole. For this effect Keaton used a real
house front weighing several tons which was calculated to miss
his head and body by only two inches. Luckily it fell straight!
The ordinary spectator may not be consciously thinking in
terms of true or fake but such an indication as Keaton always
gives by refusing to cut does have an effect on us.

The great period of silent comedy lasted only a few years:
Chaplin's *The Kid*, *The Gold Rush* and *The Circus*, Keaton's *The
Navigator* and *The General*, Langdon's *Long Pants* and Lloyd's
Safety Last were all made in the course of eight years. During
this time the four film-makers used the full comic resources of
the film medium, building not only on their own enormous
talent but also on a firm foundation of a music-hall experience.
Mack Sennett had shown the popularity of the comic short-film
and they all were able to learn the craft of film-making by
turning out ten- or twenty-minute comedies (Harold Lloyd, for
example, made nearly two hundred of these). The success of
such films and the profits that comedy could bring allowed
them for a time to work with complete freedom on all aspects
of their films. The 1920s were the great days of the independent film-maker. When these comedians set up on their
own, they could build their own studios and employ a regular
staff of actors and technicians. This gave them a freedom rarely
enjoyed by film-makers but one of vital importance to comedians: the ability to try out material on an audience and then
go back to the studio and reshape it. The characteristic polish
of their work comes from the fact that having obtained an
audience reaction they could cut the sequences that failed to
work and build up those that succeeded best. The form of
comedy in which these men excelled died when sound came,

but not really because it was impossible to make sound films on the same lines: Chaplin's *Modern Times* was made as late as 1936. It was rather that the increased costs and new budgeting methods made the freedom of a Buster Keaton seem out of place. Sound offered the chance for a new sort of comedy, one based on clever dialogue, that was popular with audiences and could be controlled by products in a way that the work of, say, Keaton could not. As film-making became a major industry the production system changed and for the new breed of executives freedom was a dubious quality and individuality a cause for alarm.

15

The Studio Era

The end of the great age of silent film comedy brings us to one of the most fascinating aspects of the cinema of the 1930s and 1940s, the studio system. It is at this point that Hollywood begins to take on a distinctive personality as a mass producer of films for a world market. To begin with, the word studio itself needs a little defining, for it covers rather a large range of meaning. Georges Méliès had built himself a studio at Montreuil in 1896 and, even earlier, Edison's kinetoscope films were shot in the black maria. Throughout the pioneering days there were studios of sorts in Hollywood – but only in the sense of an open set with props, stages and equipment. This was the context in which men like Griffith and Keaton did their best work, and nothing could be further from mass-produced objects than the films that they produced.

However, as early as 1915 the word studio took on its new meaning with the opening of the vast Universal City set-up by the producer Carl Laemmle. This pointed the way to the giants which were to come, but Laemmle himself was not a typical studio tycoon. He was known affectionately as 'Uncle Carl' because of the number of members of his family he employed. On his death in 1939 no less than seventy of his relatives were found to be on the Universal payroll, a situation that gave rise to all kinds of jokes, such as Ogden Nash's 'Uncle Carl Laemmle, Has a large Faemmle.' He was a generous, easy-going man, content to turn out unambitious pictures of no great importance for family audiences. The casual way he ran Universal City was legendary. In 1912 one of his directors shot a ten-reel film in the studio without the producer knowing anything about it (this was *Traffic in Souls* which became one of the big hits of the early cinema). Later on Lewis J. Selznick, an out-of-work jewellery salesman, is said to have become managing director simply by hanging up his hat, commandeering a desk and writing his name on the door. Certainly it is true that when Laemmle eventually went to Europe to see his family there he left in charge of his studio his shorthand-typist secretary, Irving Thalberg, a young man of nineteen totally without film-making experience. Beneath this absent-minded exterior was in fact a shrewd and able mind, for it is surely not by chance that both Selznick and Thalberg went on to become important producers in their own right. Nor was Uncle Carl as easy-going as he appeared: in the 1900s he had been one of the few producers (with William Fox) to stand up for the rights of independent film-makers against the power of the 'Trust' massed behind Edison's patent rights.

When we talk nowadays about the studio system, however, we generally think of the companies set up and run by men ten or fifteen years younger than Laemmle. These companies came into being – most of them in the late 1920s – when the big chains of film theatres and distributing companies (mostly based in New York) were linked with groups of film-producing companies in Hollywood. The result was a continual tension between the moneymen in the East and the film producers in what was now the film capital of the world.

In the 1930s, when the system was at its height, Hollywood was dominated by eight major studios, each with its own employees and stars and its own brand of film-making. Of these eight, the so-called big five all had their own distribution system, a circuit of cinemas in which their films were automatically shown. There was Paramount, which was descended from several old companies, including Lasky Feature Plays (which had made *The Squaw Man*) and Famous Players, founded in 1912 by Adolph Zukor, who was still a president of the

Paramount Company when he was in his nineties. Twentieth Century Fox was created in 1935 thanks to a merger of two very dissimilar companies. One was the virtually bankrupt company founded in 1915 by William Fox who, some years before the merger, had attempted to take over the whole film industry. Fox failed, lost a fortune estimated at one hunderd million dollars in the attempt, and died a comparatively poor man. The other company in the merger was a new and dynamic enterprise, Twentieth Century, created by Darryl F. Zanuck and Joseph Schenk. Warner Brothers, the third major company, was the product of four men, Sam, Jack, Harry and Albert Warner, who had founded it in the 1920s and made a fortune by being the first to introduce sound successfully with *The Jazz Singer* in 1927. RKO radio also had its roots in the 1920s but it is best known as the studio bought and owned after 1947 by the multi-millionaire Howard Hughes (who had already dabbled in film-making in the early 1930s). All these four companies were important, but the greatest of the big five was Metro-Goldwyn-Mayer, which was welded together in 1924. Though the new company bears his name Sam Goldwyn was already an independent producer by the time of the merger (he later became the most important independent in Hollywood) and the dominant force in the M-G-M company for over twenty-five years was Louis B. Mayer. As head of production he was for several years America's highest-paid employee with a salary of over a million dollars a year. For a good many years M-G-M, too, had its link with the world of high finance in the person of another famous multi-millionnaire, William Randolph Hearst, who put up the money for films starring the actress Marion Davies.

All the big five were combinations of production companies and cinema chains. The three lesser companies – Universal, United Artists (founded in 1919 by D. W. Griffith, Charles Chaplin, Mary Pickford and Douglas Fairbanks) and Harry Cohn's Columbia – were merely production companies. Though this made them of less importance in the 1930s, it in fact proved an advantage in the late 1940s when the film industry was thrown into disorder by a government ruling that production companies and cinema circuits had to be separately owned.

As machines for turning out films, all eight studios operated in much the same way, and to understand their methods it is necessary to know a little about the quite remarkable group of men whose names have already been mentioned, the movie tycoons, the great producers. Virtually all of these founding fathers of Hollywood were either immigrants from Europe or the first generation of children of immigrants who had come to America to seek a new opportunity and to escape poverty. This drive to escape their background circumstances gave them a fantastic energy which they soon displayed in their relentless fight to the top. Most of them had little education, no artistic background and, to begin with, no real knowledge of the entertainment industry. They tended instead to be salesmen, often connected with fashion in some minor way. Laemmle, from Germany, worked in a clothing shop; Zukor from Hungary began by sweeping out a fur store; Sam Goldfish (later Goldwyn) from Poland sold gloves; William Fox from Hungary was a cloth sponger; Lewis Selznick from Russia sold jewellery; Mayer from Minsk in Russia was a junk dealer, and so on. They found an industry offering vast possibilities and they seized their chance. Within four years in the movie business Sam Goldwyn, for instance, had made nine hundred thousand dollars, and he was by no means the richest.

The reason why men like this turned to the cinema in the years before and immediately after the First World War lay in the state of the cinema in these years. They were outsiders with no inherited fortunes and with nothing to recommend them to banks or finance houses. They were, however, well suited to the film business which at that time was not quite respectable, looked down upon even by the actors who were attracted by the money it offered. Films were still shown in penny arcades and converted warehouses so it was easy to begin at the bottom. Yet this was a booming era in which fortunes could be made overnight. The way in which Louis B. Mayer made his first quarter of a million dollars – from his share in the distribution of a single film, *The Birth of a Nation* –

showed what could be done. These men could succeed because the new entertainment form of the film was a simple, international language with no rules to be learned. The kind of tastes that were needed for success were those that the producers had by birth. Films had to be made to appeal to the poor and the working classes, the immigrant masses who had poured into America in the first years of the twentieth century and willingly paid out their nickels for a form of entertainment that did not demand a great knowledge of the English language and which nonetheless offered a good measure of laughs and thrills.

The movie tycoons are probably the most attacked and argued-about group of men in the history of the cinema. The tales widely circulated about them show them often to have been regarded as monsters by their employees. When Louis B. Mayer died, Sam Goldwyn is supposed to have said that the reason so many people turned up for the funeral was that 'they wanted to make sure he was dead'. Even this unflattering remark was capped in 1958 when, after the funeral of Columbia chief, Harry Cohn, a television comedian remarked to his audience, 'Well, it only proves what they always say – give the public something they want to see, and they'll come out for it.' There are plenty of instances on record of these producers using violence, in words or fists, to get what they wanted. If threats failed, some of them would weep or go on their knees to get their own way. If they did not succeed or were crossed, they would fire their employees quite ruthlessly and do their best to stop them getting jobs elsewhere. They were hardly more attractive when they were in a happy mood. The sense of humour of Harry Cohn, for instance, is illustrated by the fact that he had a special chair installed in the Columbia dining room in which an unsuspecting visitor could be given an electric shock when Cohn pressed a button. The titles of two biographies show the kind of men the movie tycoons aimed to be: the book on the Columbia president is called *King Cohn* and that about Mayer is called *Hollywood Rajah*. Despite their aims, their enormous salaries and their practically unlimited power in their own domains, these men were far from regal figures. Their contacts with art were usually disastrous. Sam Goldwyn's attempt to buy the film rights to George Bernard Shaw's plays gave rise to the retort, 'The trouble, Mr Goldwyn, is that you are only interested in art and I am only interested in money.' Later Goldwyn brought over from Europe the distinguished playwright Maurice Maeterlinck and set him to work, only to find that the hero of the script was a bee!

The reputation of the Hollywood tycoons is more often based on such stories than on the films they produced. Reporters loved them because of the excellent articles they provided. Jack Warner, even when he was the millionaire head of production at his own studio, used to get up at public dinners and make rambling incomprehensible speeches full of terrible puns and unfunny jokes. Sam Goldwyn's struggles with the American language resulted in such memorable phrases as 'Include me out,' and 'I can answer you in two words – im possible.' As a consequence of this, the writers he employed spent long hours making up Goldwynisms and trying to get them published as the words of the master. But how can you compete with a man who actually said things like 'You've got to take the bull between your teeth,' and 'I've read part of it all the way through'? Even more striking were the troubles of Harry Cohn. He was president of Columbia Pictures for twenty-six years, yet when, in moments of stress or argument, he was challenged to spell the company's name, he would always begin C-O-L-O . . . If the logic of making films were a simple one, the products of such men would surely be appalling. But this was not the case. In part this was due to the quality of the men whom they employed to take charge of the artistic side of production while they chased the power. Among these were the young men who shot to fame as Hollywood's 'boy wonders'. Irving Thalberg, left in charge of Universal studios as a nineteen-year-old, became Louis B. Mayer's right-hand man at M-G-M. Mayer's son-in-law, David O. Selznick (himself son of the pioneer producer Lewis J. Selznick), independently produced the greatest commercial success of the 1930s, *Gone with the Wind*. Darryl F. Zanuck, who headed production at Twentieth Century Fox for twenty years until he retired in

1956, returned to the old habit on his appointment as president in 1962 by installing his own twenty-eight-year-old son Richard as head of studio production and boss of the Hollywood end of the business.

Mayer, Goldwyn, Cohn, Warner and their like gave the world audience their own kind of film. They were tyrannical and often wasteful but they knew their own taste and that of their audience, and created films that could be seen and appreciated all over the world. This success was the result of the kind of men they were. They hated things which were obscure or 'arty' and they relied on the qualities of story, star and colour. Though they seem to have been rather disagreeable people in many ways, they could recognize the talent that would give them the kind of films audiences liked. And they were willing to pay well for it. Naturally the films they made were glamorous pictures of America, which came out as a fantastic wonderland where every story had a happy ending and good triumphed over evil ultimately. To make sure that this was always the case, and because they were afraid of censorship from other people, they created their own code of motion pictures which set limits on the kind of words that could be used and the kind of scenes that could be shown. This was easier for them to accept than for the writers and directors they employed, because they always aimed at a family audience (with all the limitations that this implies). Louis B. Mayer, for instance, always set out to produce films to which he could take his own two daughters.

Producers like Harry Cohn tried to turn everything, including script-writing, into a nine-till-five occupation in the studio, and were highly suspicious of writers who seemed to spend too much of their time sitting around 'thinking'. Cohn's method of dealing with writers gives a clear indication of the basic shrewdness of these tycoons. If he could not judge the writing, he could test the writer's involvement. After a week or two Cohn would send for the work of a new writer and tell him that the script he had written was the worst he had ever read. If the writer agreed, his days at the studio were numbered. If he argued, pointed out good bits, he would stay on. If he discovered that Cohn had not in fact read a word of the script, he might even get a rise! The writer's lot was not a happy one. Often two writers would be working on the same script quite unknown to each other, while the final script would be written by a third writer drawing on their efforts. Of course, only a certain kind of writer could work successfully in these conditions, and successful screen-writers were often former journalists or reviewers, used to working to deadline and to order. In search of prestige, the studios would invite great writers to Hollywood. Because of the very high fees which were paid, many such writers were tempted to try their hand at working for the screen, but the best scripts are not those written by the men with the greatest literary talent (F. Scott Fitzgerald or William Faulkner for instance). The idea of a novelist writing for the screen as freely as he would for publication is a far newer one in the cinema and has its home not in Hollywood but in Europe. In Hollywood many talented writers became very unhappy at the way they were treated and took revenge by writing about the place when they left. And most of the novels about Hollywood paint a very dark picture of it indeed.

The power of the studio bosses over the people they employed was enormous. Jack Warner, for instance, once claimed that he had a hand in editing every film to leave his studio. The producer had complete freedom to stamp his taste on his films and to fire anyone who did not co-operate in this. So the studios developed their own group styles which fans could recognize at a glance. At M-G-M, the studio that boasted of having 'more stars than there are in the heavens', the output in the peak years was forty-two films a year. All were of a high technical polish, for the studio could afford the designers and photographers who gave the glamorous image that made the studio's films so popular. M-G-M had the biggest stars – Mayer discovered Greta Garbo in Europe and built Clarke Gable to be the greatest male star of the 1930s – and the high-key photographic style was designed to show them off to the best advantage. Film stories tended to be tales of love that ended happily and had an uplifting effect, set in a world that was luxurious and therefore deeply exciting for audiences. But despite the luxury, the family was sacred to Louis B. Mayer and nothing was allowed to mar this. The public agreed with his views and one of Mayer's biggest hits was the sentimental Andy Hardy family series, starring the young Mickey Rooney.

At Warner Brothers the average product was very different and the stess was on action and excitement, with Errol Flynn appearing in fast-moving adventure stories directed by the Hungarian-born Michael Curtiz. The Warners took years to become really successful (only their desperate gamble with sound made them rich men), and in the stories and settings they chose there was a certain touch of the realism lacking at M-G-M. Warners became famous for its thrillers and backstage musicals, its typical players being actors like James Cagney, Humphrey Bogart, and the very unglamorous Bette Davis. Paramount was not a richer studio but its image was more upper class, with an emphasis on gloss and high living. Cecil B. De Mille made many of his biblical epics for the company; Ernst Lubitsch made fast, witty comedies there; and Joseph von Sternberg found that the Paramount designers were ideal for the beautiful films, like *Scarlet Empress,* that he directed with Marlene Dietrich. Twentieth Century Fox had Shirley Temple, but also made realistic studies of the life of the poor, such as *The Grapes of Wrath,* made by John Ford in 1940, while Universal became famous for its horror films.

The remarkable qualities of the studio movie are perhaps best illustrated by the making of *Gone with the Wind,* which had taken forty-seven million dollars at the box office even before its recent re-release in 70 mm. form. David O. Selznick, its producer and the driving force behind it, worked for over a year on the script after buying the rights of the still unpublished thousand-page novel by Margaret Mitchell for $50,000. He did not use just one writer, he needed eight in all, and not one director but three (George Cukor, Victor Fleming and Sam Wood). Together they spent four million dollars and shot eighty hours of film. The hero, Rhett Butler, could only be played, everybody was sure, by Clarke Gable, then the world's leading male star. But he was under contract to M-G-M and it cost Selznick a large share of the profits to obtain Gable's signature on the contract. For the female lead 1,400 girls were interviewed and enough film shot in screen tests to make a normal feature film. Even then filming had to begin before Selznick had his actress – eventually Vivien Leigh was signed out of the blue when on a visit to watch the filming. The resulting success with audiences everywhere justified the trouble and expense, but *Gone with the Wind* is the kind of film that could only have been made in Hollywood and at that time. It needed the confidence and experience that can only come from making vast numbers of films in a closed atmosphere where film-making is all that counts. Only the Hollywood film industry could build up the reserves of talent and create the stars on which *Gone with the Wind* relies.

16

Disney and Animation

The effect of the studio system on the development of the film medium can be studied in microcosm as it were if we turn away from the complexities of the feature film and consider what happened to animation under the influence of Walt Disney. The terms 'animated film' or cartoon are somewhat clumsy expressions, far less revealing than their German equivalent, the *Trickfilm*. The trick in question is to go one step farther than in the conventional live-action film and to give an appearance of movement without actually filming something moving. To make this possible the film is broken down, not into sequences or even individual shots, but into single images or frames, each of which is treated separately. Even if we limit ourselves to films made one frame at a time and in which all the movement is created by hand instead of by photographing natural motion, we still have an enormously wide field: cartoons of all kinds, puppet films and films that manipulate objects to show buttons dancing or match-sticks on parade. If we think of how these films have been made, frame by frame, and remember that a sound projector eats up film at the rate of twenty-four frames a second, it is immediately clear that we are dealing with problems very different from those of normal film-making. Animated films of any sort are going to need a very unusual degree of patience and ingenuity, for the sheer labour involved is enormous. A five-minute cartoon needs

7,200 different pictures, while a ninety-minute feature requires no less than 129,600. In return for this patience the animated film gives the film-maker a total control which no feature film-maker using real actors and settings can ever equal. The animator has the same total command over his creation as the painter over his canvas.

There is another important reason, apart from this mechanical difference, why the animated film should be considered separately, and this is the way in which the camera is used. Ordinary cinema grew up as the pioneers began to use the camera creatively. Whatever effects a feature film-maker is seeking – absolute truth to what is real or total fantasy – his success can be measured in the way he uses his camera (the position and angle he shoots from, the lighting he chooses for a scene, the succession of images placed one after the other). None of this is true of the animated film, which is free to employ purely graphic ways of linking shots and obtaining effects. The film cartoonist is as free to create marvels and monsters as a painter is and, as every second's action is broken down into twenty-four separate stages, he is able totally to ignore the way the laws of logic, gravity or cause and effect work in our real world. The speed of the action is not tied to what human beings can perform, and the animator can play with the rhythms of his images as a composer does with the rhythms of his musical notes. All sorts of doubts have been expressed as to whether the cinema is truly an art form. The basis of most criticism is that since the camera exists simply to photograph what is there, it is a mechanical, not a creative medium. To justify the feature film against such criticism we have to show the effect of the selection and reassembling of the parts of reality which are photographed and this can be quite difficult. But no such problem exists with the animated film, for here everything, every movement, is created artificially. Because of this the animated cinema has its own history, quite separate from that of the cinema as a whole.

The theoretical differences between the ordinary film and the cartoon or puppet film have been emphasized here because the effect of Walt Disney's application of studio techniques to the animated film was to blur these distinctions completely. Indeed, one could say that the driving force of Disney's creative life was the attempt to destroy the essential difference between photographed reality and animated cartoon, just as the basic impulse of Hollywood was to pass off a facsimile of life for life itself. It would be as impossible to talk about cartoon films and not mention Disney as it would be to ignore Chaplin in a discussion of film comedy, yet in many ways Disney's work tells us more about the workings of the Hollywood system than about the potentialities of the animated film. When he created Mickey Mouse, his first great success, Disney brought into existence a superstar to equal Charlie Chaplin in world fame. Though Mickey (originally called Mortimer, oddly enough) dates from 1928, the empire founded on the profits from his films continues today. Even now, when Walt Disney himself is dead, we still get new Disney films made and shown to audiences who know just what to expect. The size of the Disney empire is staggering and it was calculated in 1966 that every year all over the world 240 million people see a Disney film and three times that number read a Disney book or magazine. Walt Disney himself became a multi-millionnaire, one of the great figures of Hollywood, and towards the end of his life his formula had proved so successful that he could not fail to get richer. Like Chaplin he owned all the rights to every film he made, and by re-issuing his past successes from time to time he could make profits to equal those of many new films being shown for the first time. Small children going to see *Bambi* find everything new and wonderful; they are not aware that they are seeing the same film that delighted their parents when they were children back in 1942 or on a subsequent re-release.

In view of all this it seems rather sad to have to admit that Disney did not actually draw any of his cartoon characters. The original Mickey Mouse, for example, was drawn by one of his most talented employees, Ub Iwerks, and the later ones (for Mickey changed with the years) were devised by a team of artists. Indeed, it is even said of Disney that he could not draw Mickey Mouse at all, even in the autograph books of children who visited his studio. In much the same way, though his films are full of humour, no one has ever recorded a single funny remark of his made in real life. The reason for this is simple: Disney was not really an artist but a businessman like Thomas Edison or Henry Ford. What is interesting about him therefore is less his personality than the way he turned a neglected part of the cinema into a great industry and made film-making into a machine. Of course, all the great Hollywood tycoons tried to do this, but Disney could succeed better than other studio bosses because everything in a cartoon film can be controlled (and because his stars – Mickey Mouse, Donald Duck and all the rest – never gave trouble, nor asked for a rise!)

In many ways Disney was a model businessman, always eager to use new devices and techniques. When sound arrived in the late 1920s he already had plenty of problems, for he was just launching his Mickey Mouse films, but he insisted on finding a recording system and adding sound to his films. The result was that his cartoons were brilliantly successful, replacing the comic shorts in which men like Chaplin and Keaton had learned their art. In 1931 Disney was one of the first to use Technicolor and later in the 1930s his organization perfected a marvellous new device, the multi-plane camera, which allowed the camera to move *into* his cartoon scenes just as a camera can move into a real setting. Whenever cartoons are made it is usual to break up the picture into various layers – background, middleground, foreground – as well as the separate characters, so that only the parts that actually move need be changed from frame to frame. This saves an enormous amount of time and labour, and if the various layers are painted on celluloid they can be clamped together and shot as a single image. For the real illusion of depth to be achieved, the layers have to be separated to carefully calculated distances and then filmed with great precision. This sounds fairly straightforward but it is in fact a tricky engineering problem which was solved for Disney by Ub Iwerks.

Of course, none of this matters to the small children who go to see Disney films. They go to see the characters (Mickey Mouse, Donald Duck, Pluto, Goofy) or to follow a favourite story – for almost all of Disney's full-length films (beginning with *Snow White and the Seven Dwarfs* in 1937) have been based on fairy tales or popular children's stories — *Dumbo, Bambi, Cinderella, The Jungle Book*, etc. The parents can be sure of what they are getting, for Disney had very clear ideas on what he allowed in his films: nothing to frighten children, no violence or nastiness. Cartoon films are extremely expensive because of the time and talent they consume and Disney expanded his organization to take in other types of film, applying the same principles to his nature films, films mixing cartoons and live action and his television shows. Since he has given so much enjoyment to so many people, it seems unkind to criticize him but this is what one must do when one starts to think about all the possibilities of the animated film. For, though Disney has made more people see cartoons than anyone else in the history of the cinema, he limited their appreciation to just one of the innumerable range of forms of cartoon film-making.

The reasons for this lie in the kind of man Walt Disney was. He came from the American Mid-West, he did not have much formal education and he had a fixed set of beliefs. In his films he wanted to show that good triumphs over evil, that children and animals are lovable and that humour can be wholesome and still funny. He believed in work, in business and in giving value for money, but he was suspicious of things like art, great music and literature. Perhaps his least entertaining feature film is *Fantasia* in which he illustrates classical music. On seeing the rushes of the scene showing centaurs galloping about to the sound of Beethoven's Pastoral Symphony, he is said to have exclaimed, 'Gee, this will *make* Beethoven!' Disney was not interested in creating characters capable of arousing deep emotions, he had two rather different ideas in mind. He wanted the characters in his films to be cute and lovable and to look real. The first aim he achieved by basing all his principal characters on shapes derived from curved lines — plump rabbits, babies, birds — and by including tiny animals in all his stories. The second aim was more difficult to attain, for the cartoon is more suited to picturing unreal or distorted things, but Disney worked at it doggedly. He made his animators study real movement and sought devices (like the multi-plane camera) to give an illusion of depth. Though his stories might be tales of mystery and magic and his characters talking animals, he always stressed their ordinariness. He also created a cleaned-up world where there are no rough edges, no problems, no dirt. In this respect the supreme achievement of Disney is his vast amusement site, Disneyland, where the visitor can be surrounded by three-dimensional figures of the Disney imagination – even a walking, talking Abraham Lincoln – amid an atmosphere of good neighbourliness and fun.

To emphasize the limitations of Disney's work is not to deny its success in its own terms or its influence. In a sense the trouble with Disney is that he was too successful and influential. Everywhere, even in places as far away as Japan or Russia, his style was copied, to such an extent that the other possibilities of the idea of animation were ignored. In France it is Disney's influence that can be seen in the films of Paul Grimault, who made the feature-length *Mr Wonderbird* (*La Bergère et le ramoneur*) from a script by the poet Jacques Prévert in 1952. Equally Disney had a great effect on John Halas and Joy Batchelor who in 1954 made the first British feature-length cartoon, *Animal Farm,* from the novel by George Orwell. These film-makers accepted Disney's idea of what a cartoon is: fully drawn and over-polished, with attempts to smooth out the movement and make the backgrounds a photographically accurate replica of the world. It was not until some of the film-makers who had broken away from Disney set up the UPA company that it became apparent how limiting this influence was.

Walt Disney reigned supreme from the advent of sound until the early 1950s. His style caused the work of the pioneers of animation to be forgotten, and the few animated films that stood aside from his influence were seen as fringe works. Yet it was only when his relentless quest for pseudo-realism was replaced by a new awareness of materials and textures that animation could be regarded as having any real connection with modern painting or twentieth-century graphic art. While, from a present-day standpoint, one can attack the sentimentality

and false values of many Disney films, it is impossible to deny
the sheer professionalism of the animation. For modern animators – even those working furthest from the comfortable
children's world of *Dumbo* and *Snow White* – this skill and
expertise remains an awesome achievement, and a reminder
that, though Hollywood may be replaced by more modern
methods of production, its greatest achievements remain un-
surpassable on their own terms.

17

The Stars

No consideration of Hollywood is possible without reference to
the stars. They are one of the most fascinating aspects of film
history, particularly as they are a consciously and deliberately
created idea, not an essential part of what the cinema is. Films
can be made without stars. For the first fifteen years of the
cinema's history players were anonymous and the star was
unknown. Equally, as the present vogue of pop singers shows,
stars in the true sense can exist without the cinema. If we think
of the entertainment world's stars of the 1960s it is immediately apparent that a newer twentieth-century technical
marvel, the long-playing hi-fi record, has been just as efficient
at creating stars as the cinema ever was. The Beatles have
made films but they are by no means a product of the cinema,
as the idols of the young from 1910 to the 1950s tended to be.
Indeed, the cinema now no longer produces stars on the old
pattern – Elizabeth Taylor with her salary of one million
dollars a film is the last of a dying breed. Before John Wayne
there were half-a-dozen men who could claim to be western
stars, but when he makes his last western there will be no one
to replace him. As we shall see, the phenomenon of the stars is
linked up with the growth and power of the studios. Before
these latter came into being, the audience was captured by the
figures or characters they saw repeatedly on the screen – the
heroes of the serial stories, for example. But they did not go

beyond this and become deeply and totally concerned with the actors who played these roles.

Even at the height of the star era there were still roles that somehow had a greater impact than any of the men or women who played them. A dozen or more Tarzan films have been made and Tarzan is a sort of star in his own right. The magic remains attached to the character itself. Something of the same sort is also true of radio and television today. The existence of stars has to do with the way we identify with characters we see on the cinema screen, but we do not automatically turn the players we see into stars, and lately the cinema has gone back to the earlier method. Among the biggest successes of the 1960s were the James Bond films. Ian Fleming's fictional character has become something of a cult. Books have been written by learned Italian scholars about the 'semeiological importance of 007'. A woman called Mrs James Bond wrote a book about her husband – a distinguished student of ornithology – whose only real claim to this sort of fame was that Ian Fleming borrowed his name. The author himself got caught up in the excitement and tried to live like his hero with none-too-happy results. It seemed that the actor who played the role must become a star in the old sense. Sean Connery was paid a star salary for his interpretations of Bond, but none of the glamour attached itself to him. In other roles he has become just another actor (and one with more talent than he could show in his 007 films). Similarly producers in the period since the late 1950s have found their audiences to be very fickle. Julie Andrews was the star of *The Sound of Music*, which collected an unprecedented seventy million dollars at the American box office, but producers who thought she was a star of the old school received a nasty shock: her presence in other films did not ensure their success. Just as film-makers have in recent years shown independence of the studios, so too audiences have shown their freedom from the star cult. They flock in millions to see one film and yet stay away from the next one in which the same players appear. Yet for a long time in the cinema's short history the stars were the one really safe bet in a risky business. It is with this period that the present chapter is concerned: the forty or fifty years during which the stars reigned supreme, the time when, if they talked of the cinema, people meant Chaplin or Pickford, Valentino or Garbo, Bogart or Monroe.

The invention of the idea of the star can be traced with great exactness. Though we may never know what star quality is precisely, there is no mystery about when the first American star was born. It was in 1910, as the result of a publicity stunt thought up by the man who founded the first studio of the modern type, Carl Laemmle. At the time Laemmle was head of the Independent Moving Picture Company of America (IMP for short) and, like his fellow producer William Fox, was having trouble fighting the power of the Edison-backed Trust. Something extra was needed if the independents were to survive and Laemmle it was who found it. Rumours were circulated (probably by Laemmle himself) that his newly signed actress, Florence Lawrence, was dead. In the *Motion Picture World* Laemmle replied with an advertisement headed 'We Nail a Lie'. In it he wrote that the story of the death of Miss Lawrence, 'the IMP girl, formerly known as the Biograph girl', was 'the blackest and at the same time the silliest lie yet circulated by the enemies of the IMP'. To prove how silly it was, said Laemmle, he had arranged for Miss Lawrence and her leading man, King Baggott, to appear at St Louis's railway station. When she did so, the crowd which turned out to greet her was bigger than the one which had welcomed the President of the United States the previous week. The people thronged around Miss Lawrence, tore at her clothes for souvenirs . . . and the star was born.

Florence Lawrence herself did not remain an attraction for long (in this way too setting a pattern for the future), but audiences now demanded to know the names of the players they saw every week. With their personal fame secure, the latter could now demand ever-increasing salaries. Laemmle's second signing from Biograph was the actress known as Little Mary or the Girl with the Curls. She had been born Gladys Smith but we know her best as Mary Pickford. Signed by Laemmle for $70 a week, she soon became America's Sweetheart and the highest-paid actress of the time, her salary even keeping pace with that of Charlie Chaplin. By 1912 she was earning $500 a week from another great pioneer producer, Adolph Zukor, and four years later this had risen to $10,000 plus a bonus of $300,000. Even this was not enough to keep her happy and an offer of $350,000 a picture lured her away to another company. Mary Pickford is also an interesting example of the way many stars get limited in the roles they can play by an audience which will only accept the star in one sort of role. Throughout her career Mary Pickford was condemned to play the same role. At sixteen she had begun playing innocent little orphan girls of a kind you find only in Victorian novels, and at the age of thirty-two, in *Little Annie Rooney*, she was still cast to play a twelve-year-old girl from the slums. All her attempts to play adult roles were box-office failures and eventually she retired, rich but defeated. Even then the audience taste for the kind of role she played remained and in the years 1935–8 the top box office star was the (real) little girl, Shirley Temple.

William Fox's venture into star-making was if anything more interesting than that of Laemmle. There is something quite natural in the rise to stardom of an extremely gifted actress like Mary Pickford. Equally it is unsurprising that the great comic actors should become stars, taking the names suggested by their roles: Max (the Frenchman Max Linder), Charlie the Tramp (Charles Chaplin) or Fatty (Roscoe Arbuckle). What Fox did was to show that the same stardom could be achieved without any of the talent that these men clearly possessed, simply by publicity. Fox's big star of 1915 was a complete fabrication. She was a mysterious vampire-like woman called Theda Bara, a name which Fox's publicity men were quick to point out was an anagram of Arab Death. She was supposed to have been born within the shadow of the Pyramids and to spend her spare time making exotic perfumes, looking into the future and driving men mad with love. In fact she was a nice girl from Cincinnati, USA, a tailor's daughter called Theodosia Goodman. Like Mary Pickford, but even more quickly and disastrously, she found herself a prisoner of her star role and retired after forty films in three years.

One of the great secrets of the star idea comes from the fact that being a star does not need any talent (as Miss Goodman shows), for this creates a great bond between the star and the audience. A girl can be serving in a shop or working as a typist one day and on her way to stardom the next. This being so, any shopgirl or typist can relate very directly to the star, who becomes a glorified, dream-fulfilment version of herself. The reason why stars do not need any special talent lies in the nature of screen acting. To succeed on the stage an actor needs a definite acting gift. The greatest actors are, it is true, born not made, yet no-one could become Laurence Olivier overnight. A stage actor needs some technique, training, experience, the ability to move, speak, master an accent. So it is that even the best work their way comparatively slowly to the top, learning their art acting as amateurs, working in repertory theatres, tackling small parts before taking on a role like Hamlet or Lady Macbeth. In the cinema, on the other hand, such training is not needed and can indeed be a handicap. Because of the way a film is made and the manner in which it works on its audience, a screen actor is called upon not to act but simply to be. This is why film actors are always supposed to dread playing a scene with an animal or a child. Children and animals have a spontaneous gift for being natural that only a rare adult can match, and this is reflected in the success they have in the cinema. If we were making any complete list of stars, we would have to include animals like Lassie and the horses of the singing cowboys of the 1940s, as well as the child stars like Shirley Temple, Mickey Rooney, or Judy Garland, who were such a great success in Hollywood in the 1930s.

Just how little acting talent or experience is needed for successful acting is best shown perhaps by the films that do not use stars at all. In realistic films some directors have made masterpieces using people who have never even seen a movie camera before – Luchino Visconti employing Sicilian fishermen in his film *La terra trema* and Robert Flaherty turning his Eskimo friends into actors for *Nanook of the North*. In the hands of a great director anybody can play himself, or a role very close to his own personality. The camera can do everything. It can create, with effects of lighting, shadow, movement and cutting, apparent acting of a skill and subtlety that few stage actors could match. But if a director can create a performance out of nothing at all, and make anyone an actor, in the case of the star there is something that no director can give, not talent but the unique aura, the mystery, the magnetism that the star exhibits. Here the flair or sensitivity of the director is seen in his ability to discover this magnetism in an actress who, to other people, simply looks uninteresting.

The way this works is clearly shown by the examples of the two greatest female stars of the 1930s, Greta Garbo and Marlene Dietrich. When she met the director Mauritz Stiller, Garbo, for instance, was a plump, shy drama student whose only film experience was acting in two advertising shorts and playing a frisky bathing beauty in a little comedy. Already a great director, Stiller was looking for a star and already had a name in his mind (Greta's real name was Gustafsson). He uncovered her talent but ironically when they both went to Hollywood she won acclaim while he quarrelled with the studio bosses and did nothing of real merit. He began directing her first film there, but was replaced by another director at the orders of Louis B. Mayer. After Stiller's death Garbo continued working in Hollywood and in all she made twenty-four films for M-G-M. Then suddenly, at the age of thirty-six and at the height of her powers, she withdrew into total seclusion. All great stars have an element of mystery in their make-up: in the case of Garbo the mystery is complete. Marlene Dietrich was likewise created by one man who saw in her possibilities unsuspected by anyone else (she had already made several films). Josef von Sternberg discovered her in Berlin, remained her director in Hollywood for six years and wrapped her in a veil of mystery. The impact of both stars comes very much from the quality of their faces when photographed in close-up, and it is not by chance that virtually all Garbo's M-G-M films were photographed by one man, the brilliant William Daniels, or that Sternberg, as well as being a great director, was also a photographer of genius.

The quality of a star – the unique ability to exist fully in front of a camera – is not acting in the conventional sense, and to begin with it is apparent only to the rare film-maker who can sense it instinctively. (The colleagues of Stiller and Sternberg all thought they were mad when they cast their discoveries in their first starring roles.) Once established, however, the communication between the star and the audience is direct and total – to be a fan is in a way to be in love with the star. Yet as pointed out earlier in this chapter, the star and all the things he or she represents are not an inevitable part of the cinema. For stars to exist fully there must be a studio system which will organize film-making around them. The films become simply vehicles for the star's talents; they exploit the scenes and emotions which a star is uniquely gifted to present. When this happens the star becomes a real power – he or she can insist on certain writers and photographers, hire and fire directors, earn a bigger salary than the president of the film company. Yet the star is not free. He or she still remains a product, an object that the studio sells to the public. Advertising, invented news stories and romances, autographed photographs, fan clubs, personal appearances, all specially staged and arranged, contribute to the fame of the star and therefore to the value he or she has for the studio. Often the star, once discovered, is denied the chance to have a private life but has to live instead in an unreal world of glamour and publicity. For this reason the lives of many stars, despite their wealth, are often very unhappy. Their marriages end in divorce (Richard Burton is Elizabeth Taylor's fifth husband) or, tragically, they kill themselves with drink or drugs (Marilyn Monroe was a striking example). Yet such is the nature of the world of screen publicity that this only increases the public interest in stars and the public desire to see their films.

Stars, as the name itself implies, are more than just human beings of a particularly interesting type. They are figures that tell us a great deal about the society in which we live and about the basic human desires and dreams. The range covered by the term 'star' is enormous. In many ways the very early stars, particularly the actresses like Mary Pickford and Lillian Gish who began work with D. W. Griffith, are Victorian heroines. For all the wonders of the new inventions of the twentieth century – the car, the gramophone, the film itself – it is clear that many people who made up the film audience still lived emotionally in the nineteenth century. Until the late twenties silence prevented the cinema from being a mere record of the ordinary world and encouraged it to reflect our dreams, as is shown by the stars of the late silent period. Rudolf Valentino, one of the great romantic stars, built his career on being mysterious. Women fell in love with him because he was remote and unreal, yet the emotions he aroused were genuine enough for two young women to commit suicide at his funeral. In the 1920s female stars with names like Alla Nazimova and Pola Negri lived – or seemed to live – fantastic lives in princely villas where no luxury was spared. The very existence of figures like this – the sharp contrast of maidens in distress (Lillian Gish on an iceflow drifting towards the falls) and vamps (mysterious females luring men to their doom) – tells us a great amount about the role and status of women. There is mystery, but of a different kind, in Garbo and Dietrich (both, significantly enough, imported into Hollywood from Europe). But as the relationship of men and women moves to one of equality, stars become more ordinary and more human, as with Katherine Hepburn or Ingrid Bergman. The way women are treated as objects comes through in the series of pin-up girls from Rita Hayworth to Marilyn Monroe, now giving way to the more modern image of pert young women like Audrey Hepburn or Brigitte Bardot, who would never find themselves alone and helpless on an iceflow.

The arrival of sound which brought female stars down to earth also had the same effect on the men. The stars of the 1930s have solid American names – Cary Grant, Gary Cooper, Clark Gable, Henry Fonda, Spencer Tracy. Interestingly, many of these have remained popular long after their youth has gone, creating a new category of unique father figures, ageing yet attractive and manly. The core of the male stars is not the boy-next-door figure but the man of action. Lancelots and Galahads come in several brands. There are the cowboy heroes from Tom Mix to John Wayne and the swashbuckling adventurers like Douglas Fairbanks and Errol Flynn. With the sound film comes a new kind of hero, the tough guy from the modern city – Edward G. Robinson or James Cagney.

All these types have a certain indestructible quality. Their roles give them weapons with which to conquer the world – the six-shooter, the duellist's rapier, the sub-machinegun – but there are always rules governing their behaviour – the code of the West (reflected in the ritual of drawing a gun), the duellist's code of chivalry or the gunman's evil rule of shoot first and ask questions afterwards. A more modern variation is the defeated hero of whom the cinema's greatest representative is Humphrey Bogart, the battered world-weary private detective of a dozen thrillers. More recently this particular image has been revived in the figures of rebels like Marlon Brando and James Dean. Dean who died after only three pictures while driving his Porsche sports car at 160 miles-an-hour, is a figure to rank with Valentino. Even after his death his fan mail amounted to two thousand letters a week.

Such stars as these dominated the cinema for several decades, but as they die or grow older they are not replaced by similar figures. The cinema is constantly changing and developing new techniques. Modern methods of shooting, using freer camera work, real settings and more complicated stories, demand different qualities. The old stars were a product of a hot-house studio atmosphere: their names sold seats in the cinema and so film-making was built around their needs and whims. Now audiences make new demands and the stars become relics. The older people who at one time went to the cinema twice a week to see their favourite stars now stay at home to watch television. The younger audience turns its attention to the pop scene. As with the decline of the big studios, another part of the era of the cinema has come to an end.

18

The Western as a Film Genre

The creation of stars with whom the audience can identify is one answer to the film producer's fundamental dilemma of how to combine mass production with constant variety. On the one hand, he must produce a regular, unending flow of films, for the cinemas need a new work to show every week (in the early 1900s the position was even more difficult, for films were changed every day or two). Yet, on the other hand, all the films must be different, each one must offer something new, or why should audiences keep on going to the cinema week after week? This is the big difference between producing films and producing, say, motor cars. In general, film audiences are not really interested in which company has produced a given film, and equally they do not care about writers or directors, despite the influence these people have on the quality of the film (a rare exception is Alfred Hitchcock, whose films are sold on his name rather than those of the players). But audiences have, it seems, always been reassured by some elements of continuity between this week's film and last week's. Hence, stars are almost by definition players who never vary from film to film and for a star to play a part that fell outside his customary range was always considered a risky undertaking. In the same way, if the film itself can be made to fit into a certain category, so that the audience knows what to expect in general terms but is intrigued as to how the well-known ingredients will be served up this time, then a certain level of success can almost be guaranteed. Audiences like to know what is in store for them and a successful film is one which can be clearly and accurately labelled: it is a western or a musical, a horror film or a gangster movie, a slapstick comedy or a woman's picture. Even today, when lists of new releases are made in the film industry's trade papers, every film is given a one-word categorization – comedy, drama, adventure, etc. – and woe betide any director who just wants to make a 'film'.

Most of the forms which the cinema has made its own are extensions or modifications of forms already existing in other arts. There are, for example, close links between the musical on film and on the stage and between gangster films and the thrillers of men like Dashiell Hammett and Raymond Chandler. Yet one form at least, the western, is largely a new development of the cinema, though there is even here perhaps a connection with the Wild West shows of Buffalo Bill and other showmen from 1870 onwards. The western can claim to be one of the oldest of film types. Edwin S. Porter's *The Great Train Robbery* of 1904, one of the very first story films, is a western of sorts in that it tells how a group of bandits stop and rob a train and are then pursued and killed. Since 1904 hardly a year has gone by without some worthwhile western film (and any number of worthless ones) being made. The western continues to draw crowds and give exciting viewing and its range is extraordinarily wide. There have been comic westerns and musical westerns, and the form has even been successfully transferred to the television screen (though one would have thought that the absence of the wide open spaces that only the cinema screen can show would have been a crippling limitation).

The western is a further illustration of the question of film genres that has already been touched upon in the discussion of silent comedy. Because of its long history and continued popularity, the western allows perhaps the clearest analysis of the issues involved. As a form it offers the film-maker certain advantages. People like stories of adventurous open-air life that take them out of their everyday lives, away from the monotony of factory bench or school desk. They like a story that has a clear and gripping development and moves to a satisfying climax when everything is settled in a blaze of guns. The disadvantages of the western for the film-maker are equally clear. There is a certain sameness which can result in a deadened response on the part of the audience, or the automatic response may be so strong as to drown the message that the film-maker is trying to get across (spectators will tend to find the violence romantic, for example). But for a film-maker who wants to talk directly to his audience about moral values, or about themes such as male friendship or patriotism, the western can offer an unequalled freedom. We all have a pretty clear idea of what a western is, but if we try to pin down a definition it becomes obvious that we do not base our judgement on what the story is about or really where it is set. Westerns tend to be about a certain period of American history and to show the building-up of the nation, but they have an attraction that is international. We find echoes of the western in a great many Japanese films, particularly those of Akira Kurosawa, and some of the most interesting westerns of the 1960s were made in Italy. In a similar way virtually any kind of story can become the basis of a western. John Ford's classic *Stagecoach* is a version of Guy de Maupassant's story of the Franco-Prussian War, *Boule de suif*, while *The Magnificent Seven* was based on a Japanese period film, Kurosawa's *Seven Samurai*.

To define a western we have to look beyond the nominal setting and story to the visual quality of the film itself. There are certain images we expect to find in any film that calls itself a western. We look for a certain sort of costume, for example, and when a film like *The Wild Bunch* opens with the gang in First World War army uniforms we feel – as the director Sam Peckinpah intended us to at this point – a certain unease. In a western there will of course be horses (some of these have in the past been almost stars in their own right, like Champion and Trigger, the horses of the singing cowboys, Gene Autry and Roy Rogers), and the kind of pictorial compositions where horse and rider stand out against the skyline or suddenly become visible against a rocky landscape. We expect guns, elegant-looking weapons like the colt and the Winchester rifle.

which help to explain to us the sort of people the story is about. But there are other signs too: a sheriff's badge or a gambler's fancy waistcoat. Nowadays it is going too far to expect all badmen to wear black hats or the hero to be dressed all in white, though this has happened in the past in westerns, but there is a powerful symbolism present in the clothes. When in the classic western *Shane*, made by George Stevens in 1953, we catch our first glimpse of Jack Palance, clad from head to toe in black, we know immediately that he is a killer. One might include the actors as part of the visual pattern for, in addition to their star magic, there are some faces that almost automatically conjure up the world of the West. The variety of them is enormous. In the beginning there were men like Broncho Billy Anderson, William S. Hart and Tom Mix. Then came William Boyd (celebrated as Hopalong Cassidy) and the singing cowboys Autry and Rogers (whose popularity is, for us today, one of the hardest things to understand about the cinema of the 1930s and 1940s). Since the 1940s, mention of the western summons up the faces of John Wayne, Alan Ladd and Gary Cooper, Randolph Scott and Henry Fonda.

Not only are the names of the stars constant, so too are the minor players in the background and, indeed, the roles they play. The western has a varied but limited range of characters. Mexicans and Indians have traditionally been cast as villains and not until the 1950s were there serious attempts to present problems from their point of view. The slow pan to reveal the Indian hordes silhouetted on the hilltops is one of the classic images of the western, to rank with the cavalry charge or the stagecoach pursued across the plains. Women frequently have very stereotyped roles. They are either scarlet-clad saloon girls (leading a bad life but always willing to die to save the hero) or gingham-clad ladies from the East bringing the civilized values that the newly won West lacks. Though we often talk of 'cowboy' films, the really striking figures in most westerns are those with more distinctive roles – the cattle barons for ever at war with the ranchers, and the men whose professions set them off from the mass – the bankers (so often the outwardly respectable cause of so much violence), the gamblers, the gunfighters. The same scenes and settings recur in western after western. The swing doors of the saloon open and a stranger walks up to the long bar. As he orders his whisky and confronts his long-sought enemy, the crowd melts away to a safe distance. There is a poker game in one corner, usually crookedly run and often a cause of needless violence, resulting in the death of a good man or turning an impetuous youth into a hunted killer. As an aftermath of violence there are quieter moments at the funeral of the dead man or at a church service where young and old gather around a preacher who may not be ordained but who knows his bible by heart. Then the streets are cleared for the final confrontation of hero and villain, the shoot-out fought man against man with a code of rules as powerful as those of any duelling code.

The western has been called an art form for connoisseurs because it assumes that you have seen it all before. You do not spoil anyone's enjoyment of a western if you tell them how it ends. What counts is not what happens, but how it happens, the little ways in which a scene or a shot is different. It is clear in any case that we do not go to westerns to be surprised. In a traditional western it does not take us long to anticipate what is going to happen: John Wayne will outpunch the badmen, Randolph Scott will outwit them quietly, Henry Fonda will keep his honesty and integrity in the face of violence. In one way audiences like it because it is all so reassuring, but beneath the surface there are real tensions and conflicts. Generally speaking westerns deal with the years 1865–90, the years when the West was opened up and a crucial period in American history. Many of the characters bear the names of men who really lived, and here we have a whole range of humanity. We find lawmen like Wyatt Earp and reformed drunkards like Doc Holliday, men of peace like the Apache Cochise and arrogant blundering fools like General Custer. America is still a society in which men feel that they have a right to carry a gun and it is in the western that some of the implications of this attitude are examined in a succession of violent figures: the youthful Billy the Kid, the warrior Geronimo, the outlaws Jesse James and his brother Frank (often treated sympathetically), the animal-like

Dalton brothers and their cousins the Youngers. Equally, many of the incidents we find in westerns have their roots in history: the gunfight at the OK Corral, Custer's Last Stand, the Battle of the Alamo, the break-up of the great cattle ranches and the coming of the railways.

The historical setting of the western is ideal. The period is far enough away from the settings and costumes not to seem just quaint and old-fashioned, yet near enough for personal memories to remain (the director John Ford, for instance, met Wyatt Earp on several occasions when he was a young man). The questions raised are therefore far enough away to be treated with detachment and yet close enough to involve Americans of today. The matter of the treatment of the Indians is very important at a time when the position of the Negro in America is always being discussed. The questions of the way a man fits into a community and the kinds of demands it can make on him are as relevant in the 1970s as in the 1870s. Some westerns, like Fred Zinnemann's *High Noon*, which was scripted by Carl Foreman and starred Gary Cooper, are in fact political fables, in this case a treatment of political upheavals of the 1950s only nominally set in the old West.

There is another level too to the western. The plots can be extremely simple and yet remain very effective. A man rides into town, deals with the trouble there and rides out again (*Shane*), or a man whose wife has been murdered confronts and kills the men responsible (Budd Boetticher's *Ride Lonesome*). Equally, the characters, while very clear-cut in terms of good and evil, are of bigger than normal stature. They are not weighed down as we are by the needs of everyday life. They are free men called upon to defend what they believe in against powerful enemies only too willing to use a gun. For these reasons the western, for all its links with real events, is not a realistic portrayal of life. That is to say, it does not present human beings as they are with all their petty worries, but as they ought ideally to be. In this way the western becomes either myth (recording the deeds of legendary, super-human figures) or a sort of morality play, showing the triumph of good over evil.

When one thinks of film directors who make westerns, the first name which comes to mind is that of John Ford. In the course of a fifty-year directing career in Hollywood he has made dozens of westerns, including some of the best-known: *Stagecoach* (1939), *My Darling Clementine* (1946) and *The Searchers* (1956). In a trio of films with John Wayne in the years 1948–50 (*Fort Apache, She Wore a Yellow Ribbon* and *Rio Grande*) he celebrated the heroism of the cavalry in its war against the Indians, but later, with *Cheyenne Autumn* in 1964, he reversed the pattern and showed events from the Indian point of view. Ford makes his films about the romance of the West and this is reflected in his imagery. Many of his westerns have been filmed in Monument Valley, which he chose not because of its authenticity as Indian country but for its picturesque scenery. We constantly find figures silhouetted against the sky, or noble men, whether cavalry officers or Indians, facing death with a calm assurance. In Ford's work ideas like honour, duty and nobility have a real meaning.

In his films we also find a strong sense of the community. Seeing them we become aware of the pioneering spirit of the men and women who went out to settle in the new land and of the values on which they built their townships. When these people gather to dance or pray the warm sentiment that colours all Ford's work is clearly apparent. In the cavalry which plays an important part in so many of his films Ford shows both his respect for discipline and his sense of comedy. The films are almost always given passages of knock-about farce and far more stress is placed on loyalty than on the moral issue of killing. The values which Ford celebrates are virtues such as courage in the face of death, respect for the weak and for women, obedience to orders. There is no one Ford hero – the civilized restraint of Henry Fonda, the warmer vitality of John Wayne and the cynicism of James Stewart all contribute to the picture he builds up – but always these men are shown in their relationship with their fellows and with the community.

When we consider a younger specialist in westerns like Budd Boetticher (twenty years Ford's junior) we find quite a different sort of style and method of approach. Here the hero is a sort of bull-fighter, alone in an arena, facing an enemy whom he must outwit by bluff or cunning. The hero of Boetticher's best films of the 1950s — westerns like *The Tall T*, *Ride Lonesome* or *Comanche Station* — is the lean, ageing figure of Randolph Scott, who plays a man lacking all family ties or special skills of any kind. Though his behaviour is quite matter-of-fact, he is a man with a mission which absorbs him totally. In Boetticher's films one of the common themes of many westerns — the long journey to seek revenge on a past enemy — comes very clearly to the foreground. The avenging Scott, relying totally upon himself, settles down to even odds, outwits those who have disarmed him and splits his enemies so that he can deal with them one at a time. He succeeds, but there is no joy at the end — he kills but takes no pleasure in it. The images in a Boetticher film reflect the drabness of the hero's life. The setting is a desert of rocks and scrub, not at all picturesque and offering little shelter or sign of habitation. Everything is scaled down and even the stagecoach tends to be drawn, not by elegant horses, but by mules. In Boetticher's world simply staying alive is an achievement that few characters manage.

In the hands of newer directors in the 1960s the western changes yet again. Sam Peckinpah, ten years younger than Boetticher, takes a new look at the West and finds new things to stress. He sets his films in a precise historical setting, often — as in *Ride the High Country* or *The Wild Bunch* — the end of an era as the gunman begins to be out of date and the motorcar comes to replace the horse. Similarly, where Boetticher pares down the story to its bare essentials, Peckinpah builds up the drama and stresses the realism of the character's clothes, guns and behaviour. There are no innocents left in Peckinpah's world — the women are as bad as the men, and the children amuse themselves by tormenting and roasting scorpions. In the end, most notably in *The Wild Bunch*, there comes a great burst of savagery, with dozens of men dying in slow motion, technicolor blood spurting most convincingly and a ballet of total destruction being created.

There are many other film-makers who have made westerns that merit attention — Anthony Mann with his epic westerns,

Howard Hawks, whose films tend to be studies of groups of men welded together under pressure, and Delmer Daves, who sets out to show what the West was really like. Yet even the three we have looked at show the multiple possibilities of a form or genre and what varied ideas can be expressed with virtually the same materials: a man, a horse and a gun. A genre can develop as the attitudes of the men who use it change. Without fixed forms like the western and the stars who help bring them to life, the Hollywood cinema would never have functioned so effectively, had so much impact on the world film industry and given us so many good films. Now that the cinema is giving way to television as the normal visual entertainment for the vast mass of people, so television too is developing its own patterns of storytelling, particularly the endless series of episodes recounting each week the adventures of the same group of characters. It is an indication of the richness of the western as a genre that even here – as series like *Wells Fargo, The Virginian* and *High Chapparal* show – it can play its part.

19

Hitchcock and Authorship in Hollywood

Just as a novel mirrors the thoughts and feelings of its writer or a piece of music those of its composer, so too a film can be the expression of a single person and a reflection of his views on life and human experience. At first sight this seems an unlikely idea. The making of any normal feature film involves the collaboration of dozens of people, all with special talents and viewpoints. Moreover, the cinema is, undeniably, a very mechanical medium – the camera photographs what is put in front of it and there does not seem to be much freedom left to the film-maker. But in fact this is to underestimate the importance of such things as the choice of how you shoot something, what you leave out, the angle of the camera from which you shoot it, the length of time you leave it on the screen, and the shots you choose to precede and follow it. Together these allow a great freedom to a film-maker and permit the film to be a genuine expression of his feelings. Sometimes the key man is the actor (Buster Keaton's films are an example of this), sometimes it may be the writer, though even this is comparatively rare. In general the man who has the greatest control over a film is the one non-specialist, the director. It is he who has the possibility of working with the writer on the preparation of the material for shooting, who is in charge of the actors and camera during the actual filming, and who may well also supervise the editing of the film (putting together the individual shots in their ideal order and rhythm). Because, in this way, the director can play a part at all the vital stages, he has the chance to make the film his own, to make it express what he wants it to. The writer cannot do this so easily because he does not control the images, the colours, the acting style or the players. The actor himself cannot shape the film through his performance, as he might do on the stage, because a film is nearly always shot out of order and in tiny fragments, so that a whole day's shooting may be pruned or re-ordered in the editing. So it is the director who is the key man. Stars like John Wayne and Bette Davis obviously have a great importance and stamp their personalities on the films in which they appear, but if a film is a really good one, it will express more than just an actor's performance and character: it will become the vehicle for a view of life, a moral concern, an analysis of some chosen facet of human experience.

In Europe it is not uncommon for the most important directors to be granted the kind of ideal freedom which we have described here, and consequently the question of who is the author of a film directed by Luchino Visconti or Federico Fellini never arises: it is self-evidently the director. The Hollywood system on the other hand has traditionally been geared to a quite different scheme of priorities. The aim is not personal expression but the production of dozens of films simultaneously so as to provide a never-ending stream of films for the world's cinemas. In Hollywood therefore specialization became the keynote. The studios employed a great many talented craftsmen, teams able to build and costume a Persian city one week and an eighteenth-century villa the next. That such men should be specialists is unsurprising, but the studios took the idea a stage farther and tried to turn the creative men into narrow specialists as well. A film director might not become involved in a film until the script has been fully written and every word of dialogue composed, and when the shooting finished, he would hand over the film to a specialist editor. Even the writing would not be the work of one man. Thus one writer, regarded as good at shaping a story would compose the basic construction of a film, while another would write in the dialogue. A third might then add a few scenes to give greater impact to a dull section, while a fourth would quickly revise and polish the script ready for shooting. It was not uncommon, in the great days of Hollywood, for a writer to be given a script and be told to write in half-a-dozen laughs in the first ten minutes, to create, out of nothing, a part for some female star who had suddenly become available. Of course, only a certain kind of film-maker could work creatively within the confines of the studio set-up. Directors of great but unwieldy talent like Erich von Stroheim or Orson Welles could never find a place there. But there are film-makers of another kind who work happily in this sort of situation, men like John Ford, Howard Hawks or Douglas Sirk, the master of the glossy woman's picture.

The careers of men like these are at the heart of what we mean by the word Hollywood, but the question of how to deal with them critically is quite a difficult one. To begin with, the issue of who is responsible for what and who should be credited with the authorship of a film is often dubious in the Hollywood context. In the case of a great many films there is no clear answer, and there will probably always be the problem of the isolated, inexplicably brilliant film in the career of a director or writer otherwise doomed, it seems, to total mediocrity. Where more consistent film-makers are concerned, it is almost always helpful to look at a whole series of the man's works. Even if it is not wholly successful, any film by a great director demands critical investigation and will reward the critic who is seeking to understand some of the basic impulses behind the film-maker's work. A bad film may even be more revealing than a good one, simply because the ambitions and intentions behind it are more obvious. Re-evaluation must be constant, and there are many instances of films which were neglected when they first appeared but which now, after twenty years or more, look infinitely better than other more celebrated works of the period. A way of looking at films that takes a director's output *en bloc* and considers each film to be, initially at least, worthy of the same critical attention, can do far more than merely uncover a handful of neglected masterpieces. It can change our whole sense of values in the cinema. The manner in which this occurs becomes clear if we look at the career and reputation of one of Hollywood's most successful directors, Alfred Hitchcock.

In a career extending over fifty films and an equal number of years in Britain and Hollywood, Hitchcock has always been a professional. He has often contributed to the writing of his film scripts, sometimes served as his own producer and constantly made tiny cameo performances (as a sort of trademark), but nevertheless he remains the epitome of the pure professional movie director. For thirty years his films have been major Hollywood productions backed by the resources of a big studio. Generally too they have been based (often fairly remotely, it is true) on popular novels and plays, and acted by leading Hollywood stars (names like Ingrid Bergman and Grace Kelly, James Stewart and Cary Grant recur in the credit titles of his films). He himself has fostered the image of the shrewd but smiling professional. Yet his films show that there is still, beneath the surface of the bland, rotund figure of the mature Hitchcock, more than a trace of the child of four terrified by being sent by his parents to spend a night at the police station as a punishment for some minor misbehaviour, and of the twenty-three-year-old aspiring director who had written his first film script (*Woman to Woman*) but never touched alcohol or been out with a woman. For a long time, however, the outward image was all that concerned audiences and critics, as attention was focused on his skill and adroitness as a director. After ten years as a film-maker in the British studios these qualities were strikingly apparent as he made an international reputation with half-a-dozen thrillers for the Gaumont-British company, including films like the first version of *The Man who Knew Too Much* (1934), *The Thirty-Nine Steps* (1935) and *The Lady Vanishes* (1938).

It was clear from these films that Hitchcock was above all a narrative artist. He was perfecting his way of telling stories through images and sounds, so that his films became compulsive viewing for an audience. Much of the pleasure to be got from these films (as from many of his later ones) comes from the way the story element is handled. Events are piled one upon the other at such a pace that the implausibilities of the story pass unnoticed. The British national character is gently mocked through the figures of chattering landladies, dim-witted policemen and the ever-resourceful upper-class characters who keep the foreigners at bay with their pistols, while caring most deeply about the outcome of the current test match against Australia. He avoids the stereotyped hero-heroine situation with some sharply drawn couples whose bickering gives way to real respect, and at the same time delights in playing with clichés of setting and background. If the film unfolds in Scotland, a flock of sheep and a mist will allow the hero and heroine to escape (*The Thirty-Nine Steps*), just as in later films the traitor falls from the Statue of Liberty (*Saboteur*, 1942) and the hero saving the nation's secrets is pursued over the giant faces of the Mount Rushmore national monument (*North by Northwest*, 1959). Striking proof of Hitchcock's sheer skill as a narrator is his use of the device he himself christened the MacGuffin. He realized early in his career that, if the mechanics of the plot were properly handled, the MacGuffin – the vital document, evidence or secret for the possession of which the characters chase, kill and cheat each other – could be reduced to a mere shadow without harming the suspense. Thus, in two of his best films, *The Lady Vanishes* and *North by Northwest*, the complex action revolves around something quite small, in the one case, a little tune (allegedly a code message) and, in the other, a roll of microfilm.

The 1930s British thrillers took Hitchcock – almost inevitably – to Hollywood, where he remained for thirty years, with only brief visits to England to make two shorts for the British Ministry of Information in 1944 and to direct two features, *Under Capricorn* and *Stage Fright*, in 1949–50. When, in 1971, he came back once more to the British studios to make *Frenzy*, he included some striking echoes of his 1930s style, almost as a kind of affectionate homage to his own past. In 1940, however, when he was trying to establish himself in Hollywood, his Englishness caused some difficulty, and he found producers dubious about giving him the stars and budgets he needed. But gradually he affirmed his reputation as the master of screen suspense, creating as it were a genre of his own. His thrillers are quite distinct from both the American gangster films which have their roots in social criticism and the Agatha Christie-style whodunnits which he dislikes as mere cold puzzles that do not deeply involve an audience. His films show his concern not with what disaster may happen next, but with how the hero or heroine will avoid an impending disaster. For Hitchcock the distinction is crucial. If a character enters a room in which, unknown to him and to us, there is a bomb, the explosion will give perhaps fifteen seconds of exciting cinema. But if we know the bomb is there when he enters, our attention can be held for perhaps fifteen minutes. Always Hitchcock is careful to make us identify closely with his innocent heroes, so that we share emotionally the danger he places them in. If we do this, another of his maxims comes true: the bigger the villain, the better the movie. Taken in this way Hitchcock's films seem to have a surface but no depth, and their director appears as a clever, even cynical manipulator of audience reaction.

The director himself, in his public statements, seems happy to talk simply about technique (how effects were achieved), even if it means accepting this level of interpretation. For, unlike European film-makers such as Antonioni or Bergman, he has never talked about any profound significance in his films, and his interviews offer few clues as to the reasons why they are so powerful. *Psycho*, for example, is a highly complex film however we approach it: probing, ruthlessly effective, highly ambiguous and shot through with a macabre sense of humour. To describe it, as Hitchcock does, as simply a 'fun' picture is hardly enlightening. It is therefore, not to the director, but to his critics – particularly those who have looked at his whole output – that we must look for starting-points if we are to talk meaningfully about his films.

In a book published in 1957 the Frenchmen Claude Chabrol and Eric Rohmer (both later to become noted directors) found all kinds of moral issues hidden beneath the thriller surface.*

---

* Claude Chabrol and Eric Rohmer, *Hitchcock* (Editions Universitaires, Paris, 1957).

Taking as their starting-point Hitchcock's Catholic background (he was educated by the Jesuits), they looked at the themes of guilt and innocence, accusation and punishment, good and evil. In films scripted by many different writers and adapted from a diversity of sources, they found that Hitchcock deals with the same preoccupations, many of them indicated by the film titles themselves: *Blackmail, Suspicion, Shadow of a Doubt, I Confess, The Wrong Man, Vertigo.* Viewed in this way the films allow a Hitchcock universe to be defined, in which the characters live in a perplexing network of deceit and betrayal, doubt and suspicion. Murder or violent death are among the few unchanging constants, and there is no immediately obvious way of escape. Blind confidence in others is disastrous, curiosity is relentlessly punished and only confession may lead to a sort of salvation. Here innocence cannot be taken for granted: it has to be proved, and this often entails the hero in a considerable ordeal. Characters tend to polarize into embodiments of purity or evil, but their roles are interchangeable. Because of this Hitchcock's films abound in instances of the transfer of crime, guilt or punishment. In *Blackmail* (1929) the blackmailer, by the manner of his death, throws suspicion on himself and frees the heroine who is the real guilty party. *Shadow of a Doubt* (1943) shows an innocent girl responsible for the destruction of her uncle who is intent on murdering her, while *Strangers on a Train* (1951) is built around one character's suggestion to another that they swop crimes – he will kill the other's wife in exchange for the murder of his own father.

More recently the English critic Robin Wood has looked at Hitchcock's films in terms of the nature and depth of the relationship binding the hero and heroine.* He stresses the growth of contact as each film unfolds and the way in which the characters overcome their weaknesses and problems by living through difficult situations together. This is a theme that he finds common to such otherwise widely different films as *Suspicion, Vertigo* and *The Birds.* If Wood's argument is accepted, then the customary dismissal of Hitchcock is turned

* Robin Wood, *Hitchcock's Films* (A. Zwemmer, London, and A. B. Barnes, New York, 1965).

upside down and he emerges as a deeply moral artist concerned with many of the great problems of the twentieth century. *Psycho*, for example, becomes 'one of the key works of our age'.

Both these critical approaches have their limitations: the one overemphasizes the Christian ideology and symbolism, while the other tries to force the director into a scheme of moral values which the critic sees all great art as embodying. But both make us go back and look at the films again. A full evaluation will entail a consideration not only of these themes, but also of all the many shaping forces at work in the Hollywood system – producers, stars, genre conventions. In the case of Hitchcock we must also take into account the fact that his roots lie in the silent film, which he sees as the purest form of cinema. His preoccupation throughout his career has been to tell stories by means of images and virtually all the most admired set pieces of suspense in his films can be analysed in exactly the same terms as a sequence by a master of silent cinema like Eisenstein. A film like *Shadow of a Doubt*, if looked at simply as a series of images, can be seen to comprise a whole series of visual parallels and duplications. For example, not only are the innocent niece and the evil uncle both called Charlie, they are also both introduced in the same pattern of shots, the only difference being that one is the mirror image of the other (Uncle Charlie is first seen lying fully dressed on a bed with his head to the right, his niece Charlie in an identical position, but with her head to the left).

If emphasis is placed on such patterns of imagery and the symmetry that they create, then it becomes increasingly difficult to force Hitchcock into a straitjacket of Christian or moral concerns. His films affect us not because they show the working out of divine grace or the therapeutic impact of love, but because they involve us in questioning the very way we look at cinematic images. As the cinema is, for Hitchcock, a visual medium, so his films are about the way his characters see each other, the way they are forced to doubt their own eyes and senses, the way they intrude on each other by looking and probing. We, the audience, are deeply involved in this because the films make us share the characters' perspectives. In *Suspicion* we share Joan Fontaine's doubts about Cary Grant, in *Rear Window* we are involved in James Stewart's spying on his neighbours, in *Vertigo* we are caught up in the mystery of Madeleine's behaviour. But Hitchcock does not stop there. Most of his films have a moment when the mask is removed, when we and the characters see clearly an unsuspected truth. The use made of this moment varies from film to film – it may be a surprise ending (as in *Suspicion*), a revelation of basic sanity (*Under Capricorn*), a punishment of our own voyeurism (*Psycho*) or an upsetting of our sense of reality (*Vertigo*). But, whatever the case, Hitchcock's films send us back to fundamental questions about the cinema: how do patterns of images on the screen affect us? and how can we translate these patterns into verbal terms to explain the meaning of what we have seen? Hitchcock's art, like that of a great many directors of the Hollywood studio days, revolves essentially around the problem of reality becoming illusion and illusion turning to reality, and thus plays on the paradoxical nature of our response to the film image.

20

Hollywood's Heritage and Influence

By the beginning of the 1970s the position of Hollywood was totally different from what it had been in the great years of the 1930s and 1940s. The arrival of television had taken away the unreflecting masses who had traditionally been the cinema's main audience. Instead of being able to assume the interest of habitual filmgoers, producers had to make films for audiences who would pick and choose. As Sam Goldwyn said, who wants to go out and see a bad movie when you can stay at home and see one on television? Therefore film-making had to change and tended to split into, on the one hand, what the industry calls blockbusters – massive spectacles that no television programme could equal – and, on the other, smaller less expensive works made independently with a real personal involvement on the part of the film-maker. Neither sort of film needs the kind of production set-up that the Hollywood studios at the peak represented. As a result, though the names still remain, the studios are no longer there. Their films sold to television, their studio lots developed for housing and their props auctioned off to interested fans, they are now no more than shadows to remind us of a past era of film history. But this past itself continues to pose all kinds of questions crucial for an understanding of the cinema. If Hollywood no longer exists as a geographical entity, the many thousands of films produced there are still – even increasingly – a part of our general cultural awareness. Movies are no longer subject to the old rhythm of one week's general release and then long years of oblivion. In the more fluid situation of the present more and more films are available to the public – the National Film Theatre in London, for example, shows over a thousand different films each year. Film societies are proliferating, and scores of items from the Hollywood repertoire have been bought for showing by the television companies. The newly exhumed wealth of the American studios has had the same degree of impact on cinematic awareness as the major archaeological uncovering of the civilizations of Greece and Egypt had on wider European culture in the past.

Once it was easy to be certain about what Hollywood represented. The writers whom the studios lured with exorbitant salaries and then ruthlessly exploited to turn out an unending stream of trivia took their revenge in the image they painted of the studio world. Novels like Scott Fitzgerald's *The Last Tycoon*, Nathaniel West's *The Day of the Locust* and Budd Schulberg's *What Makes Sammy Run*, together with a whole host of minor works, tell the same depressing story. The literary attitude to Hollywood is exemplified by the novelist Graham Greene, whose novels and stories provided the source material for a dozen films and who himself scripted eleven others including Carol Reed's highly successful *The Third Man*. From our present-day perspective the late 1930s are often seen as one of the golden ages of Hollywood. Yet at the time Greene, who was film reviewer for *The Spectator* for five years from 1935 onwards, could find little to enthuse about. In an article about the role of the film critic he asked plaintively what he was supposed to write about, since no more than two or three films a year could be treated with respect. The only approach he saw possible was a satirical one, and like a great many lesser writers he set out to purge the cinema with laughter. But when he complains of the picture postcard quality of the sunsets in *The Garden of Allah* or the pasteboard desert and stunted cardboard trees of *The Petrified Forest* he is clearly setting up a system of values which cannot allow the Hollywood cinema of illusion its proper place. Standards appropriate for judging literature or the documentary are inadequate to cope with this type of film-making, and it is not surprising that, despite his success as a screen-writer in the 1940s and 1950s, Greene should always have felt ill at ease with the cinema. Looking back on his career in 1958 he concluded that adapting material for the screen, even reshaping one of one's own novels, was an 'ambiguous toil' because it meant using words for a cause not believed in by the writer. The best he could bring himself to say of the cinema was that, like a psychiatrist, it enables one to do without it.

Greene's view of Hollywood as a devourer of talent and a snare for the gifted is typical of his generation, but today Hollywood fulfils quite a different function. For writers, artists and film-makers it is now less of a threat to their independence than an outstanding example of achievement. The ruthless machine which dominated and controlled those who, like Greene, were drawn into its net, can now be seen to have given a remarkable body of works. What is most striking and influential for artists of today is that very professionalism and efficiency which once filled all serious-minded critics with horror. Film-makers of the 1960s and 1970s are concerned to make films of a very different kind, but lessons learned from American movies have often been crucial in their development. The emergence of what was known as the 'New Wave' in France in 1959 marks the first appearance of a generation of film-makers weaned on the works of Hollywood's peak years. In film magazines, particularly the influential *Cahiers du cinéma*, young would-be directors had looked again at the American film scene and reversed all the critical opinions of their elders. Directors who had worked successfully for long periods within the studio system – men like Alfred Hitchcock or Howard Hawks – were no longer pitied as victims of an impossible creative situation but seen as artists who, if different in kind, were nonetheless of equal stature to independents like Orson Welles or the European directors like Ingmar Bergman or Luchino Visconti. These views were very apparent when the young critics turned to film-making. Jean-Luc Godard, for example, has explained how he made his first feature by conscious reference to shots and scenes he admired in the films of George Cukor and Otto Preminger. *A Bout de Souffle*, which appeared in 1960, is full of explicit connections: the casting of Jean Seberg (who had been Preminger's *Saint Joan*) and the one-minute silence observed by the hero in memory of Humphrey Bogart, to take but two examples. The whole film with its countless Hollywood echoes shows the force and novelty that could be obtained by reinterpretating the gangster theme in a new European context. Godard's *Une Femme est une femme*, made the following year, is an equally direct homage to the American musical, and references to Hollywood recur constantly throughout the next few years of Godard's work.

Godard's contemporary, François Truffaut, shows an equal involvement with Hollywood. Truffaut's lifelong obsession with Hitchcock has led him not only to write a long interview book but also to attempt, in several films, to emulate the American master of suspense. Truffaut even goes to the extent of employing Bernard Herrmann to write the score of one film and basing two more on novels by William Irish, author of *Rear Window*. A third member of the same group of French film-makers, Claude Chabrol, is, however, the one who comes nearest to creating works that could take their place as equals alongside Hollywood products.

These New Wave directors are merely the most obvious examples of a whole tendency among young film-makers of the past decade to draw on the American experience of the cinema. Such a development must lead us to reassess the whole of this tradition and now books are pouring out filled with enthusiastic analyses of Hollywood movies. But the kind of study of authorship which is so fruitful when applied to Hitchcock is perhaps less relevant to some of those to whom it has recently been applied. Men like Allan Dwan, Sam Fuller and Roger Corman, who would once have been given no more than the briefest of mentions in a film history, are now analysed at book length as major artists, but many important areas are still unexplored. There is little worthwhile writing on the studio structure which is so crucial to an understanding of the American cinema, and the contributions of writers and producers are passed over in the current cult of the director. But our knowledge of Hollywood is continually growing and ultimately we can no doubt expect a full-scale reassessment which takes into account social and economic pressures and faces the critical problems posed by Hollywood as a popular art. Instead of the customary derogation of Hollywood films as escapist, what is needed is a deeper analysis of their function of reinforcing as well as reflecting moral values, and offering models of behaviour and basic reassurance to the audience.

PART THREE

Film Modernism

21

Film's Space-Time Potential

The realism which has dominated European thinking about the cinema and the narrative style of the Hollywood movie are the two most developed tendencies of the cinema. As we have seen, both have their origins in the very earliest days of film and both are in addition international phenomena. The industries of Japan and India pose the same kinds of questions as Hollywood and realism has its adherents the world over. Both share, too, a basic rootedness in the nineteenth century and are offsprings of the same impulse that gave rise to the nineteenth-century novel and music drama. Film realism adopts a conception of reality as mere surface appearance which is quite at variance with twentieth-century thinking, while the Hollywood film deals with plot and character in terms which would have been quite acceptable to any late-nineteenth-century novelist or playwright. This basic conservatism of the film medium bears out Marshall McLuhan's assertion that any new medium begins by taking over the content of its predecessor and has resulted in a certain failure to develop the full potential of the cinema. The modernist possibility has never had anything like the same coherence and weight as either of the other tendencies, and the works with which we are concerned here are, for all their novelty and audacity, isolated experiments which never constitute a tradition. They represent, however, an equally valid and important aspect of the cinema's relationship to reality and probably point the way to the future development of the film medium. The arrival of television has already destroyed the studio system in which the Hollywood movie was born and flourished and is also taking over many of the documentary and naturalistic functions formerly the prerogative of the cinema. The underexplored modernist potential is therefore free to assert itself as a major tendency of filmic development.

At this point it would perhaps be as well to look back briefly at the characteristics of modernism as it first emerged in the arts over sixty years ago. In general terms the importance of modernism lay in the fact that it disputed certain centuries-old traditions in art and literature; perspective in painting, realism in the novel, tonality in music. The necessity of modernism derived from the fact that each of these traditions, though in itself only one specific style chosen from a whole range of possible approaches, had come to be seen as the only possible mode. Explored by successive generations of creators, such modes had ceased to constitute a challenge to the artist's skill and technique and had become instead a set of blinkers keeping his eyes fixed on only one aspect of reality. In its origins the modern movement is rooted in the work of the preceding generation and constitutes a further development of qualities inherent in late-nineteenth-century styles. Thus the music of Schoenberg stems from a dissolution of tonality already apparent in a late-romantic composer like Gustav Mahler; Joyce takes to an extreme some of the concerns of the naturalistic novel; and the cubists draw new lessons from the conclusions of Paul Cézanne. Equally, modernism did not succeed in totally replacing older forms of tonality or realism: Sibelius and Schoenberg were roughly contemporary, as were Kafka and Thomas Mann, Joyce and E. M. Forster (the position being still further complicated, as far as these particular examples are concerned, by the fact that in each case the slightly older traditionalist outlived his modernist counterpart). Often too the concern with experiment of this generation has produced a reaction from younger artists and writers. As an instance of this one might cite the English novel's retreat into provinciality since the death of Joyce.

Though it was in this way an artistic movement with its own antecedents and a definite place in the continuing development of art, the modernism of the pre-1914 era was also part of a wider pattern. It reflected the dawn of an age which questioned the old certainties under the impact of new scientific and pseudo-scientific discoveries. Here one thinks of the new view of the nature of man that derives from Freud's investigation of the subconscious mind, the critique of bourgeois capitalist society expressed in Marx's analysis of man and society, and the revolution in our insight into man's place in the universe which we owe to Einstein's theory of relativity. This is not to say that these discoveries were a direct influence, but they are symptoms of a changing pattern of belief. As has been observed, the truly contemporary artist is always slightly in advance of science, for he is conscious of the atmosphere about him in a way that the scientist or critic is not: Picasso painted *Guernica* long before Hiroshima was annihilated. Dostoyevsky plumbed the unconscious before Freud. Equally important was the impact of technological discoveries from the turn of the century onwards. The pace of life changed, as new forms of transport and communication (among them, of course, the cinema itself) altered men's social experience of their own environment and brought in influences from previously alien cultures. The rapidity of this social change and the upheavals caused by war helped foster a quest for novelty. The new mass media – brilliantly characterized by Marshall McLuhan as extensions of man which institute new ratios both among themselves and among our private senses – created fresh ways of thinking and of perceiving reality. Changes of this magnitude were bound to have a profound influence on art and literature, even if they did not determine the specific paths followed by the modernists.

Though modern movements mushroomed in the early years of the century – cubism, constructivism, futurism, expressionism, dadaism, surrealism, etc. – and soon began to contradict each other as much as they contradicted the traditions of the past, there are certain broad generalizations one can make about the early modernists. Firstly, modernism was an art of abstraction which refused to involve itself in mimesis. Artists shed that desire to reproduce realistically the surface of life which had been so important to men like Courbet and Zola, and turned their attention more to new areas like the subconscious. Modernism may not have turned its back completely on reality, but it certainly sought a new relationship with it. Moreover, it widened the sphere of what had traditionally been considered art by using the principles of distortion and dislocation to great effect, and by producing works which were often ugly and shocking to the untutored eye and ear. The rejection of tonality led to new dissonances and rhythms in music, the rejection of perspective gave rise to a new use of paint and material in art, while novelists needed new linguistic textures for their explorations of the stream of consciousness. Modernism was also, in reaction to nineteenth-century romanticism, a highly intellectual art which refused the principle of the untrammelled flow of emotion. Often there is something which initially seems cold, even dehumanized, in many modern works, for though the emotion is there, it is ordered in new ways. The early modernists were generally men very aware of their relation to past styles, often aiming at synthesis with other arts and disciplines and frequently attempting to build new systems on the ruins of the old (one thinks of Schoenberg's twelve-tone system or Le Corbusier's modulor).

The connection between the cinema and the modernist impulse as it was expressed in these art movements of the early years of the century is both intricate and intimate. Arnold Hauser, in *The Social History of Art*,* dubs the postimpressionist period, embracing cubism, expressionism and surrealism, the Film Age. In his view, the agreement between the technical methods of film and the characteristics of the new twentieth-century concept of time in art is so complete that the time categories of modern art can be said to derive from the

*Arnold Hauser, *The Social History of Art* (Routledge & Kegan Paul, London, 1951).

spirit of cinematic form. If this view is accepted, then it becomes possible to see the entire pattern of modernism in relation to the cinema, which, as one of the new electric media, released art from what Marshall McLuhan has called the single descriptive and narrative plane of the written word. Not only is this relationship a general one; even specific modernist tech- niques can be connected with filmic methods. McLuhan, for example, notes that the stream of consciousness is really man- aged by the transfer of film technique to the printed page.

The paradoxical nature of this interaction of a modernist art which drew its lessons from the idea of film and a cinema which was, in its practice, limited to aping nineteenth-century realist methods, is clearly shown by the confrontation of cubism and the cinema. The cubist movement in painting, last- ing from 1907 to about 1914, runs exactly contemporary with D. W. Griffith's creation of a film grammar between *The Adven- tures of Dollie* (1908) and *Judith of Bethulia* (1913). Both cubists and film-makers were engaged in creating a new way of perceiving reality and achieving artistic impact by breaking down the single viewpoint (perspective in painting; the camera placed immovably in the 'best seat in the stalls' in film). By approaching objects and situations from several angles simul- taneously and fusing the fragmental images into a new syn- thesis (full-face and profile in the same painting; long shot, medium shot and close-up all used to analyse a single film scene), they created new relationships between space and time, between objects among themselves and between objects and the spectator, who was called upon to look at the resulting work – painting or film – in a new way.

On one level the essential unity of the two forms of ex- pression is so total that Siegfrid Giedion's definition of cubism in *Space, Time and Architecture* can be applied word for word to the cinema:

It views objects relatively: this is from several points of view, no one of which has exclusive authority. And in so dissecting objects it sees them simultaneously from all sides – from above and below, from inside and outside. It goes around and into its objects. Thus to the three dimensions of the Renaissance which have held good as constituent facts throughout many centuries, there is added a fourth one – time . . . The presentation of objects from several points of view introduces a principle which is intimately bound up with modern life – simultaneity.*

Yet despite this shared identity, it would be impossible to name a single cubist film and absurd to seek any close connection between Griffith and the cubists. In a recent thesis on cubism and the cinema† the author was able to define many theoretical similarities between the two, but quoted only one specific example. From Griffith's *The Birth of a Nation* he selected the shot of John Wilkes Booth, immediately after he has entered through the doorway into the passage outside Lincoln's box. In his view, this 'yields an amazing congruence with cubist paintings. The linear quality of the door frames and the railing on the left taken as abstract lines yields a cubist arrangement of planes; and because of the lighting, the figure seems to fuse with the background.' What is surely more amazing still is that this tiny and irrelevant example, lost in a work utterly remote from cubist aspirations, was the only practical proof he could furnish of the conjunction he had so admirably demonstrated in theory.

* Siegfrid Giedion, *Space, Time and Architecture* (OUP, London, 1956), p. 432.

† David De Smit, *Cubism and the Cinema* (Film Studies No. 4, Boston University Communication Arts Division, no date).

22

Silent Experiment

Though its connections with a modernist movement like cubism are tenuous and purely theoretical, the silent cinema did evolve its own original narrative patterns. Its achievements during its short existence were great and various. It is probably the only art form for which we can give the exact date of birth and death. Strictly speaking, there was no cinema before 28 December 1895, when the Lumières showed their first little films, and the silent form of cinema was doomed on 6 October 1927, when, in a not very good Warner Brothers film called *The Jazz Singer*, Al Jolson uttered the memorable phrase, 'You ain't heard nothin' yet folks. Listen to this.' These words spelt the end of an art which in little over thirty years had become an immensely complex means of visual communication. On the foundations laid by Griffith and Sennett a whole mass of works came into being, ranging in Hollywood alone from the sombre realism of Stroheim to the comic masterpieces of Chaplin, Keaton and the rest. In Europe, aside from the Soviet masters, we find works as divergent as René Clair's comedy, *An Italian Straw Hat*, and Abel Gance's epic *Napoleon*, Carl Dreyer's probing study of *The Passion of Joan of Arc*, shot almost entirely in brilliant close-up, and Friedrich Murnau's atmospheric *The Last Laugh*. If Murnau's film *Sunrise*, in which he combined German experiments into visual style with the whole resources of a major Hollywood studio, is perhaps the supreme achievement of the silent cinema as an art of movement, light and shadow, it is the films of Sergei Eisenstein which show most clearly the new form's struggle for autonomy.

Eisenstein completed only seven films in a creative life of twenty-four years, but he ranks as one of the cinema's greatest innovators as well as one of its profoundest theoreticians. His approach is characterized by a series of contradictions. Though deeply influenced by the Southerner D. W. Griffith, Eisenstein remained totally committed to Marxism. Yet his political views co-existed with an almost obsessive concern with religion and religious imagery. Despite a background of bourgeois comfort, he was driven by a desire to reach out to the ordinary people, workers and peasants, with his work. His training as an engineer was balanced by his work in avant-garde theatre groups and his intellectual approach did not prevent the images of his films from being among the most sensuous in the history of the cinema. He is very much a part and product of the cultural upheaval that followed the success of the revolution in Russia. His first film, *Strike*, was made in 1925 when he was twenty-five and reflects his interest in the theatrical ideas of Meyerhold and his own experience in the Proletkult Theatre, where he mixed elements drawn from such varied sources as the circus, the *commedia dell'arte*, silent film comedy and oriental theatre. *Strike*, described in *Pravda* when it appeared as 'the first revolutionary film of our cinema', told the story of the birth and failure of a strike in Tsarist Russia. The bosses are caricatured in the bloated, loathsome figure of the factory owner, and the faces of the police spies who overhear the workers' discussions about the need for a strike are intercut with the heads of animals. The strike, triggered off by the suicide of a worker, runs its course, as the men's initial enjoyment of an unaccustomed leisure gives way to hardship and the authorities respond with threats, bribes and provocations. It is a tiny incident involving a small child who strays amid the Cossacks' horses which sparks off the final confrontation. Here Eisenstein's mastery of crowd movement is most apparent, and he indulges in some ambitious cutting by linking the massacre of the workers by troops with shots of a butcher hacking up meat.

Eisenstein was later unhappy about some of the theatrical elements of this superbly vigorous film, and his next and most famous work, *Battleship Potemkin* (1925) was more obviously a development of theories of the Soviet film pioneers. Drawing on Kuleshov's ideas of editing and Vertov's documentary approach, Eisenstein had elaborated what he called in a 1923 article the 'montage of attractions'. Behind this theory lay the understanding that in the cinema two shots properly linked could provide an impact greater than that which they could produce alone. In his later theoretical articles Eisenstein was to relate this idea to Pavlov's theories about our response to stimuli and find parallels for it in Japanese art and the writings of James Joyce. But in *Potemkin* his concern remains primarily a narrative one: to tell in the most effective terms the story of a mutiny provoked among the sailors of the battleship Potemkin in 1905 when they are forced to eat rotten meat. The Odessa steps sequence in the middle of the film constitutes perhaps the best-known and most influential eleven minutes in film history. The mutineers, having disposed of their officers, have sent ashore the body of one of their leaders, killed in the fighting. In the peaceful sunshine the people of Odessa come out to watch the sailors and wave their encouragement. Then suddenly and without warning the Tsarist soldiers appear and fire indiscriminately into the crowd. By cutting between the ordered march of the soldiers with their machine-like discipline and the confused mass of people under attack Eisenstein created novel filmic tensions. By means of carefully chosen details – a woman running *towards* the soldiers, a pram bouncing unattended down the steps, eyeglasses shattered by a bullet – he created great emotional impact. Moreover, by the subtle way in which he joined these details together, he showed how the attention could be gripped in the cinema even though events might be stretched out to take longer than they would in real life. In doing so he showed film's freedom from the constraints of time and its originality as an art of *montage* or editing. Eisenstein had originally set out with this film to cover the whole range of revolutionary actions in 1905 but in the course of shooting had become aware that the revolt of the sailors of the *Potemkin* alone offered sufficient material for a whole film. And even within this deliberately restricted canvas he found that he could take the single incident of the Tsarist soldiers' attack and make it stand for the whole history of oppression and violence.

Eisenstein's next two films could hardly have been more diverse in their stylistic approach. In *The General Line*, begun first but not completed until 1929, he set out to show in the simplest terms the advantages of collectivization. He told the story of a woman, Marfa Lapkina, who develops from a defeated, cowering peasant into a self-confident modern woman thanks to the benefits brought by Bolshevik ideas and the mechanization of agriculture. The film is not a reasoned argument in favour of the thesis it puts forward, but a naïve and very simplified hymn of praise for the new forces sweeping away the dark stagnation of age-old traditions. Eisenstein's exuberant delight in his own mastery of the cinema goes hand in hand with Marfa's childlike devotion to the bull she buys and the new machine whose advent she helps to make possible. In contrast to the deliberate simplicity of this film, *October*, made in 1927 to commemorate the events of 1917, is a work of immense intellectual complexity. Eisenstein was faced in this film with the problem of reconstructing just a decade later the 'ten days that shook the world'. He had both to conform to the current party line and make an authentic record, convincing to the thousands who knew the events at first hand. The overall structure of the work shows the version which the party claimed as the truth in 1927 (the part played by Trotsky, for example, goes unmentioned), and in this sense *October* fails as an objective historical document. Where it does succeed, on the other hand, is in capturing the feel of the revolution. The use of authentic settings and the masterly manipulation of the scenes of mass action bring such sequences as the popular demonstrations on the streets, the storming of the Winter Palace and the smashing of the Tsar's wine cellar vividly to life.

But aside from these realistic preoccupations, *October* also has a great importance as the most extreme example of Eisenstein's use of the possibilities of *montage*. Indeed, it is one of the films which most clearly demonstrate the silent cinema's claim to be considered as an authentically modern art with its own formal language. Some of Eisenstein's devices develop ideas tried out in the Odessa steps sequence of *Potemkin*. Thus the effect of a machinegun being fired is conveyed by rapidly intercut shots of various details of the gun. The opening of a bridge to cut off workers who have been fired on in a peaceful demonstration receives a new pathos as we see a dead girl's hair stretched across the widening gap. Eisenstein plays around with time and space in other ways too to convey the futility of the leader of the Provisional Government, Kerensky. As the latter adds title after grandiloquent title to his name, we see him slowly climbing the same staircase, over and over again. The angling of shots has an ironic effect as a statue seems to crown him with a laurel wreath. The same effect is also obtained by intercutting Kerensky preening with a mechanical peacock spreading its tail and Kerensky deep in thought with Napoleon in the form of a small porcelain figure. The advance of the counter-revolutionary General Kornilov leads Eisenstein to even more audacious devices. The statue of Alexander III symbolically smashed at the beginning of the film pieces itself together as Kornilov's power grows. The derisoriness of his slogan 'For God and Country' is demonstrated by a whole series of images illustrating the concept. Eisenstein brings together in swift succession images from many civilizations, moving from our conventional image of God – a baroque Christ – to Indian statues, Chinese gods and finally to primitive sculptures. Not all of this intellectual *montage* is totally successful, but the imagery of *October* has a sensuousness and intellectual complexity scarcely equalled in the cinema for thirty years, until in fact Michelangelo Antonioni used a similar series of abstract images to complete his study of contemporary neurosis in *The Eclipse*.

In 1929 Eisenstein signed a manifesto welcoming the coming of sound and pointing out some of the possibilities it offered, but nine years passed before he completed another film. In the meantime he spent some months in Hollywood studying sound techniques and elaborating scripts which were never filmed. Then, with the backing of the socialist novelist Upton Sinclair, he embarked on a disastrous Mexican venture. He shot thirty-five miles of film for *Que Viva Mexico*, but quarrelled with Sinclair and was never allowed to edit the footage. On his return to the USSR he found his artistic preoccupations and Western tastes out of tune with the current demands for socialist realism and the first film he shot, *Bezhin Meadow*, was banned for ideological reasons. When, after years of teaching, he returned to directing with *Alexander Nevsky*, an epic of Russian resistance to the Teutonic invaders in the thirteenth century, his style had changed completely. This film and the two completed parts of the projected trilogy on *Ivan the Terrible* represent quite a new preoccupation. Eisenstein now saw the cinema as the genuine and ultimate synthesis of all the arts, and these films are an attempt to fuse into a unity 'all those separate elements of the spectacle once inseparable in the dawn of culture and which the theatre for centuries has vainly striven to amalgamate anew'. Eisenstein gave these spectacular studies of the moulding of ancient Russia an operatic dimension by his use of symbolic decor, expressive lighting and stylized acting, and his work here with the composer Sergei Prokofiev constitutes one of the most successful attempts to bring together images and music in the cinema.

23

Expressionism

The relationship between the cinema and the major modernist movements such as surrealism and expressionism is more tangible than that with cubism, but it is equally subject to important limitations. 'Expressionist' and 'surrealist' are terms frequently applied to films but rarely, if ever, is a specific connection implied with the art movements of the early twentieth century. More commonly the terms are used in an extremely diluted sense to give a spurious importance to works more properly designated as simply fantastic or bizarre. Expressionism as a literary and artistic movement had been ably characterized by Walter Sokel as the existential or proto-existential form of modernism, nearer to surrealism than to cubism, in that it is 'subjective, dreamlike, visionary rather than object-centred, intellectual and linguistically experimental'.* In this precise sense expressionism finds comparatively little echo in the cinema, even in the German cinema of the period immediately following the First World War. Much of what is generally termed film expressionism is in fact rooted in German romantic and *Sturm und Drang* literature. In her fascinating study of German cinema, *The Haunted Screen*, Lotte Eisner finds closer connections with E. T. A. Hoffmann and Jean Paul Richter than

---

* Walter Sokel, *The Writer in Extremis* (Stanford University Press, Stanford, California, 1959), p. 30.

with Kafka, Toller or Trakl.* She also notes very pertinently that certain chiaroscuro effects, so often thought expressionist, existed long before *The Cabinet of Dr Caligari*, and demonstrates that Max Reinhart, whose theatre exercised a decisive influence on the composition and lighting of much of the German silent cinema, was the very opposite of an expressionist.

The Cabinet of Dr Caligari, which was directed by Robert Wiene in 1919, does, however, remain a remarkable demonstration of the possibilities of an expressionist cinema. The writers, Carl Mayer and Hans Janowitz, apparently based their script on personal experience (Janowitz had been at a fair one day when a murder took place and thought he could sense who the killer was). But in turning the script into a film the filmmakers replaced real locations with painted sets and backcloths which were specially produced by a group of artists much concerned with expressionist approaches. In this way the film adds the atmosphere of the expressionist theatre – an atmosphere dominated by distorted perspectives and shadowy phantoms – to a story line reminiscent of Poe and E. T. A. Hoffmann. The story envisaged by Mayer and Janowitz dealt with a lucid young man who solves the mystery of the murder of his friend and the abduction of his fiancée. At the end he is able to unmask the doctor in charge of the local asylum as the frightening Dr Caligari, who uses the hapless somnambulist Cesare as a funfair attraction and as the tool to carry out his murderous intentions.

The meaning of this anti-authoritarian script is reversed in the actual film by the framework in which the story is set. The hero is shown at the beginning to be himself an inmate of the asylum and at the end Dr Caligari, far from being a murderous villain, emerges as a sympathetic doctor who, now that he knows the nature of his patient's delusions, will be able to cure him. Despite this apparent reversal, the film still maintains much of its bite. At the end, for instance, the sanity of the resolution is undercut by the fact that we still see the nightmare decor. The

*Lotte Eisner, *The Haunted Screen* (Secker & Warburg, London, 1969).

totally stylized acting of Werner Krauss as Caligari and Conrad Veidt as Cesare is very powerful and the film remains, as Parker Tyler says, a fantastic modern exploration of the black forces of sex, and as such a forerunner of many a modern underground film. *The Cabinet of Dr Caligari* is also a perfect example of a film which turns its back on photographic possibilities and creates its own reality. It captures perfectly a subjective view — a madman's vision of the world — and fulfils the ambition of its designers who wanted films to be drawings brought to life.

In essence expressionism proper in the cinema can be reduced to this one major work, and to a handful of attempts to repeat the formula, such as Wiene's own *Genuine* (1920) and *Raskolnikov* (1923) and Karl Heinz Martin's *Von Morgens bis Mitternachts* (1920), together with a number of German films of the period which take elements of expressionism but use them as part of a style which cannot be defined as purely expressionistic (Paul Leni's *Waxworks*, Friedrich Murnau's *Nosferatu*, etc.). More recent study has done nothing to refute the conclusions of Rudolph Kurtz writing in 1926 who saw the expressionist movement in the cinema as a history of repetitions which did not get beyond its brilliant beginning and failed to bring about a total upheaval and transformation.* We can, however, use the term expressionism in a wider sense, to denote any tendency to subordinate realism to the demands of the symbolic expression of the artist's inner experience. If we do this, we can indeed talk of an expressionist cinema. An expressionist use of light and shadow was as important an ingredient in the classic American gangster film of the 1930s as the sociologically precise portrayal of organized crime. This American tradition was renewed by Orson Welles with *Citizen Kane*, and Welles's own later thrillers are brilliant examples of expressionism in this sense. In *Lady from Shanghai*, for instance, we find the grotesque characters of the evil Bannisters and a final climactic gunfight in a hall of mirrors. The figure of Hank Quinlan played by Welles in *Touch of Evil* is a figure of nightmare proportions, and this film too has its classic

* Rudolph Kurtz, *Expressionismus und Film* (Verlag der Lichtbildbühne, Berlin, 1926; reprinted Verlag Hans Rohr, Zurich, 1965).

expressionist sequence, that in which Charlton Heston trails Quinlan and his assistant through an urban jungle of scaffolding and oil derricks. Carol Reed's *The Third Man* and Robert Aldrich's *Kiss Me Deadly* are both, in their very different ways, a part of this black tradition. The horror film too often has expressionist overtones – the Gothic excesses of Alfred Hitchcock's *Psycho* are an excellent example. All these are, however, films made within the conventional narrative film structure and, despite the visual style, the total meaning of the work may be far from expressionist. The true heir of *Caligari* would seem to be rather the Swedish director Ingmar Bergman, many of whose films are expressionist in the anguish they reveal as much as in the use of light and shadow.

The range of Bergman's work as writer-director in the course of thirty years of film-making is enormously wide, ranging from the naturalistic dramas, such as *Port of Call*, made in the 1940s to the totally stylized television play, *The Rite*, completed in 1969. But a number of his most significant films are a part of the expressionist heritage and show the growing independence of his work as it develops away from borrowed expressionist devices to a fully mature and modern manipulation of filmic potential. The opening of *Sawdust and Tinsel*, which he directed in 1953, shows his debt to the silent cinema. The long prologue depicting the agony and humiliation of the clown, Frost, when his wife bathes naked with a group of soldiers is particularly interesting in this respect. The sound is unsynchronized and the lighting harsh and full of sharp contrasts. The cutting-together of such shots as the guns opening fire and the officers bellowing at the men is done in conscious imitation of Eisenstein and the whole sequence is a vivid portrayal of anguish and despair. In *Wild Strawberries*, made four years later, the film as a whole still has a rational structure, depicting an old man going to the University of Lund to receive an honorary degree. But as he travels the old man is disturbed by memories and nightmares. The film opens with one such dream, of a strangeness recalling *Caligari*. Isak Borg finds himself in a totally empty and silent city where clocks and watches have no hands and where the funeral he follows turns out to be his own. Later, a return to the house where he lived as a child brings fresh floods of dreamlike images. In these dreams real and imaginary scenes of isolation and humiliation are inextricably entangled and Isak finds that he can even converse with the figures of his own past. The film finds its resolution too in the world of memory as Isak, purged of his tormenting thoughts, takes comfort in the remembered vision of a summer day, shimmering water and the nearness of his parents and childhood sweetheart.

The Face, made in 1958, is described by its author as a comedy, but in fact it makes great use of the conventions of the horror film. It opens, for example, with the classic shot of a coach passing the gallows in a lonely wood and stopping to pick up a dying man. Twice in the film an apparently dead man comes back to haunt the living, and a key scene is one in which a coldly rational medical counsellor is scared out of his wits when an eye appears in his inkwell, a severed hand places itself upon his and the man he has just dissected stands suddenly before him. Within this framework, however, Bergman is concerned to do more than merely terrify his audience. The whole film is a meditation on illusion, deceit and pretence. In the figure of Albert Emmanuel Vogler Bergman puts to us his own doubts about the film-maker as conjurer playing on our human weakness of seeing life and movement in a succession of projected images. Bergman has traced his interest in the cinema back to his experiences as a child: the picture on the wall which seemed to come alive in the sunlight and blended with the piano music heard from next door, or the shadows on the nursery wall at night, not so much men or beasts as 'something for which no words existed'.* This is the atmosphere recaptured in *The Face*. Vogler is an impressive Christ-like figure at the beginning – mute, bearded, claiming mysterious healing powers. But the beard and the silence are both fake, and to avoid imprisonment as a menace to society he has to pass himself off as a cheat and swindler. His illusions need elaborate

*Interview with Ingmar Bergman in *Films and Filming* (September and October 1956); reprinted in Andrew Sarris, *Interviews with Film Directors* (Bobbs-Merrill, New York, 1967).

equipment, but they succeed in terrifying. He is reduced to begging for payment, yet at the end is summoned to play before no less an audience than the king himself. Throughout the film we are constantly deceived as to what is real and what is illusory, but the anguish of the artist in his self-questioning torment is all too evident.

If *The Face* draws on the conventions of the horror film for its pattern, the films of Bergman's maturity, like *Persona*, which he made in 1966, are totally original. In *Persona* the whole atmosphere is dreamlike and subjective. Gone is the comfortingly rational structure of *Wild Strawberries*, and instead we find an intellectual play with illusion and reality and constant reminders that what we are watching is not a slice of life but a film. The breakdown of the form mirrors perfectly the breakdown of the characters who form the film's subject. Yet these characters themselves are not the rounded figures of a naturalistic narrative. As the film's title indicates, they are, like Vogler in *The Face*, in essence the masks they assume. Alma, a nurse, and Elisabeth, a distressed actress, are complimentary halves of a single personality, yet their growing intimacy has all the true tenderness and anger of a relationship between real women. We are never sure of how real or imaginary any scene is. If the core of the film begins fairly rationally, it still contains perplexing scenes. Does Elisabeth utter the words we hear as the two women are at table? Does she visit Alma in the night? Or are these simply Alma's imaginings? Later the film discards even this framework and the scenes between the women take on an even more troubling aura. The visit of Elisabeth's husband is clearly imagined, but we have no clue as to which of the women is imagining it. The women can read each other's deepest thoughts and their faces merge into one. Thus the action of *Persona* moves away from the story and characters and into our own minds, and we share in the subjective vision on an equal footing with the author and the figments of his imagination.

24

Buñuel and Surrealism

If we turn now to surrealism we find that many of its key elements as a movement in art and literature are accessible to the cinema: dreams and hallucinations, imagination and the investigation of the unconscious, chance and spontaneity. But surrealism aimed to be more than just a movement like any other – to constitute, in fact, a way of life – and in this its ethos is totally at odds with the commercial structure of the film industry. Patrick Waldberg offers a useful definition of the artistic aims of the movement which shows its compatibility with filmic methods. Among all surrealist artists there is 'a desire to find, over and beyond appearances, a truer reality, a kind of synthesis of the exterior world and of the interior model . . . Human figures and objects are divorced from their natural function and placed opposite one another in a relationship which is unexpected – perhaps shocking – and which therefore gives each of them a new presence.'* Techniques such as these aims require are very much a part of our experience of cinema. Religious artists such as Carl Dreyer and Robert Bresson have successfully depicted the reality they see beyond the world of appearances, and the use of *montage* juxtapositions for shock effect lies at the heart of Eisenstein's conception of cinema. Moreover, the surrealists' enjoyment of games and jokes which

* Patrick Waldberg, *Surrealism* (Thames & Hudson, London, 1965), p. 8.

are not 'art' in the traditional sense might have been expected to bring them close to a form like the cinema which, in the 1920s, was not quite respectable artistically. Certainly the cinema exercised an initial attraction, and in 1929 André Breton and Louis Aragon uttered their celebrated dictum that 'it is in *The Exploits of Elaine* and *Les Vampires* that it will be necessary to look for the great reality of this century. Beyond fashion. Beyond taste'.

Yet what attracted them was the kind of diffuse and involuntary surrealism that can be found in a great many otherwise bad films and which Ado Kyrou documents in his book, *Le Surréalisme au cinéma*.* The attitude of the photographer and film-maker Man Ray is perhaps typical when he says that in the most banal film there are always ten interesting minutes and that even in the very best films there are hardly more than this, for him at any rate. At first sight the cinema may seem to be the ideal medium for surrealist thought and creation, a rich and supple means of communication allowing the artist to disregard totally the constrictions of weight, space and time. But the basic methods of professional film-making are alien to the vital surrealist notion of automatic writing, and film producers are always likely to be hostile to the expression of pure surrealist attitudes. Even in Paris in the period of the avant-garde three of the key experimental works – Man Ray's *Le Mystère du Château de Dés*, Luis Buñuel's *Un Chien andalou* and Jean Cocteau's *Le Sang d'un poète* – were all made aside from the system and financed by a single patron, the Vicomte de Noailles.

Ultimately one is led to the same conclusion as Gabriel Vialle, that the true surrealist poets of the screen can be counted on the fingers of one hand. In the wake of surrealists like Ernst, Masson and Miró who put the emphasis on calligraphy, animation and movement there is some experiment with 'pure' cinema in the 1920s. But how much of this is directly surrealist? Even Hans Richter, who was closest to the group, has said that at the time of *Filmstudie* (1926) he was not sure that he really 'understood' surrealism. The abstract

* Adou Kyrou, *Le Surréalisme au cinéma* (Arcanes, Paris, 1953).

cinema of men like Richter and Fernand Léger has a definite place in film history, but it remains marginal, and was even attacked at times by the surrealist polemicists. Films, which use the alternative surrealist method – that adopted by Magritte, Delvaux and Dali – of using faithfully reproduced beings and objects to make a totally unreal scene, are more numerous. But if we are to use the term surrealist with any precision we need to separate films of dadaist inspiration (such as René Clair's *Entr'acte* and the films of Man Ray and Duchamp) and those whose authors were never part of the movement (one thinks of Jean Vigo, whose films the surrealists in general liked, and Jean Cocteau, who was for a time the surrealists' public enemy Number One). If we do this we are left with virtually nothing from the late 1920s and early 1930s apart from *La Coquille et le clergyman*, directed by Germaine Dulac from a script by Antonin Artaud, and the two Buñuel classics, *Un Chien andalou* and *L'Age d'or*.

These two latter films are, however, a total vindication of the idea of a surrealist cinema. Luis Buñuel, one of the most complex and original directors in the history of the cinema, was born in Spain in 1900. When, at the age of twenty-five, he went to Paris, he rejected for ever his middle-class background and Jesuit education. As a young unknown on the fringes of the surrealist movement he made his first film with another unknown Spaniard, Salvador Dali. *Un Chien andalou* was born out of discussions the pair had about their dreams, and was scripted jointly in a matter of three days. Buñuel, alone responsible for the direction, was well served in his leading actor, for Pierre Batcheff had all the qualities of the film's tormented hero (he was to commit suicide three years later). Dali and Buñuel replaced the conventional story line with a succession of dream happenings and gags, choosing only images and events which they could not explain rationally. In this way the film illustrates better than any other the surrealists' basic belief in what André Breton called the superior reality of certain forms of association hitherto rejected, in the omnipotence of dream and in the disinterested play of thought. There is an element of mystification in the choice of titles for the various sequences:

'Once upon a time', 'Eight years later', 'About three o'clock in the morning' and 'In spring'. But a deliberate structure can be unravelled. This consists of a prologue, a lengthy sequence built around the problems of a couple hampered by culture, upbringing and sexual fears, and a concluding ironic after-thought (the couple buried up to their necks in sand). The prologue – the slow and graphic slitting of a girl's eyeball by an enigmatic male (played by Buñuel himself) intercut with a cloud passing across the moon – remains as shocking as it was intended to be forty years ago. The problems of the couple are handled through images which are partially explicable in Freudian terms but still remain striking and effective: the hand caught in the door and seen to be teeming with ants; the young man's attempt to assault the girl though weighed down by the past (represented by two priests, two grand pianos and two dead donkeys).

Two years later Buñuel, this time without Dali, completed his second masterpiece, *L'Age d'or*. This is a longer, more didactic work, an indictment of our whole western civilization and a call for revolt and total freedom. Like *Un Chien andalou,* the film has no story line, simply a series of apparently random episodes. The opening documentary-style account of the fighting prowess of scorpions and rats is followed by a sequence showing the battle between starving guerillas and bishops. The founding of a great city (referred to as Imperial Rome) is interrupted by the frenzied coupling of a man and a woman in the mud. Throughout love is set against convention and freedom is seen at its most extreme (as the kicking down of a blind man for instance). At a reception the wealthy guests are amused by the senseless shooting of a child by his father and remain indifferent to a fire in the servants' quarters and to a farm cart passing through the room. The lovers, frustrated at every meeting despite their longing for each other, turn to mutual mutilation and the hero ends by tossing from an upstairs window such things as a plough, a giraffe, a burning Christmas tree and two bishops. In a final, apparently disconnected, episode the degenerate Duc de Blangis – who bears an uncanny resemblance to conventional portraits of Jesus –

murders a girl in the midst of an unspeakable orgy.

Buñuel's protest is no mere literary revolt. Its roots lie in the condition of his native Spain, as his next film, the documentary, *Land without Bread*, makes plain. This study of a backward region of Spain shows that images of horror equal to anything that Buñuel or Dali can imagine exist in reality. It is enough to observe life, to study disease and poverty and to note the irrelevance of the church's wealth and the state education system to the real needs of the people. *Land without Bread* is also remarkable in the way it anticipates later modernist cinema by its triple impact. It combines devastating images of poverty, starvation and idiocy with a dry, matter-of-fact commentary and a musical score filled with romantic idealism (Brahms's Fourth Symphony).

After these three films Buñuel vanished from sight for eighteen years, working in a minor capacity on the production and dubbing of films in Paris, Madrid and Hollywood. Then he managed to re-establish himself as a director in Mexico and burst back on to the world scene in 1950 with a masterly study of slum life in Mexico City, *Los Olvidados*. From this date onwards he has been able to continue his career without interruption and has made a whole series of films, mostly in France and Mexico, which are in a more conventional narrative style, but which show clearly that he kept true to his surrealist and anarchist beliefs. The range of this later work is enormous: commercial potboilers, adaptations of the classics (including *Robinson Crusoe* and *Wuthering Heights*) and a whole series of more personally conceived films exposing the contradictions of Christianity and bourgeois society. *Nazarin*, set in the Mexico of 1900, is the story of a priest who attempts to follow Christ's example absolutely, only to bring death and disaster to all around him and to shake even his own belief. *Tristana*, made twenty years or so later, is an equally ruthless exposé of the fallacy of bourgeois liberalism. *The Exterminating Angel* showed an upper-class group reminiscent of the characters in *L'Age d'or* disintegrating when they are trapped by mysterious forces in a luxurious apartment. The veneer of civilization cracks and the violence, superstition and hypocrisy shows through, as they turn the flat into a kind of primitive pre-historic cave. *Viridiana*, made in Spain in 1961, is one of Buñuel's most striking studies of sexuality, telling the story of a novice whose sexual instincts are aroused by a particularly sordid rape, and of her uncle, one of the many fetishists in Buñuel's work, who is obsessed by the death of his wife on their wedding night thirty years before. All Buñuel's films contain scenes of surreal beauty and strangeness, but none surpasses the orgy staged by a group of beggars in *Viridiana* and set to the sublime music of Handel's *Messiah*. The mixture of real and imaginary is inextricable in all Buñuel's work. *Belle de jour*, for example, deals with a beautiful and wealthy society woman who spends her afternoons working in a Parisian brothel. The ending might seem to indicate that the whole film is in fact a rendering of the young woman's fantasy about herself, but this in no way undermines the force and bite of the film's depiction of masochistic self-annihilation.

These later films of Buñuel represent perhaps the most striking linking of the surrealist belief and narrative style to be found in the cinema. But as with expressionism, there is a residue of surrealist influence which extends to younger directors of the present day. Film-makers like Roman Polanski and Alain Resnais, for instance, admit to a strong surrealist influence, and use the movement's methods and ideas as a vital part of a more broadly based style.

25

Post-Disney Animation

Just as Disney's work gives us a picture of the Hollywood production method in miniature, so too the progress of animation in the 1950s and 1960s anticipates the development of the feature film towards more modernist patterns of construction. The work of Disney tends to make us overlook the fact that animation has its own history, quite separate from that of the ordinary cinema. Whereas realism has its roots in Lumière's work and Hollywood looks back to Edison, animation's originator was a man called Emile Reynaud. From 1892 onwards – before the first Lumière screenings, that is to say – this Frenchman was showing hand-drawn cartoon films to audiences at the Musée Grevin (the Paris equivalent of Madame Tussaud's). These were in all respects but one the forerunners of modern cartoons. The difference was that Reynaud did not use the camera or indeed any photographic means of recording his work. For this reason he could not reproduce his little films and was limited to single showings. He continued his work until the end of the 1890s but without much financial success. Ultimately he could not compete with Lumière's cinematograph and, like Georges Méliès, he died a ruined man. Reynaud's example of independence, if not his production method, was followed by a number of animators in the early years of the twentieth century: Winsor McCay, with *Gertie the Dinosaur*, Emile Cohl with his *Fantoche* series and Max Fleisher, originator of *Popeye*. All three used simple animated line-drawings and their work retains a great freshness and charm, but with the advent of Disney their example was forgotten.

The American UPA film-makers who led the revolt against the Disney style in the early 1950s found that simply by leaving lines and rough textures in their work they could free themselves from the Burbank studio point of view. With their work the cartoon film began to be something that adults could enjoy, as when an adaptation was made of James Thurber's ironic study of married life, *Unicorn in the Garden*. UPA's most popular character, the short-sighted, dumpy little Mr Magoo, was not lovable at all. John Hubley left the brush strokes apparent in his cartoons and used this style later to make films with a serious message about the bomb (*The Hole*) and about frontiers (*The Hat*). Ernst Pintoff's character, Flebus, was just an outline figure against blank backgrounds, and as such he echoed the methods of pioneers like Cohl. On other sides, too, Disney's methods were assailed. The Warner Brothers' Bugs Bunny took over as the leading cartoon character, with a far richer personality than Mickey Mouse, and a whole host of American cartoonists – such as William Hanna and Joseph Barbera with the Tom and Jerry series – put back all the violence that Disney had left out. In a typical five-minute offering poor Tom might be beaten to pulp, sliced by wires, fried and finally blown up by his tiny rival. Along with the violence came a new freedom to use distortion and completely unreal things in cartoons with genuine zest.

Of course, there had always been individualists working independently in their own styles but before the 1950s they had little effect. One limitation is the great expense of animation in Disney style. His feature films cost several million dollars each, and even with his brilliant reputation and organization not many of them covered their cost on their first release. Independents had to make smaller films, often for government departments. In this way, Len Lye, who seems to have been the first man after Reynaud to get rid of the camera and to draw directly on film, made his *Colour Box* (1935) and *Trade Tattoo* (1937) for the GPO , so that the postal slogans ('Post Early in the Day') are mixed with abstract patterns of dots, lines, squiggles and colours. Norman McLaren, who followed in Lye's footsteps, went to work for the National Film Board of Canada where he experimented in every sort of technique. He used normal cartoon methods, drawings made direct on films, animation of live actors (posed twenty-four times every second!) and cut-out shapes. Tiny films like *Blinkity-Blank* (1954) – the encounter of a bird and an explosive worm – show his great skill in giving life and wit to the simplest of subjects. The importance of a man like McLaren is that he makes personal films independently (and this is surely the ideal for the cinema of animation), whereas by the 1950s Disney had turned animation into the equivalent of a factory production line with men spending their lives specializing in one tiny piece of the whole process. While few animators have tackled so wide a range of styles as McLaren, many have shown an equal independence of approach. In the 1930s there were several interesting experiments in France. The architect Bertold Bartosch used woodcuts and crude animation with great effect in the short *L'Idée*, which showed the fate of truth in a world dominated by big business and torn by war. Hector Hoppin and Anthony Gross by contrast used flowing line-drawings in their best-known film *Joie de vivre*. Beginning with *Night on the Bare Mountain*, a visualization of Mussorgsky's music, in 1933 and working always in collaboration with Claire Parker, Alexandre Alexeieff has experimented with a wholly individual technique, the 'pin board'. This consists of a large board covered with small nails. When the height of these is varied and light shone on them from different angles, all kinds of strange shapes and effects can be achieved. Given the immense range of methods available to animators, only a few have so far been really exploited. Only one animator, Lotte Reiniger, for instance, has used the possibilities of animated silhouettes.

In Eastern Europe since the war there has been progress in other neglected fields of animation. The Czech Jiri Trnka, who began as a cartoonist, gave the puppet film a new force and intensity from 1947 onwards. Trnka's range is very wide: a parody of the western (*Song of the Prairie*), a bitter political parable (*The Hand*) and even a feature-length version of Shakespeare (*A Midsummer Night's Dream*), and his importance is that he makes his puppets provoke more than childish amusement. In his hands a puppet can express deep emotions and have a force equal to that of a live actor. Around Trnka has grown up a whole school of animators of whom perhaps the most striking is Karel Zeman, whose films like *The Invention of Destruction* (1956) and *Baron Munchhausen* (1959) are a unique mixture of animation, tricks and live action, all blended in a style that echoes nineteenth-century engravings. In Yugoslavia, too, the animated film has taken a firm hold and the Zagreb studio has turned out dozens of bright, inventive little cartoons. The best known are those of Dusan Vukotic, such as his *Concerto for Sub-Machinegun* (a parody of gangster films) and the splendid *Ersatz*, in which a man surrounded by inflatable gadgets is shown, in the last shot, to be an inflatable gadget himself.

Poland's greatest animators, Walerian Borowczyk and Jan Lenica, have both done most of their work abroad, Lenica uses collage techniques in most of his films, with the cut-out figures heavily outlined in black and simply animated against engraved backgrounds. What emerges is a black, poetic vision of life. In *Monsieur Tête* the little man hero, after innumerable adventures, is loaded down with decorations, but as each new medal is pinned on he loses one of his features (his nose, an eye and so on) to end up a faceless nonentity. In *Labyrinth* a bowler-hatted, winged little figure flies into a strange city, full of Victorian-style monuments and peopled by nightmare monsters, and is destroyed as he tries to leave. *Rhinoceros* is a virtuoso piece, an eleven-minute rendering of Ionesco's play about the power of conformity, where everyone, including the hero, eventually joins the mad rush to become an animal, in order to be just like everyone else. Lenica's world is a bleak place where no one is safe. In *A*, for example, a happy little man is secure in his room when he is suddenly assaulted and terrorized by a gigantic letter A. Eventually he manages to get rid of it, but his rejoicing is cut short by the sudden appearance of an equally large letter B . . .

Disney was principally a storyteller and not a draughtsman. He ignored the style of illustration in the books he animated – Sheppard's drawings for *Winnie the Pooh* and Tenniel's for *Alice in Wonderland* were both boiled down to the same old Disney style, familiar for twenty or more years. But with the new animators it is becoming possible to relate the cartoon (as it should be related) to the graphic arts. If we find the influence of Dufy in a UPA cartoon or an echo of Seurat in Alexeieff or Yves Tanguy in McLaren, it is because these film-makers are artists aware of what has been going on in art. In this way the animated film has come of age and we can now expect it to do more than just amuse. As an example it is only necessary to compare with Disney's work that of Walerian Borowczyk. Working in France, Borowczyk has made cartoons that are totally adult in their approach. The mood is set in the early film *Dom* in which a wig comes to life and slowly eats the other objects on a table, including an apple and a bottle of milk, finally crunching up the glass itself. *Renaissance* is a brilliant example of the idea of using film backwards. It opens with a shattered room which slowly puts itself together: a hamper, some books, a doll, a trumpet, a stuffed owl and finally the bomb which, reconstructed, blows the whole room up again. His drawn films are equally strange and he has invented a spikey and horrific couple called the Kabals. His masterpiece, *Les Jeux des anges*, has an intensity quite equal to that of any surrealist painting of Max Ernst, a nightmare vision of a prison world of suffering and cruelty. Where Disney gave the cartoon its economic value and showed that it can be big business and quite as profitable as any other film-making venture, Borowczyk and his contemporaries have shown it to be a powerful art form. Thus the idea of what animation is has been totally reversed, and there can be little doubt that in the future it will be one of the most exciting forms of cinema, for adults as well as children.

26

New Narrative Structures

One of the great differences between the modernist cinema of
the 1960s and the traditional form of the film in the 1930s is
the handling of the story element. The treatment of the flashback is perhaps the device which makes this distinction clearest. As early as the time of Griffith, film-makers discovered that
if they were given some warning, audiences were quite prepared to accept that scenes shown them were 'in the past',
showing, for example, how the heroine came to be in her present predicament of lying tied to the railway line. Sometimes
the warning to audiences was a spoken one: 'You remember
how we used to . . .' Later it became accepted that if the screen
went blurred for a moment or two, this was to indicate that the
hero or heroine was remembering. The use of the flashback
became a regular part of film storytelling and a great many
films used it to great effect. A typical example is *Le Jour se
lève*, a film made in 1939 by the French director Marcel Carné
from a script by Jacques Prévert. It opens with a shooting incident and closes with the suicide of the man responsible, played
by Jean Gabin. In between we follow not only the actions of
Gabin trapped in his attic room and the efforts of the police,
but also the series of events that led to the shooting. The order
and placing of these flashbacks within the unified frame of a
single night's activity gives a great emotional power to the
story.

Le Jour se lève represents what we might call the classic use of the flashback simply as a time device to tell a story out of chronological order so as to make an added impact. This is a method used in dozens of films and it continues to be valid today. Beginning with the climax and then working through the events that led up to it seems to be a pattern particularly suited to the cinema. Probably the reason for this is that we get completely caught up in a film which is shown to us in a darkened room without the interruptions and distractions that television has to cope with. So a film does not need the more extreme type of suspense ('How is it all going to end?') to keep us involved. As forms like the western show, it is enough for us to ask ourselves *how* the things we know will happen are going to be arranged. In any case, the happenings in *Le Jour se lève* could be re-edited in a chronological order and the result would be a film that would make sense, even if it did not seem so gripping.

More interesting for the future perhaps are films in which events are not told from a single point of view by a sort of godlike storyteller who knows all the answers. For a film can use a flashback not only to go back in time but also to go into someone's mind. If this happens, the film begins to show all kinds of doubts and uncertainties, for the same events look very different seen through another person's eyes. Then the time in a film is not that of a clock outside the action but the personal time, as it were, of a character and a whole new range of ideas is opened up for the cinema.

The film which first pointed the way towards this new use of the flashback and which, thirty years after it was made, remains one of the most original films of all time in terms of the ideas it contains, is *Citizen Kane*, made in 1941 by Orson Welles. At the time Welles was only twenty-five years of age but he had already made a name for himself in the theatre and on radio. His radio production of H. G. Wells's *The War of the Worlds*, for example, was so realistic that it caused widespread panic, with many people thinking it was an authentic news programme and taking to the hills in terror. So when he went to Hollywood to work for RKO he was given complete freedom to work as he pleased, a massive salary and a quarter of the eventual profits. These were unheard-of terms and it would be nice to be able to say that the company thought it got value for money. But in fact the film was so original that it frightened the company bosses and provoked a scandal when the millionnaire William Randolph Hearst, who thought the film a caricature of himself, tried to buy it for the cost price of $800,000. To tell the life story of his fictitious newspaper magnate, Charles Foster Kane, Welles chose a totally novel form not only in the photographic style but also in the handling of time. Giving up the idea that a film should try to tell the literal truth, 'what really happened', Welles told Kane's story from six different angles and left us to sort out the truth. The film begins with a very real-looking newsreel of Kane's life – the official portrait of what his career looks like from the outside. Then the same events are gone over again in interviews with five people who talk about slightly different, but overlapping periods of his life. In this way we see how complicated it is to sum up a man like Kane, for each of the five – his banker, his business manager, his best friend, his second wife and the butler who runs his fantastic mansion, Xanadu – sees him in a different way. To give unity and a little suspense to the film these six 'episodes' are put within a framework. A reporter, told to discover the meaning of Kane's last word, Rosebud, carries out the five interviews. He fails to get the answer he is seeking, but in the final images of the film we in the audience learn it – Rosebud was the name of Kane's boyhood sledge, a reminder of the days before he knew he was one of the richest men in the world.

The resolution of the 'Rosebud' mystery is perhaps the only thing which separates *Citizen Kane* in terms of structure from films made twenty years later. This is because the story element which it represents has generally been abandoned by modernist film-makers. An excellent example of the new attitude is that of Michelangelo Antonioni. Brought up in the midst of Italian neo-realism – he was a critic and screenwriter in the late 1940s – Antonioni gradually moved away from the basically nineteenth-century approach to storytelling which that movement represents. The first break – which can be seen in a film like *Le amiche,* made in 1955 – was to abandon the depiction of the social and economic problems of a single character. Instead Antonioni fragmented the narrative by dealing with a whole group of characters and offered a more introspective picture of their thwarted loves and aspirations. The landscape of urban streets and deserted autumnal beaches is used to convey the mood of melancholy frustration. *L'avventura* in 1960 carried these preoccupations a stage farther. A beautiful and highly original film, it told of a yacht trip along the Sicilian coast undertaken by a group of wealthy Italians, and of an ensuing emotional involvement. The plot is reduced virtually to nothing and, though its form is shaped by the search for a girl, Anna, who disappears from one of the islands visited, the mystery is never resolved. Instead the film follows the pattern of the characters' emotions. Anna is forgotten as her lover and best friend, drawn together when they set out in search of her, fall in love. Antonioni never tries to fit his characters into a formally dramatic film story, rather he allows the shape of the narrative to grow out of their irresolution and neurotic self-involvement. The visuals, mixing minute observation with subjective images, are crucially important in all Antonioni films. An acute sensitivity to landscape is a recurring feature: the industrial setting of *The Red Desert,* the trendy London of *Blow-Up* or the American desert of *Zabriskie Point.* Increasingly the logic of plot is replaced by a sensuous response to imagery. The last ten minutes of *The Eclipse* – shots depicting the place where both lovers fail to turn up for their last meeting combined with more abstract images of emotional aridity – constitute a *montage* sequence of a complexity unequalled since Eisenstein's *October.* In similar fashion *Zabriskie Point* ends with a long slow-motion vision of the destruction of a dream house and its luxurious contents. Image here has replaced story as the focal point of interest.

A further step away from a naturalistic storytelling is shown by the films of the French director Robert Bresson. His work maintains many surface links with the neo-realist style: he shoots on location with non-professional actors and avoids all explicitly imaginary sequences. But in his work these elements take on a quite new meaning. His refusal of a conventional dramatic approach and omission of the customary linking passages is illustrated by *Diary of Country Priest* (1951), in which he took a novel by Georges Bernanos and recreated it in film terms. He pared down the narrative to a simple line of classical austerity, removed all the minor climaxes and clashes of character and linked the images with a narrator's voice. The result was a unique kind of interior cinema deriving its power from the counterpointing of word and image. In *A Man Escaped* he obtained similar effects by combining scenes of sordid life in a Nazi prison with the music of a Mozart mass. Elsewhere he has set up new tensions by a deliberate use of anachronism. He is happy to take the mechanics of a plot set in 1774 (*Les Dames du Bois de Boulogne,* adapted from Diderot) of 1876 (*Une Femme douce,* after a story by Dostoyevsky) and transpose it without modification into the present. The resulting strangeness points to the underlying meaning in Bresson's work. As a Catholic artist he is intent on showing the divine grace at work through everyday reality, and his juggling with plot and time allows him to do this in an exceedingly effective manner.

The work of Antonioni and Bresson, while moving away from conventional storytelling, still retains a basic narrative framework. There are some forms of modern film-making, however, which reject this dimension altogether. A fine example of this is furnished by the work of Jean-Marie Straub. In his *Chronicle of Anna Magdalena Bach* Straub traces in sequence the events leading up to Bach's death, but the only real tensions in the film are not narrative ones but those arising from the interplay of image, sound and music. The images are static and longheld, depicting conventional documentary pictures: manuscripts, engravings and figures in period costume. Yet Gustav Leonhardt, who plays the composer, seems to have been chosen for his lack of resemblance to the real man. He does not impersonate Bach, he merely presents him without involvement or motion. While Bach's music itself soars to noble heights, it is continually undercut by the sound of a voice purporting to recite from Anna Magdalena's diary. The endless

babble about domestic trivia throws into fresh relief the religious sentiments of Bach's music, just as the unreal lighting
makes one question one's acceptance of the images.

The clash of levels of reality on which *The Chronicle of Anna
Magdalena Bach* depends for its impact is even more important
in a later Straub film, *Orthon*. Here we have a seventeenth-
century French classical play by Corneille performed in its en-
tirety. But the rhythms of the dialogue are destroyed by being
spoken by Italian non-actors and played in the open air.
Straub's chosen setting is not the theatrical space for which
the play was written but modern Rome. We hear traffic noises
and see cars and telegraph poles throughout, yet the figures are
not contemporary – they wear ancient Roman togas and speak
seventeenth-century French. Straub probably represents the
most extreme revolt against conventional film forms, but his
work demonstrates very clearly how a ninety-minute film
structure can be based on something other than a story or a
transcription of reality.

27

Resnais and Time

The ability to juggle with time is as important to the cinema and as wide-ranging as its ability to explore physical reality. Films can bring together stories from four different epochs (as in Griffith's *Intolerance*) or range, as Stanley Kubrick's *2001* does, from the primitive past when men were little more than apes to a distant future, indeed can leave our scale of time altogether. They can give the impression of moving about in time as freely as a novel does, switching to and fro among the happenings of a man's life. The film is only an illusion of life: twenty-four flashes of picture every second and the same number of tiny pauses of darkness (as the image is changed). So it can play around with time as we can do only in our dreams or imagination. A film-maker can repeat time, as Luis Buñuel does in *The Exterminating Angel*. There the director shows the guests arriving at a luxurious villa twice over with exactly the same sort of shots. This gives an odd air of mystery to the beginning of the film and prepares us for the supernatural happenings that occur later. (This is one way to explain it. When Buñuel himself was asked why things happened twice, he just replied that the film would have been too short otherwise!) Time can also be reversed in a film simply by projecting the images in the wrong order – as occurs with great force in Wale-rian Bórowczyk's *Renaissance*, which was mentioned in an earlier chapter. Time can be slowed down, by making the speed of the camera greater than that of the projector, or accelerated by the opposite procedure – filming at, say, twelve frames a second for projection at twenty-four. This always remains a special effect but it can be used in all sorts of ways. Sam Peckinpah, in his western *The Wild Bunch*, makes the violent ending seem even more violent still by filming it in slow motion, while speeding up the action can add interest to nature documentaries (showing the opening of a flower) or add humour to comedy (speeding up a mad chase, etc.).

The editing of a film also affects the time pattern. The cinema has a number of what we might call punctuation marks. As well as simply replacing one image with another by a straight cut, a film-maker has the chance to do several other things. He can fade (slowly darken the image till the screen is black) or dissolve (replace one image as it fades away with another growing steadily clearer, so that they overlap) or wipe (that is pass a line across the picture that removes one image and replaces it with another). All of these devices can indicate the passing of time, but most films like to give the impression that they follow real time. It is true, however, that it is rare for the events on the screen to last exactly the running time of the film. Audiences are happy to accept jumps from one part of the action to another – one brief shot of the sun setting is enough to convey the passing of twelve hours or so. When suspense is built up, it seems quite natural for events to take longer than in real life. In *Battleship Potemkin* the famous flight down the Odessa steps of the crowd rushing headlong as the Tsarist guards advance relentlessly takes much longer than would really be the case. By picking out details in close-up, Eisenstein lengthens the episode but builds up a greater tension. This sort of thing happens in any thriller: a gloved hand reaches out for the door handle, cut to the heroine looking up at the slight noise, cut back to the door handle slowly moving down, the heroine looking frightened, the door slowly opening, the heroine screaming . . . Lengthened like this the film is built up as an emotional experience. And in a similar way the unimportant parts of a narrative – the hero unlocking his door or making a telephone call – can be shortened by cutting, so that they last only a fraction of their real time.

The film's range is enormous but there is one thing that all the uses of time have in common. This is that whatever the cinema shows, it shows it as if it were happening in the present. There are no tenses in film as there are in language, no past tense and no future. If the film shows events that happened in 1900, it takes us back to that year and shows us the events as they unfold. The ability to make us feel we are there when an action happens, to involve us in this way, is one secret of the film's power.

Virtually all modern film-makers are concerned to some extent with time. But the director who returns again and again to this theme and whose films exploit brilliantly the present-tense quality of the image is Alain Resnais. Resnais once defined the cinema as the art of playing with time, and all his films show a startling originality. He began his career by making documentary films for eleven years before he was enabled to make a full-length feature film. Among his short films two are of particular interest here in that they show different aspects of the cinema's exploration of time. In *Guernica* (1950) he made a study of the large fresco painted by Picasso in 1937 as a protest against the destruction of the Basque village of Guernica by Fascist bombers during the Spanish Civil War. Instead of simply allowing his camera to wander over the painting, Resnais adopted the more ambitious idea of separating the various details that go to make up the picture and dealing with them one after the other in the film. In this way the separate images of suffering which made a composition in space in Picasso's original painting now make a composition in time in the film. Five years later, in a film called *Night and Fog* (*Nuit et brouillard*), Resnais made a powerful study of the Nazi concentration camps. In this he brought together material from the various archives (black and white photos, newsreels, etc.) and colour images of Auschwitz as it is today. The effect of using two layers of time is very striking; the horrors of the 1940s are put into perspective. Yet at the same time we are reminded how easily we forget (the images of the past are grey and already seem to be fading). As documentaries these two films are remarkable for the way in which they use voices and music as an essential part of the picture, as well as the manner in which they take second-hand images and make something totally original out of them, thanks to the idea of using the cinema's special abilities to deal with time.

These same attitudes are to be found too in the five feature films Alain Resnais completed between 1959 and 1968, each of which deals with a different aspect of time. In *Hiroshima Mon Amour* (1959), scripted by Marguerite Duras, he was concerned with the idea of memory. How does what we remember of the past affect the way we live now? Are our memories private things that are spoiled if we tell them to a stranger? Does our life have to follow certain patterns, so that we continually get into the same sort of awkward situations? It was with questions like these that the film dealt. It told of a woman, an actress, who is in Hiroshima to make a film about peace. The very fact of being in this city brings up the question of the atomic bomb, a past disaster from which we must learn if humanity is going to survive in the future. But the problems are not only of this dimension. The woman (we never learn her name) has fallen in love with a Japanese architect. While she is with him, filling in the long hours before the departure of the plane which will take her back to Europe, she remembers being in love before. That was in Nevers, a little town on the Loire in France, fourteen years ago. The man she loved then was a German soldier who was shot on the very day that the Germans withdrew, and his loss is something she has never yet come to terms with. The film is shaped more like a piece of music, with themes and variations, than a normal story. The heroine constantly moves from the present (Hiroshima) to the past (Nevers) and back again. In the film, the two time levels become one – we see images of France but hear the sounds of Hiroshima.

Resnais's second full-length film, *Last Year at Marienbad* (1961), was scripted by the novelist Alain Robbe-Grillet and remains his most puzzling work. It is difficult to talk about because it has none of the usual things we expect in a film: no characters, real settings or story. It is set in an imaginary world, an elegant hotel with endless corridors and park-like gardens. Here, cut off from the world of cars, newspapers and television, a man tries to persuade a woman that they met last year. Eventually she agrees and they go off together. This is all that happens on one level, the one at which we usually look at films. But from another point of view the film is packed with questions and tensions. The images and sounds keep contradicting each other. We see a string quartet, but hear the sound of an organ. The narrator describes a scene or an action, but we see something else. The characters in the film refuse to play their parts, and so on. Perhaps the film is best understood as an attempt to show how our minds work. Most films that deal, for example, with two people falling in love show the outside happenings. The two stare at each other, kiss, run hand in hand through a field of daisies, and we all understand: they are in love. What *Last Year at Marienbad* does is show the same experience, but from the inside. When we are emotionally concerned about anything, hundreds of thoughts flash through our minds. If we have to make a speech, for instance, we may manage it very well outwardly. But inside we may well have been imagining being booed by hostile faces, or finding the hall empty because we have come on the wrong night or standing helpless at the front, unable to say a word. *Last Year at Marienbad* shows this kind of wild and contradictory imagining as it depicts an experience from the inside. In this way it opens up areas of possibility for the film which have so far hardly been explored.

Having made one film about the past and another about the timeless world of our minds, Resnais returned firmly to the present for his third feature film, *Muriel* (1963), which was scripted by Jean Cayrol who had previously written the commentary of *Nuit et Brouillard*. Everything in the film is perfectly chronological and in the published script every scene is precisely timed and dated between 29 September and 14 October 1962. But the film is broken up into such tiny fragments that it is quite difficult to follow at a first viewing. The strangeness of

Muriel comes from this and from the way it is quite the opposite of *Last Year at Marienbad*. Here we see only the outside
of the characters without any explanation, the everyday happenings in their lives over a period of weeks, and can only guess
what has gone before. So we are astonished when the characters
react violently or show strong feelings. Despite its real location
of Boulogne, its lack of special colour effects and its everyday
tone, *Muriel* is far removed from a documentary. The realistic
recording is balanced by the elements that show this is a
shaped work of the imagination. The angles are chosen with
great care, the sound overlaps for added effect, we hear a
wordless soprano aria and see acting that is deliberately
theatrical.

The nearest of Resnais' films to a realistic work is *La Guerre
est finie* (1966) which recounts three days in the life of a Spanish exile working for the overthrow of the Franco government.
Scripted by Jorge Semprun, it goes into the details of revolutionary politics, the arguments for and against violence. Most
of it is in tone with the dull grey of the Parisian suburbs in
which the revolutionaries make their endless plans. From the
point of view of the handling of time, what is most interesting
is the way the film looks forward. Instead of flashbacks, Resnais
often uses flashes forward in time, recording the hero's antici-
pations. He imagines a dozen possibilities as he goes to meet a
girl he has never seen, foresees the beating he fears is in store
for his friend Juan at the hands of the Spanish police, and
anticipates the funeral of his dead colleague Ramon.

In *Je t'aime, je t'aime* (1968), which was written by Jacques
Sternberg, much of the ordinariness of *La Guerre est finie* is
still there and a great part of the film is about the most banal
situations. We see scenes in the life of a very ordinary man: his
seaside holidays, hours spent with his wife, his daydreams.
Little moments, all of them, chosen at random from sixteen
years of a man's life. What is startling in *Je t'aime, je t'aime* is
the framework in which they are placed. The hero, Claude
Ridder, is a man who has been projected through time by scientists to relive one minute of his past, and the flow of images we
see of scenes from his earlier life represent his frantic efforts to

get back to the present. From this fact comes the double tension of the film. As well as showing the hero's struggle to get out of his nightmare prison of time, we also relive the story of his marriage, which ended with his wife's death and his own attempted suicide.

One reason why Resnais, more than any other director, has made such startling use of filmic possibilities of time is that he sees the film as an art of collaboration, linked with the other arts. All his features have been made in collaboration with a novelist of repute and reflect modern ideas of what a narrative is. It must be remembered that, as a way of telling stories, the cinema has always been behind the novel. In the years when literature was producing the elaborate works of James Joyce and Franz Kafka, film-makers were still trying to tell the simplest of stories effectively. The cinema has much to learn from the years of experiment in art and literature and Resnais' working methods make this possible. He is not content to adapt an existing play or novel but always insists on an original film script composed by the writer in close collaboration with him. As a result the writers with whom he has worked have become deeply involved in the whole mechanics of film-making, and the first three have already become film directors in their own right. In this respect the most important 'by-product' of Resnais' methods has been the work of Alain Robbe-Grillet, who has followed his script for *Last Year at Marienbad* with a number of striking and original films.

28

Film and the Modern Novel

The cinema has always employed writers of great talent, but as we have seen, under the Hollywood system this gave generally bad results, because the writers were not as involved in the scripting of films as they were in the writing of their books. Hollywood did not employ the Nobel prize-winner William Faulkner to write the film equivalent of one of his novels about the Deep South – he was simply invited to help knock the script of *Land of the Pharaohs* into shape for Jack Hawkins. To a great extent this attitude towards writers persists, particularly in Britain.

The British cinema has traditionally been a literary one but with a fairly rigid division of creative roles separating the directors (usually recruited from the stage or, more recently, television) and the scriptwriters, whose first commitment remains to literature. The 1940s and 1950s were the great age of the adaptation of plays, dominated by a succession of versions of Noel Coward, Terence Rattigan and the classics (Shaw and Wilde, Shakespeare and Dickens). A crucial change occurred in the 1960s in that a whole new generation of vigorous young novelists and playwrights – John Osborne, Alan Sillitoe, David Storey and Shelagh Delaney – were brought in to adapt their own works to the screen. But the promised revolution never occurred because only one of these writers went on to produce an original screenplay conceived totally for the cinema. Shelagh Delaney's *Charlie Bubbles* was a strikingly inventive piece of work, but unfortunately it was one of the biggest commercial disappointments of the decade and the idea of using original screen material was never followed up.

The whole problem of relating experimental work in other media to the cinema is exemplified by the film career of Harold Pinter. His plays are among the most brilliantly inventive in the whole modern theatre, breaking totally with the conventional notions of action, character and naturalistic presentation. But in the cinema he has been limited to turning two of his own plays into not very successful films and otherwise scripting film versions of novels by other writers. In collaboration with the director Joseph Losey, Pinter has been responsible for some of the most striking British films of the past ten years: *The Servant*, *Accident*, *The Go-Between*. But all of these have retained a basic naturalistic form, a totally coherent and unambiguous story line, and such experiment with time and characterization as they contain seems timid when compared to Pinter's work in the theatre.

On the continent, however, writers have been able to get a greater involvement in the cinema and direct their own original scripts. Working in Sweden, the American critic and novelist Susan Sontag has been able to make two sombre studies of the paradoxical interaction of a small group of characters, *Duet for Cannibals* and *Brother Carl*. In France the screenwriter of *Hiroshima Mon Amour*, Marguerite Duras, could move on to direct a film with all the ambiguities and unresolved tensions to be found in her prose writing, *Destroy She Says*. These are interesting films for they are totally personal works made with the same commitment as a book or play would be, and they raise some fascinating questions about the role of the director. They are introspective exercises, not spectacles designed to communicate with an audience. There is a deliberate de-dramatization and the attitudes of the characters are simply stated, not realized in emotional and dramatic terms. As a result there is a gap between what the film represents for its maker and what is actually conveyed to the audience – a gap that the presence of a director should fill. The visual flatness of both *Duet for Cannibals* and *Destroy She Says* is emphasized by their extreme austerity. Such literary film-making is much more fascinating than the dreary routine of conventional adaptation, but it remains a strictly limited form, lacking the unmistakable if indefinable touch of pure direction that a film-maker like Alain Resnais can give his films.

Two writers-turned-directors to whom these strictures do not apply are Alain Robbe-Grillet in France and Pier Paolo Pasolini in Italy. Since writing the script of *Last Year at Marienbad* for Resnais, Robbe-Grillet has made a number of extremely original films: *L'Immortelle, Trans-Europe-Express, L'Homme qui ment* and *L'Eden et après*. One thing that clearly fascinates him in the cinema is the way in which the medium allows the author to play on two senses — the eye and the ear — at once. This is a luxury which the writer cannot find in literature and it opens up new possibilities of expression. Another difference between writing and film-making is that whereas a novel can use words which are by nature abstract symbols to build up a powerful impression of reality (one of the great strengths of the nineteenth-century novel lies in this), a film by contrast uses direct images of reality as its basic material. But these images of reality can be undercut by the fictional context in which they are placed. Robbe-Grillet's novels such as *Jealousy* and *The Voyeur* are hallucinatory word patterns in which there is frequently an unseen narrator who tries with words to create a pattern or construct an alibi. In his films, however, the method of approach is quite the opposite. Robbe-Grillet takes real people and settings and casts doubt on their reality by showing them as they are filtered through the eyes and mind of a narrator. He continually plays with the mixture of reality and falsehood, truth and fiction. Passing through the mind of the character whose angle of vision we share, the settings turn to mere picture-postcard representations of exotic locales and the women become the exquisite but mindless and inhuman figures of our dreams — advertisement hoardings come to life. Robbe-Grillet has the crime fiction writer's taste for mystification and the re-order of events. *Trans-Europe-Express*, for instance, perhaps the most approachable of his films, shows a group of film-makers on a train to Amsterdam. As they travel they make up a film story about a drug smuggler using this very train, and the 'real' images of them get mixed up with the scenes they have invented for their hero. The plot twists and turns, following an impossible sequence as they continually change and question what the hero is doing. The material which the authors within the film are forced to throw out of their planned work because of its inconsistency or irrelevance forms, however, a very real part of the film as we experience it. In the end the 'authors' in the film (two of whom are played, to add yet another layer of confusion, by Robbe-Grillet himself and his wife) reject the story they have been making up as unsuitable for a film. But as they leave the train at Amsterdam their fictional characters are among the crowds, as if defying them and us, for the confusions of the discarded film story have kept us engrossed for an hour and a half. The crossword puzzle side to Robbe-Grillet's approach is very apparent here, but it is balanced by his sense of humour and his fascination for eroticism and sexual perversion.

Pier Paolo Pasolini does not have the same interest in novel structures and formal patterns of plot, but he does share Robbe-Grillet's involvement in the ambiguities of film's relation to reality. A poet and novelist before he turned filmmaker, Pasolini uses pastiche as his principal stylistic device. All his work contains striking juxtapositions of ideas and image borrowed from all kinds of cultural fields. His first two films, *Accatone* and *Mamma Roma*, made in the early 1960s, were basically realist studies of Roman slum life, but the sordid events were filmed in a camera style full of visual allusions to the fifteenth-century painter Masaccio and accompanied by the music of Bach and Vivaldi. Since then he has shown a particular interest in making film versions of religious and mythical stories. Among his best films is a version of *The Gospel According to Saint Matthew*, handled with an eclectic mixture of Piero della Francesca and newsreel shooting, *cinéma-vérité* techniques and Prokofiev. In addition Pasolini has filmed adaptations of Sophocles' *Oedipus Rex* and Euripidies' *Medea* as well as *The Decameron* and *The Canterbury Tales*.

Like Robbe-Grillet, Pasolini sees strong differences between film and novel. The most important of these, in his view, is the lack of metaphor in film language. Film expresses reality with reality. Although he was brought up in Italy during the years when neo-realism was the dominant form of cinema and literature, and despite an admiration for realists like Rossellini, Pasolini is very distrustful of naturalism as a form of expression. He rigorously avoids the mere imitation of life. He likes using, in neo-realist fashion, actors chosen from the streets because of the appropriateness of their faces and figures. But he does not use them naturally. In his film, *The Gospel According to Saint Matthew*, he poses them in positions taken from the paintings of Piero della Francesca and dubs them with actors' voices. For him the only means which allows the cinema to compensate for the lack of metaphor (and hence, at a certain level, of poetry itself) is the notion of analogy. If the film-maker must always use what is real in the way of people, settings, etc., these can be chosen to represent indirectly the reality with which the film-maker is concerned. Thus Southern Italy can give an image of Christ's Palestine for *The Gospel* and Morocco the colours of Sophoclean Greece in *Oedipus Rex*. New resonances are set up by this means and a quite unique effect created by the remove from naturalism. Where most of the Marxist-orientated Italian film directors aim to demystify, to remove the aura of respectability from the capitalist exploitation of workers, for example, Pasolini is concerned to rediscover the mythical element of reality. He does not show Christ to be simply a man (as a Marxist might be expected to do), but instead gives in *The Gospel According to Saint Matthew* Christ and two thousand years of Christian art and legend. Similarly, he does not unravel Greek legend in terms of modern psychology: he gives us in *Oedipus Rex* the mystery of Sophocles plus the ambiguities of Freud and his own personal involvement. In *Medea* the primitive sense of the sacred and the oneness of nature exists alongside a sophisticated intellectual awareness. Coming from literature Pasolini is able to bring in this way a new understanding of the way film and reality can be brought together and, like Robbe-Grillet, shows the quite new combination of the basic elements of image and sound which a poet or novelist can find if he becomes involved with the cinema. Thanks to writer-directors like these two, film and literature are becoming more closely related as equal and modern forms of artistic expression.

29

Godard – The Self-Conscious Film-Maker

Of all the film-makers who have changed the look of the cinema in the 1960s, none has had more influence than the French director Jean-Luc Godard. When, among the credits of his film *Bande à part*, made in 1964, he included the credit to himself: 'Cinema by Jean-Luc Godard' he was doing no more than stating a truth. In many ways the cinema of the 1960s *is* Jean-Luc Godard, and if we want to understand what the cinema stands for today, there is no one who can give us more insight. Godard is one of the people who have made the cinema modern in the way that the novels of Alain Robbe-Grillet, the stories of Jorge Luis Borges or the musical compositions of Pierre Boulez are modern. One of the most remarkable things about the cinema, even in the years since the Second World War, has been the extent to which it has refused to belong completely to our own century. The world sees the Russian Revolution and two world wars, the atom is split, new countries and continents have become centres of world interest, men reach the moon and a new generation grows up surrounded by technological marvels undreamed of by their grandparents, yet in much of the cinema we still see a nineteenth-century world. Though it is so very much a product of our own times, the cinema has always been cut off by its position as a mass form of entertainment from the influences of other, more inventive art forms.

In the past, experimental cinema has been no more than a fringe activity and has had as little influence on the cinema as a whole as the equally specialized form of the cartoon. The commercial cinema, typified by Hollywood, was always seen to be simply a form of storytelling, as the popular novel had been in the nineteenth century. D. W. Griffith, it may be recalled, poured all his efforts not into rivalling the most up-to-date literature of his day, but into finding the film equivalents of the storytelling methods of Charles Dickens. While James Joyce was producing *Ulysses* or T. S. Eliot writing *The Waste Land*, the cinema's favourite forms like the western and the gangster film continued to tell their stories of the clash of good and evil with a straightforwardness quite lost in serious literature. The cinema could continue in this way because the audience for which it catered was one that liked good stories excitingly and grippingly told. But times change, the cinema has a different (and much reduced) audience, and a new generation of freer film-makers with wider horizons has arrived. This change is typified by the films of Jean-Luc Godard. He does not try to persuade us to lose ourselves in the swiftly unfolding events of his stories or to make us identify with his heroes (as we do when John Wayne leads a cavalry charge). Instead he keeps reminding us that what we are seeing is no more, and no less, than a film.

Godard is a very difficult film-maker to talk about, for several reasons. His enormous output of films in the first ten years of his career as a director of feature films – eighteen features and seven short films – far exceeds that of any other major director of the time. And these were not mass-produced works fitting neatly into existing categories or genres, but all of them personal films breaking new ground. It would require a whole book to trace Godard's development, his choice of material and methods, from one work to another. Moreover, the way in which his discoveries have influenced other younger film-makers makes it often difficult to sort out what is Godard himself and what is just influence or imitation. Bearing all this in mind, what can we say about his work? Firstly and most obviously that it is personal in a way that films produced within the commercial framework seldom are. Though film-making is big business and involves dozens of people in the making of one film, all the film-makers who are worth thinking or writing about have their own style which we can recognize. We can see this style in the choice of subject, the way the actors are handled, the type of compositions used, the manner of editing, and so on. Whether the film is a spy drama or a murder mystery, whoever wrote the script and whoever the stars may be, we can always recognize the signature of Alfred Hitchcock, for instance. We do not need the little appearance he always makes in his films to tell us who the director is. Godard's personal cinema, however, is of a rather different kind. He is not a man who wants to tell a story and in so doing express his personality in the way he narrates it. His early films, like the parody gangster film *Breathless* (*A Bout de souffle*) made in 1960, do have stories it is true, but only as a way of holding the ideas of the film together. By the time he reached *One Plus One*, also known as *Sympathy for the Devil*, in 1968, all pretence of a story had vanished. What Godard has been really interested in from the very first is talking directly about himself. For this reason he crams all kinds of things into his films, just as you might make up a notebook into which you put all the ideas that occur to you, stories your friends tell you, a few lines of a poem you have read and liked, some particularly atrocious pun you have just heard or invented, and so on.

These are the kind of things we get in Godard's films, and, as one of his characters says about Petrarch somewhere, all the art lies in the digression. Godard's references and asides fit so well into the whole pattern of his films because of the startling way in which he makes them. He does not work from a fixed script, but jots down a few ideas immediately before he starts shooting. Sometimes his actors are left to give their own answers. In a film called *Deux ou trois choses que je sais d'elle* (1967) he even talked to his leading actress, Marina Vlady, by means of a little microphone hidden in her hair while he was filming. He questioned her, probed her ideas, argued with her – and filmed her reactions.

Godard does not like the make-believe that actors somehow become the story characters they are impersonating, and in most of his films real people turn up as themselves. The philosopher Brice Parrain talks about what language is in *Vivre sa vie* (1962), Fritz Lang discusses what it is like being a film director in *Le Mépris* (1963), the Rolling Stones rehearse a number in *One Plus One*. Actors who are playing parts are encouraged to keep their own gestures and personalities. One very interesting aspect of this is the way Godard's own personal emotions are visible in his works. In the early 1960s he was married to the actress Anna Karina, and this is reflected in the films of the period. In *Le Petit Soldat* (1960) his fascination with her is seen in the sequence during which she is photographed from every angle. Further portraits of Karina are drawn in the musical *Une Femme est une femme* (1961), in *Vivre sa vie*, which is set in the gangster world, and in *Bande à part*. Godard invites us to make direct connections in these films in the way he shapes his material. In *Vivre sa vie*, for example, he substitutes his own voice for that of the actor in the scene where a fragment of an Edgar Allan Poe story about a man who falls in love with the portrait of a young woman is read. But Godard's marriage broke up and *Pierrot le fou* (1965) is all about this, full of questions, doubts and differences.

One of the reasons for the new kind of films which Godard makes is his background before he became a film director at the age of thirty (he had previously made a few not very important shorts). He had spent ten years as a critic, writing film reviews, interviewing film-makers and helping to run the magazine *Cahiers du cinéma*. This is an increasingly common background for film-makers these days. In Godard's case it meant that he had a great knowledge of the film-making of the past, in a way that few directors twenty years ago did. He had spent many hours in a cinema attached to the film museum in Paris, the Cinémathèque, where it was the policy of Henri Langlois to show hundreds of films without sorting them in any way. There were old films and new ones, good and bad, French and American classics and unknown films from distant countries, all shown without being forced into any pattern. In this way

Godard acquired his idea of the cinema, and he refers to film history in as natural a way as James Joyce refers to literary history in *Ulysses*. The Cinémathèque made Godard see films not as stages in a historical development but as part of a great fund of experience that the present-day director can draw on as he wishes. Though he makes his films very much for the 1960s (and taken together his films give a very clear picture of the period's attitudes and problems), he parodies Louis Lumière in *Les Carabiniers* (1963) and the American gangster movie in *Breathless*, and includes clips of the silent classic *The Passion of Joan of Arc* (made by Carl Dreyer in 1928) in *Vivre sa vie* and Resnais' documentary *Night and Fog* in *Une Femme mariée* (1964). This awareness that the cinema has its own glorious past with which some at least among the audience would be familiar is typical of the younger film-makers of today and contrasts strongly with the attitude in Hollywood only a generation ago where a man was only reckoned to be as good as his last film – all the others having been forgotten. The ability to pick at random among past film styles also puts the film-maker on the same level as a painter who, thanks to the museums and art galleries of today, can draw his influences from the art of all countries and periods. Godard himself is also very like many modern pop painters in the way he uses the manufactured images in the world around us. His films are full of posters, advertisements, neon signs, magazine pages, book titles and the like. He juggles with these just as he juggles with words in many of his films. His characters use quotations, make speeches, rattle off sentences at random, even speak each other's lines. *Made in USA* (1967), for example, is full of puns and word games: 'The barman is in the pocket of the pencil's jacket' or 'The counter is kicking mademoiselle'. One effect of this mass of bits and pieces is that Godard's films have a strange, jagged rhythm – very much like that of life in any big city. The apparent jumble has a meaning and shows Godard's view of human life. The posters scream down at us, but we are not really at home in the city. Our minds are full of little fragments of knowledge, but we are as far as ever from the truth.

For Godard, indeed, life is very much like a prison. Several of his heroes are killers on the run or gangsters fleeing from the police, reporters or private detectives investigating some crime. These are familiar figures in the cinema but Godard uses them in a new way. His vision is usually a black one. When in *Alphaville* (1965) he makes a film about the future, he sees a time when the computer reigns. Words like tenderness have been removed from the dictionaries and a man can be executed for the 'illogical behaviour' of weeping at his wife's funeral. The force of the film is even more powerful because, refusing to build futuristic sets, Godard made his film among the ultra-modern buildings of Paris today. When in *Weekend* (1967) he looks at the world of today directly, he chooses a married couple as his subject. Each is deceiving the other and when they go to visit her mother it is to kill her for her money. Travelling they find nothing but traffic jams and senseless slaughter on the roads. Society is a hopeless place, but going back to Nature is no better. In the woods reign gangs of hippies who have opted out and now live as killers and cannibals. But human beings can reconcile themselves to anything, and the last we see of the wife is when she sits down to a meal that she knows contains stewed husband.

In the late 1960s Godard became more and more involved with political questions as students and young people all over the world have done. *La Chinoise* (1967) was about left-wing students and *One Plus One* dealt with, among other things, Black Power. In the arguments of these films Godard shows a considerable awareness of the realities of the situation. But political films of this kind run up against a blank wall, for the workers whom Godard would most like to influence are the very last people who would go to see them. Nevertheless for three years following the making of *Le Gai savoir*, a television film which contains his immediate reactions to the student revolt of May 1968, Godard worked outside the confines of the industry. Together with a group of students calling themselves the Dziga-Vertov group he made 16mm. films designed for showing to political groups and not for normal cinema distribution. It was not until 1972, with *Tout va bien* starring Yves Montand, that he returned to the commercial industry. While this three-year diversion is readily understandable in terms of the director's own personal development, it is in other ways ironic, for in the 1960s it was Godard more than anyone else who showed the enormous amount of freedom that could be obtained by working cheaply and quickly within the normal structure of the film industry. In these years he made films of every kind – gangster and science-fiction films, musicals and anti-war fables, social studies and films of personal confession. The way in which he went to extremes in his rejection of the rules and conventions has often led his imitators to make films that are rough and hard to follow. But he helped to give a fresh sense of life to the film. As far as techniques are concerned, he showed from the very beginning that the cinema has now developed far enough to do without all the props that have been used to help the audience understand what was happening. He showed that audiences can follow jumps in the story and are not worried if finally he does not tie up all the loose ends. It was Godard after all who defined what modern film-making is all about when he agreed, in a discussion, that a film should have a beginning, a middle and an end, but added that they did not need to be in that order. His inventive use of what can be done with images and sounds has helped change our idea of what a film is. He has demonstrated that it is possible to admit that a film is just a film, that the actors are simply acting and that the corpses are covered with tomato ketchup and not blood – and still move and excite the spectators.

30

Anger and the Underground

In moving away from the commercial film industry in the late 1960s Godard draws attention to the existence of a whole alternative cinema which now flourishes alongside the conventional one. Earlier avant-garde film-makers such as Buñuel and Cocteau had worked largely in isolation and both (like so many other makers of such independent films) were eventually absorbed into the normal film industry. Transfer to the commercial cinema may not harm an avant-garde film-maker's talent, but it does tend to have the effect of taking the edge off his attack on the system. In America during the postwar years, however, the development of cheap 16mm. equipment has allowed one form of experimental film, the underground cinema, to flourish quite independently – with its own financial structure, distribution system and audience – and even to influence the conventional cinema.

Instead of producing movies for the millions, the underground film-makers are producing private films for themselves, their friends and a few like-minded supporters. There is plenty of scope for them for a great range of subjects is left untouched by the normal cinema. The latter, hampered by censorship and the need to cater for a family audience, has neglected all kinds of aspects of life. Underground film-makers can explore our dreams and fantasies, the bits of life we do not talk about because they are private. They can also experi-

ment with ways of using pure forms and images with no concern to tell a story or create characters. By using their freedom
in this way these film-makers – men like Stan Brakage, Gregory
Markopoulos and Ron Rice – have brought the cinema round a
full circle. When Brakage uses the camera to photograph his
own family, he brings us back to Louis Lumière picturing his
brother and sister-in-law feeding their baby in the garden. It is
to the underground too that we must look for a naïve delight
in the possibilities of film to compare with that of Georges
Méliès. For all the size and colour of *Gone With The Wind* and
The Sound of Music part at least of the cinema remains what it
has always been: the record of a man's life. Now that the rules
of film-making are all known they can be forgotten, and the
cinema, while remaining a vast entertainment industry, can also
become a truly personal form of expression no more remote
from the individual than poetry or painting. The change is symbolized by the fact that film-making, instead of being a salaried
occupation carried on in the factory-like atmosphere of the
studio, can be a direct part of the film-maker's whole life, pursued in his own home or workshop.

The taboos broken by underground film-makers fall into two
broad categories. The first are those concerning technique.
Even the decision to work with 16mm., though made partly
because of financial considerations, represents a reaction
against the Hollywood format and the concern with professional standards that has traditionally accompanied it. But
it does not end there. In addition to the kinds of animation
techniques already described in the earlier section on post-
Disney developments, we find a whole range of new devices,
most of which stem directly from the underground film-
maker's method of working. Since he no longer has teams of
assistants and cameramen to come between him and the physical material he uses – the film stock itself – his work shows a
new awareness of this. Instead of attempting to construct
plausible fictions, many underground artists are concerned
with film itself as the physical reality. So we find film-makers
using clear film, black leader, focusing marks, even splices as an
integral part of their films. Anthony Scott has made what he

calls the longest, most meaningless movie in the world simply by joining together every bit of film on which he can lay his hands. Whole films may be made out of individual aspects of film technique – single frames, a zoom in and out again, a take limited only by the length of the reel and so on. Perhaps the most striking examples of this kind of approach are those furnished by the 'structuralist' films of Mike Snow, whose *Wavelength* comprises a single forty-five-minute zoom across an eight-foot room.

The second type of taboos are those related to subject matter. On the one hand, this may simply imply a refusal of the conventions of the naturalistic film and a concentration on rhythmical movement – as in the balletic dramas of Maya Deren or the poetic fantasies of James Broughton. More recently, however, the underground has seen its role as that of providing a super-realism with regard to sex. Explicit and forthright expositions of such subjects as homosexuality, sexual intercourse, masturbation, group sex and transvestism are common. Examples are such films as Jack Smith's *Flaming Creatures*, Ron Rice's *Chumlum* and many of the Andy Warhol films. Warhol, pioneer of the immensely long film in which the camera never moves and nothing perceptible happens (*Sleep* and *Empire,* for example), moved on to more complex films in which a minimal technique is combined with nudity and frankly observed sexual sparring. These later films, among them *Bike Boy* and *Lonesome Cowboys,* brought Warhol wider audiences and contributed to the movement of the underground away from the private statement and towards greater audience concern (a change explicit in a film like *Flesh,* made by Warhol's assistant, Paul Morrissey).

This is the context in which the work of a film-maker like Kenneth Anger should be seen. He has all the typical hallmarks of an underground film-maker, combining technical originality (particularly his use of editing and superimposition) with taboo subject matter (homosexuality and the occult). In addition, however, Anger's work shows clearly the relationship between the independent and the Hollywood cinema. He was born in California and at the age of four appeared as the changeling in the version of *A Midsummer Night's Dream* which Max Reinhardt directed for Warner Brothers in 1934. Anger mixed with Hollywood people in his childhood and wrote a book, *Hollywood Babylon*, about the scandalous side of life there. His vision of the lost splendour of the movie capital is combined with a taste for horror films, B pictures in general and serials of the *Flash Gordon* type. *The Cabinet of Dr Caligari* also has a place in his mythology, and a figure recalling the sleep-walker Cesare appears in *Inauguration of the Pleasure Dome*. Yet despite this background, Anger's own films are very much underground ones. They are conceived as personal expression, not as works designed specifically for an audience, and the films we know are only part of his output. He has been using film cameras since he was seven, and the films he does release are generally fragments of longer films subsequently abandoned or, in one case, stolen after a first showing.

Much of Anger's work seems to be an attempt to recreate the illusory world of the Hollywood studio and the magical setting of the Reinhardt film in particular (he quotes a few moments of Mickey Rooney's performance as Puck in *Scorpio Rising*). A concern with the paradoxes of light and fire is constant and the vision of a sparkling tinsel paradise is a recurring one, particularly in the early films. Examples of this are the decorated Christmas tree which bursts into flames as a climax to his first film, *Fireworks*, the Pierrot's moon worship and play with the magic lantern amid a tinsel forest in *Rabbit's Moon*, and the glittering reflections of light on the Roman fountains of *Eaux d'Artifice*, which give an impression of cold fire. Anger has confessed to having indulged in arson as a child ('Nothing big, a few fields . . . and a church') and the figure of Lucifer is a key one in the personal mythology he has evolved in his later films, including his most recent work, *Lucifer Rising*. Often this play with light and fire has sexual overtones, as in the famous image of the incandescent Roman candle bursting from a sailor's trousers in *Fireworks* and the routine of asking for a 'light' which recurs as a way of making personal contact in several films. *Fireworks*, which Anger made in 1947 at the age of seventeen, is perhaps the most explicit exposition of his homosexuality. Shot in his home in three days while his parents were away, and using film stock stolen from the Navy, this fifteen-minute work depicts the sexual frustrations of a young man (played by Anger himself), his survival of a savage ordeal at the hands of the sailors he entices and his eventual, magical contact with another youth. A prefatory note in the film states that these 'imaginary displays offer temporary relief', but Anger's subsequent work continues this probing of the male face and body, uncovering the latent sexuality.

Anger's films never use the camera to go out and explore or transcribe reality. His is a claustrophobic world of mental images and occult ritual. There are some echoes of the work of Jean Cocteau in *Fireworks* (particularly the use of the photographs at beginning and end), and Anger, like Cocteau, is always intent on expounding his own private myths. Virtually all his films have a ritual structure. In *Fireworks* there is the graphically depicted beating of the hero, while in *Puce Moment*, which shows a 1920s movie star of ambiguous femininity preparing to go out, we find the first of several sequences of dressing and making-up, with clothes and jewels taking on a life and meaning of their own. In *Scorpio Rising* and *Kustom Kar Kommandos* the same ritualistic approach is applied to the bike boys and their motorcycles and to a car enthusiast slowly stroking the gleaming chromework with a white feather duster. In the later Anger films this element is developed into full-scale restagings of magic rituals – Shiva's feast in *Inauguration of the Pleasure Dome*, Anger as the magus performing to Mick Jagger's music in *Invocation of my Demon Brother* and the still incomplete *Lucifer Rising*. The reason why these rituals are powerful even to those who do not share his belief in the validity of Aleister Crowley's Magick is that Anger's own sense of evil and spiritual presence is so strong. This is apparent even in the early films. In *Fireworks* the longed-for partner materializes in a flash of light (all the more noticeable for being scratched on to the film), in *Rabbit's Moon* there is a magical conjuring-up of a beautiful woman who prefers Harlequin to the hapless Pierrot, and *Eaux d'Artifice* is an invocation of the spirits of the fountains. Anger has stated that he regards the movies as an evil medium because they use the capturing of a person's image as a means of stealing his soul. Evil is a quality he conveys astonishingly well, particularly in his film on the bike boys, *Scorpio Rising*.

The other key to the success of Anger as a film-maker is his sheer technical ability. Like many other leading underground film-makers he shows an enormous professional skill though his work is shot through with private meaning. This skill is apparent in the editing of images to music in the films up to *Scorpio Rising* and the often quintuple exposures of the later rituals. The result is a great complexity of meaning. There are the startling juxtapositions – the classic mime and modern pop in *Rabbit's Moon* or the intercutting of the priest moving round the magic circle and the baboon chasing round a tree in *Lucifer Rising*. The fusion of his images and his chosen pop music tracks is often brilliant, as when he brings together the song 'She Wore Blue Velvet' with shots of a pretty boy in tight jeans in *Scorpio Rising*. This film in fact provides some of the best examples of the complexity of many of Anger's sequences, as when he builds up the myth of the motorcyclist as Scorpio by bringing together pop music ('You look like an angel . . . but you're the devil in disguise'), images of James Dean and Hitler, comic-strip cartoons, a television clip showing Marlon Brando in *The Wild One* and staged images of the desecration of a church, and then intercuts a wild homosexual orgy with stagey scenes of Christ entering Jerusalem taken from the old De Mille epic *King of Kings*. But even a quieter work like *Eaux d'Artifice* shows great complexity if looked at in detail. On the surface a mere linking of a lady in eighteenth-century wig and costume and the fountains of Rome, it throws up all kinds of tensions and conflicts of meaning. The woman is in fact a dwarf dressed up and there is a sense of real connection between her and the carved stone faces which come alive in the half darkness. She emerges from and fuses into the water, and the movements of her fan and the spurting water are equated. And above all there is a link between water and fire (the title is a pun on the French word for fireworks: *feux d'artifice*). Visually the play of light on the fountains has the same impact as that on the tinsel streamers of his earlier films, and the light itself is but a symbol of the bursting liberation of life. With Anger the modernist impulse to use film to create an alternative reality and express a personal subjective vision is totally vindicated.

Bibliography

The arrangement of the bibliography which follows corresponds to the order of the chapters of this book. It is of necessity selective, being designed to offer suggestions for further reading on the various topics treated. Subjects not dealt with directly in the book are ignored, as are rare or out-of-print volumes. At the time of writing, however, a large number of long-unavailable classics of film literature are becoming available thanks to a programme of expensive reprints inaugurated by the Arno Press of New York.

INTRODUCTORY

There is now no broad concensus of opinion on the overall perspective in which film is to be viewed of the kind furnished some twenty years ago by such volumes as Ernest Lindgren's *The Art of the Film*, Roger Manvell's *Film*, Paul Rotha's historical survey, *The Film Till Now* and the influential Soviet theoretical writings of Eisenstein (*Film Form* and *The Film Sense*) and Pudovkin (*Film Technique and Film Acting*).

The contemporary approach is reflected in works of a more fragmentary nature: the anthology or the book of interviews. Among the first variety, the best are perhaps Richard Dyer MacCann's *Film – A Montage of Theories* (Dutton, New York, 1966) and Daniel Talbot's *Film – An Anthology* (University of California Press, Berkeley and London, 1966), while an excellent example of the interview book is Harry M. Geduld's *Film Makers on Film Making* (Indiana University

Press, Bloomington, 1967; Penguin Books, Harmondsworth, 1970) which covers the whole field, from Lumière to Anger.

One of the few critics to attempt a comprehensive reassessment of film theory is Peter Wollen in *Signs and Meaning in the Cinema* (Secker & Warburg, London, 1969), a difficult but rewarding book that deals with Eisenstein's theories, the *auteur* concept and semeiological aspects of film.

Among recent attempts to offer a history of the cinema two studies may be recommended: *A Concise History of the Cinema*, with contributions by thirty writers, edited by Peter Cowie (Barnes, New York, 1970; Zwemmer, London, 1971), and a valiant solo effort, *A Short History of the Movies* by Gerald Mast (Bobbs-Merrill, New York, 1971).

Film reference books are becoming increasingly popular with publishers. The most useful paperback is Leslie Halliwell's *The Filmgoer's Companion* (Paladin, London, 1972). By far the best of the large-scale encyclopaedias is Dr Roger Manvell's *The International Encyclopaedia of Film* (Michael Joseph, London, 1972), a major work of film research.

FILM REALISM

Theoretical Statements

SIEGFRIED KRACAUER, *Theory of Film: The Redemption of Physical Reality* (Oxford University Press, New York, 1960; as *The Nature of Film*, Dennis Dobson, London, 1960).

An outspoken statement of film's realist potential, sometimes forcing material into a theoretical straitjacket but thought-provoking.

ANDRÉ BAZIN, *What is Cinema?* (University of California Press, Berkeley; Cambridge University Press, London; Volume One, 1967, Volume Two, 1971).

These collections of Bazin's essays (translated by Hugh Gray) provide fine examples of a critical method rooted in an appreciation of realist film-making.

Documentary Film and its Background

PAUL ROTHA, *Documentary Film* (Faber & Faber, London, 1935; 3rd edn, 1952; Hastings House, New York, 1964).

Though undoubtedly dated now in its critical views, it offers useful insight into 1930s documentary approaches.

FORSYTH HARDY (ed.), *Grierson on Documentary* (William Collins, London, 1964; Faber & Faber, London, 1966; Praeger, New York, 1966).

A collection of key articles by the driving force behind the British documentary movement.

JAY LEYDA, *Kino: A History of the Russian and Soviet Film* (Allen & Unwin, London, 1960; Hilary House, New York, 1960).

Invaluable for background to the context in which film-makers like Vertov and Eisenstein worked.

LEWIS JACOBS, *The Documentary Tradition: From Nanook to Woodstock* (Hopkinson & Blake, New York, 1971).

A comprehensive survey of documentary style from 1920 to 1970.

ALAN LOVELL and JIM HILLIER, *Studies in Documentary* (Secker & Warburg, London, 1972).

A useful survey of British documentary, seen from a 1970s perspective.

Individual Documentarists and their Work

ARTHUR CALDER-MARSHALL, *The Innocent Eye: The Life of Robert J. Flaherty* (W. H. Allen, London, 1963; Harcourt, Brace, Jovanovich, New York, 1966).

A very useful biography, based on research material assembled by Paul Rotha and Basil Wright.

ROBERT L. SNYDER, *Pare Lorenz and the Documentary Film* (University of Oklahoma Press, Norman, 1968).

A detailed study of the career of one of the leading American documentarists of the 1930s.

JORIS IVENS, *The Camera and I* (International Publishers, New York; Seven Seas Books, Berlin, 1969).

The personal story of the Dutch-born documentarist whose career took him to the USSR, Belgium, Spain, the USA, Eastern Europe and, more recently, Vietnam.

Silent Realism

JOEL W. FINLER, *Stroheim* (Secker & Warburg, London, 1967; University of California Press, Berkeley, 1968).

A chronological analysis of Stroheim's work, concentrating especially on the genesis of *Greed*.

THOMAS QUINN CURTISS, *Von Stroheim* (Farrar, Strauss & Giroux, New York, 1971; Angus & Robertson, London, 1972).

A personal memoir and biography of Stroheim.

The script of *Greed* is available from Lorrimer (London) and Simon & Schuster (New York), and an expensive shot-by-shot reconstruction with 400 stills – *The Complete Greed* – is published by the Arno Press (New York).

French 1930s Poetic Realism

PIERRE LEPROHON, *Jean Renoir* (Crown, New York, 1970).

A translation of a very useful book by a distinguished critic, first published in French.

LEO BRAUDY, *Jean Renoir – The World of his Films* (Doubleday, New York, 1972).

An enthusiastic study of Renoir's style and beliefs.

P. E. SALES GOMES, *Jean Vigo* (Secker & Warburg, London; University of California Press, Berkeley, 1972).

First published in French and for a long time the standard work on its subject, now available in an English translation.

JOHN M. SMITH, *Jean Vigo* (November, London; Praeger, New York, 1972).

A new and detailed analysis of Vigo's rich but tragically short career.

French scripts of the 1930s which are readily available in English include Renoir's *La Grande Illusion* and *La Règle du jeu*, René Clair's *A Nous la liberté* (with *Entr'acte*) and Carné's *Le Jour se lève*, all from Lorrimer (London) and Simon & Schuster (New York).

Italian Neo-Realism

ROY ARMES, *Patterns of Realism: A Study of Italian Neo-Realist Cinema* (Tantivy Press, London; Barnes, New York, 1972).

A detailed study of the movement from *Rome Open City* in 1945 to *Umberto D* in 1951.

JOSE LUIS GUARNER, *Roberto Rossellini* (Studio Vista, London; Praeger, New York, 1971).

A film-by-film analysis of the great Italian director's work.

GEOFFREY NOWELL-SMITH, *Visconti* (Secker & Warburg, London, 1973; Doubleday, New York, 1968).

A comprehensive study of Visconti's work from *Ossessione* to *Vaghe stelle dell'orsa*.

Lorrimer (London) and Simon & Schuster (New York) have published the script of de Sica's *Bicycle Thieves* and the Orion Press of New York have issued de Sica's *Miracle in Milan* and Visconti's *La Terra Trema* and *Senso* (together as *Two Screenplays*).

Realism outside Europe

MARIE SETON, *Portrait of a Director: Satyajit Ray* (Dennis Dobson, London, 1971).

A detailed study, based on personal contact and much research, of the Indian director who drew inspiration from neo-realism.

ROBIN WOOD, *The Apu Trilogy* (November, London; Praeger, New York, 1972).

Analyses of three of Ray's greatest films, written with all Wood's customary insight and moral seriousness.

DONALD RICHIE, *The Films of Akira Kurosawa* (University of California Press, Berkeley and London, 1965).

An immensely detailed film-by-film study of Kurosawa's career up to *Red Beard*.

The script of Kurosawa's *Ikiru* (*Living*), one of the greatest of realist films, is published by Lorrimer (London) and Simon & Schuster (New York), while *Rashomon*, his modernist masterpiece, has appeared in a Grove Press (New York) edition.

Cinéma-Vérité and Television

G. ROY LEVIN, *Documentary Explorations* (Doubleday, New York, 1972).

Interviews with fifteen documentarists, including Rouch, Franju, Wright and Leacock.

ALAN ROSENTHAL, *The New Documentary in Action: A Casebook in Film Making* (University of California Press, Berkeley and London, 1971).

Interviews with twenty-two *cinéma-vérité* and television documentarists, American, Canadian and British.

FILM ILLUSION

General Books about Hollywood

ANDREW SARRIS, *The American Cinema: Directors and Directions, 1929–1968* (Dutton, New York, 1968).

Well-documented and brilliantly provocative notes on the whole range of directors active in Hollywood over four decades.

PARKER TYLER, *Magic and Myth of the Movies* (Henry Holt, New York, 1947; Secker & Warburg, London, 1971).

This is an original and thought-provoking account of the 1940s cinema, far ahead of its time when first published.

PAUL MAYERSBURG, *Hollywood and the Haunted House* (Allen Lane The Penguin Press, London, 1967; Penguin Books, Harmondsworth, 1969; Stein & Day, New York, 1968).

A useful, fairly light, introduction, with plenty of interview material.

IAN CAMERON, *The Movie Reader* (November, London; Praeger, New York, 1972).

A collection of some of the best writing from *Movie* magazine, with pieces on Hitchcock, Preminger, Hawks, etc.

KEVIN BROWNLOW, *The Parade's Gone By* (Alfred Knopf & Son, New York; Secker & Warburg, London, 1968).

The best of the interview books, a nostalgic picture of Hollywood based on original material, lovingly edited and beautifully illustrated with rare stills.

CHARLES HIGHAM and JOEL GREENBERG, *The Celluloid Muse: Hollywood Directors Speak* (Angus & Robertson, London, 1969; Regnery, Chicago, 1971).

A dozen or so interviews, mostly with men prominent in the 1940s.

JOSEPH GELMIS, *The Film Director as Superstar* (Doubleday, New York, 1970; Secker & Warburg, London, 1971; Penguin Books, Harmondsworth, 1973).

Interviews with directors of the 1960s, including Mailer, Penn and Kubrick.

ANDREW SARRIS (ed.), *Hollywood Voices* (Secker & Warburg, London, 1972).

A reprint of the American interviews collected in Sarris's more comprehensive book, *Interviews with Film Directors* (Bobbs-Merrill, New York, 1967; Avon Books, New York, 1969).

CHARLES HIGHAM, *Hollywood Cameramen: Sources of Light*

(Thames & Hudson, London; University of Indiana Press, Bloomington, 1970).

Interviews with seven cameramen from the golden days of Hollywood.

BERNARD ROSENBERG and HARRY SILVERSTEIN, *The Real Tinsel* (Macmillan, New York; Lollier-Macmillan, London, 1971).

A collection of interviews with a whole host of Hollywood old-timers (not simply directors).

The Beginnings of Hollywood

LEWIS JACOBS, *The Rise of the American Film* (Harcourt Brace, New York, 1939; Teachers College Press, New York, 1968).

Remains a useful account, though it has not been updated since its first appearance.

LILLIAN GISH, (with Ann Pinchot), *The Movies, Mr Griffith and Me* (Prentice-Hall, New York; W. H. Allen, London; 1969).

A good picture of life and work in early Hollywood by one of the great stars of the period.

ANTHONY SLIDE, *Early American Cinema*.

PAUL O'DELL, *Griffith and the Rise of Hollywood* (both Zwemmer, London; Barnes, New York; 1970).

Two well-documented studies giving the basic facts in a digestible form. Part of a series covering the whole history of Hollywood decade by decade. Other volumes (variable in critical stance and value) are *Hollywood in the Twenties* by David Robinson, *Hollywood in the Thirties* by John Baxter, *Hollywood in the Forties* by Charles Higham and Joel Greenberg, *Hollywood in the Fifties* by Gordon Gow, and *Hollywood in the Sixties* by John Baxter.

The Comedians

DAVID ROBINSON: *The Great Funnies: A History of Film Comedy* (Studio Vista, London; Dutton, New York, 1969).

Basically a picture book, but lively and well-written.

CHARLES CHAPLIN: *My Autobiography* (The Bodley Head, London; Simon and Schuster, New York, 1964; Penguin Books, Harmondsworth, 1966).

Chaplin's account of his own career is naturally of interest, but this is very much a public portrait with little personal insight.

THEODORE HUFF: *Charlie Chaplin* (Henry Schuman, New York, 1951).

A useful study of the great comedian.

ISABEL QUIGLEY: *Chaplin: Early Comedies* (Studio Vista, London; Dutton, New York, 1968).

Covers Chaplin's career up to the end of the First World War in loving detail.

DAVID ROBINSON: *Buster Keaton* (Secker & Warburg, London; Indiana University Press, Bloomington, 1969).

An excellent survey of the whole of Keaton's career and style of comedy.

RUDI BLESH: *Keaton* (Macmillan, New York, 1966; Secker & Warburg, London 1967, Collier Books, New York, 1971).

A useful supplement to Robinson's more critical work, providing plenty of biographical detail.

CHARLES BARR: *Laurel and Hardy* (Studio Vista, London, 1967, University of California, Berkeley, 1968).

A useful guide, well documented and packed with stills.

ALLEN EYLES: *The Marx Brothers: Their World of Comedy* (Zwemmer, London; Barnes, New York, 1966).

A film-by-film account of the Marx Brothers' film career.

The Studios

NORMAN ZIEROLD: *The Hollywood Tycoons* (Hamish Hamilton, London, 1971, published in the USA as *The Moguls*, Coward-McCann, New York, 1969).

A well-researched account by the author of a noted biography of *Garbo*.

PHILIP FRENCH: *The Movie Moguls* (Weidenfeld & Nicolson, London, 1969; Penguin Books, Harmondsworth, 1971).

Informal and amusing account of all the major Hollywood producers.

LILLIAN ROSS: *Picture* (Holt, Rinehart & Winston, New York, 1952; Gollancz, London, 1953; Penguin Books, Harmondsworth, 1962).

The now classic account of the production battle behind the making of John Huston's *The Red Badge of Courage*.

JOHN GREGORY DUNNE: *The Studio* (Farrar, Straus & Giroux, New York, 1969; W. H. Allen, London, 1970).

A devastatingly amusing piece of reportage on the day-to-day workings of Twentieth Century Fox in the late 1960s.

RICHARD SCHICKEL: *Walt Disney* (Weidenfeld & Nicolson, London, 1968; as *The Disney Version*, Simon & Schuster, New York, 1968; Avon Books, New York, 1969).

An excellent account of the real Disney behind the legend, the production genius obscured by nostalgia for Mickey Mouse.

BOB THOMAS: *King Cohn: The Life and Times of Harry Cohn* (Barrie & Rockliff, London; Putnam, New York, 1967).

Thalberg: Life and Legend of the Great Hollywood Producer (Doubleday, New York, 1969; W. H. Allen, London, 1971).

Selznick (Doubleday, New York, 1970; W. H. Allen, London, 1971).

Thomas has made himself something of a specialist in the study of the idiosyncrasies of the Hollywood producers and all his books are knowledgeable and packed with anecdote.

MEL GUSSOW: *Darryl F. Zanuck* (W. H. Allen, London, Doubleday, New York, 1971).

A further biography much in the Bob Thomas mould.

The Star System

There are a great many studies of individual stars and ghosted autobiographies. The Citadel Press (New York) have also brought out innumerable picture books on stars of past and present. Serious studies of the system are much rarer.

ALEXANDER WALKER: *The Celluloid Sacrifice* (Michael Joseph, London, 1966; Hawthorn Books, New York, 1967; Penguin Books, Harmondsworth, 1968).

A good introduction to the star system and its principal victims, the female sex symbols, by a leading journalist. Atrociously titled as *Sex in the Movies* in the Penguin version.

ALEXANDER WALKER: *Stardom* (Michael Joseph, London; Stein & Day, New York; 1970).

A sequel to the previous work and a thorough investigation of the star system.

The Western

JIM KITSES, *Horizons West* (Thames & Hudson, London; University of Indiana Press, Bloomington, 1969).

A sometimes tortuous but always interesting study of Mann, Boetticher and Peckinpah.

PETER BOGDANOVITCH, *John Ford* (Studio Vista, London; University of California Press, Los Angeles, 1967).

Basically a long interview with Ford and a thorough filmography; good background material.

JOHN BAXTER, *The Cinema of John Ford* (Zwemmer, London; Barnes, New York, 1972).
An analysis of Ford's career to date.

The script of Ford's *Stagecoach* is published by Lorrimer (London) and Simon & Schuster (New York).

Authorship in Hollywood

Renewed interest in Hollywood film-making has given rise to a whole flood of director monographs and interview books, some of them profound, many rather trivial. The following list in alphabetical order of subject omits studies already mentioned in previous sections.

Roger Corman – The Millenic Vision, ed. David Will and Paul Willemen (Edinburgh Film Festival, Edinburgh, 1970).

Allan Dwan – The Last Pioneer, Peter Bogdanovitch (Studio Vista, London; Praeger, New York; 1971).

The Cinema of John Frankenheimer, Gerald Pratley (Zwemmer, London; Barnes, New York; 1969).

Samuel Fuller, ed. David Will and Peter Wollen (Edinburgh Film Festival, Edinburgh, 1969).

Samuel Fuller, Nicholas Garnham (Secker & Warburg, London, 1971; New York, 1971).

Samuel Fuller, Phil Hardy (Studio Vista, London; Praeger, New York; 1971).

Howard Hawks, Robin Wood (Secker & Warburg, London; Doubleday, New York; 1968).

Hitchcock, François Truffaut (Simon & Schuster, New York, 1967; Secker & Warburg, London, 1968; Panther Books, London, 1969).

Hitchcock's Films, Robin Wood (Zwemmer, London; Barnes, New York, 1965).

Stanley Kubrick Directs, Alexander Walker (Harcourt, Brace, Jovanovitch, New York, 1971; Davis-Poynter, London, 1972).

Fritz Lang in America, Peter Bogdanovitch (Studio Vista, London, 1967; Praeger, New York, 1968).

The Cinema of Fritz Lang, Paul M. Jensen (Zwemmer, London; Barnes, New York; 1969).

Losey on Losey, ed. Tom Milne (Secker & Warburg, London, 1967; Doubleday, New York, 1968).

The Cinema of Joseph Losey, James Leahy (Zwemmer, London; Barnes, New York; 1967).

The Lubitsch Touch, Herman G. Weinberg (Dutton, New York, 1968).

Rouben Mamoulian, Tom Milne (Thames & Hudson, London; University of Indiana Press, Bloomington; 1969).

Arthur Penn, Robin Wood (Studio Vista, London, 1967; Praeger, New York, 1969).

The Cinema of Roman Polanski, Ivan Butler (Zwemmer, London; Barnes, New York; 1970).

The Cinema of Otto Preminger, Gerald Pratley (Zwemmer, London; Barnes, New York; 1971).

The Films of Robert Rossen, Alan Casty (Museum of Modern Art, New York, 1969).

Sirk on Sirk, ed. Jon Halliday (Secker & Warburg, London, 1971; Viking Press, New York, 1972).

Douglas Sirk, ed. Laura Mulvey and Jon Halliday (Edinburgh Film Festival, Edinburgh, 1972).

George Stevens: An American Romantic, Donald Richie (Museum of Modern Art, New York, 1970).

The Cinema of Josef von Sternberg, John Baxter (Zwemmer, London; Barnes, New York; 1971).

Josef von Sternberg, Herman G. Weinberg (Dutton, New York, 1967).

The Cinema of Orson Welles, Peter Cowie (Zwemmer, London; Barnes, New York; 1965).

The Films of Orson Welles, Charles Higham (University of California Press, Berkeley and London, 1970).

Orson Welles, Joseph McBride (Secker & Warburg, London; Viking Press, New York; 1972).

Orson Welles, Maurice Bessy (Crown, New York, 1968).

Billy Wilder, Axel Madsen (Secker & Warburg, London, 1968; University of Indiana Press, Bloomington, 1969).

Comparatively few Hollywood scripts are ever published. The M-G-M Library of Film Scripts has, however, got under way with Lubitsch's *Ninotchka*, Cukor's *Adam's Rib* and Hitchcock's *North by Northwest* (Viking Press, New York, 1972); Wilder's *The Apartment* and *The Fortune Cookie* have appeared as one volume (Studio Vista, London, 1970); and *The Citizen Kane Book* (Secker & Warburg, London; Little, Brown, New York, 1971) has the script of Welles's first feature preceded by a long and provocative essay by Pauline Kael.

FILM MODERNISM

General Books

DAVID CURTIS, *Experimental Cinema: A Fifty Year Evolution* (Studio Vista, London; Universe Books, New York; 1971).

An excellent survey of the whole field of modernism, from the European avant-garde and American independent cinema to the underground.

JOHN RUSSELL TAYLOR, *Cinema Eye, Cinema Ear* (Methuen, London; Hill & Wang, New York; 1964).

A good introduction to some of the key film-makers of the 1960s including chapters on Fellini, Antonioni, Buñuel, Bresson, Bergman, Hitchcock and the French New Wave.

ROY ARMES, *French Cinema Since 1946*, 2 volumes (Zwemmer, London; Barnes, New York; 1966, 1970).

The first volume contains a section on Bresson and the second deals with Resnais, Godard and their contemporaries.

IAN CAMERON (ed.), *Second Wave* (Studio Vista, London; Praeger, New York; 1970).

Contains useful essays on film-makers of the post-Godard generation including Straub.

Silent Experiment

IVOR MONTAGU, *Film World* (Penguin Books, Harmondsworth, 1964).

A comprehensive survey of the cinema's potential which draws many of its examples from silent films.

SERGEI EISENSTEIN, *Film Form* and *The Film Sense* (Meridian Books, New York, 1957).

Eisenstein's writings remain among the most valid as well as the most influential in the history of the cinema.

MARIE SETON, *Sergei M. Eisenstein* (The Bodley Head, London, 1952; Grove Press, New York, 1960; Dennis Dobson, London, 1970).

The definitive biography of the Soviet director.

IVOR MONTAGU, *With Eisenstein in Hollywood* (International Books, New York; Seven Seas Publishers, Berlin; 1968).

A vivid account of Eisenstein abroad, with the scenarios of two unmade films, *Sutter's Gold* and *An American Tragedy*.

The scripts of *Battleship Potemkin* and *Ivan the Terrible* have been published by Lorrimer.

Expressionism and Ingmar Bergman

LOTTE EISNER, *The Haunted Screen* (Thames & Hudson, London, 1969; University of California Press, Los Angeles, 1970).
Brilliantly written and beautifully produced book on expressionism and German silent cinema.
SIEGFRIED KRACAUER, *From Caligari to Hitler* (Dennis Dobson, London; Princeton University Press, Princeton; 1947).
A closely argued psychological history of the German cinema from its origins to 1933, with a supplement on the Nazi propaganda film.

The script of Robert Wiene's classic, *The Cabinet of Dr Caligari*, is published by Lorrimer (London) and Simon & Schuster (New York).

PETER COWIE, *Sweden: An Illustrated Guide*, 2 volumes. (Zwemmer, London; Barnes, New York; 1970).
The second volume is a historical and critical survey of Swedish cinema, devoting much of its space to Ingmar Bergman's career.
JÖRN DONNER, *The Personal Vision of Ingmar Bergman* (Indiana University Press, Bloomington, 1964).
An original and idiosyncratic study by the Finnish-born film critic and director.
ROBIN WOOD, *Ingmar Bergman* (Studio Vista, London; Praeger, New York, 1969).
A perceptive analysis of Bergman's whole output.

Many of Bergman's scripts have been published: *Smiles of a Summer Night*, *The Seventh Seal*, *Wild Strawberries* and *The Magician* (the film released as *The Face* in Britain) together as *Four Screenplays* by Simon & Schuster, New York, 1960; *Wild Strawberries* and *The Seventh Seal* as separate volumes by Lorrimer; *Through a Glass Darkly*, *The Communicants* (*Winter Light* in Britain) and *The Silence* as *A Film Trilogy* by Orion Press (New York) and Calder & Bovars (London, 1967); *Persona* and *Shame* as one volume by Calder & Boyars (London, 1972).

Buñuel and Surrealism

RAYMOND DURGNAT, *Luis Buñuel* (Studio Vista, London, 1967; University of California Press, Berkeley, 1968).

A lively, involved analysis of the underlying themes and motifs of Buñuel's work.

The Orion Press have issued a collection of *Three Screenplays* (*Viridiana, The Exterminating Angel* and *Simon of the Desert*) and Lorrimer and Simon & Schuster have published *L'Age d'or* (with *Un Chien andalou*), *Belle de jour* and *Tristana*.

Post-Disney Animation

RALPH STEPHENSON, *Animation in the Cinema* (Zwemmer, London; Barnes, New York; 1967).

A useful survey of the range of contemporary animation.

RONALD HOLLOWAY, *Z is for Zagreb* (Tantivy Press, London; Barnes, New York; 1972).

Well-illustrated survey of the output of the Yugoslav studios.

New Narrative, Time and the Novel

IAN CAMERON and ROBIN WOOD, *Antonioni* (Studio Vista, London, 1968; Praeger, New York, 1969).

A detailed analysis by two experienced critics.

The Orion Press have published a collection of *Four Screenplays* by Antonioni (*L'avventura, Il grido, La notte* and *The Eclipse*) and Lorrimer have issued *Blow Up*.

IAN CAMERON (ed.), *The Films of Robert Bresson* (Studio Vista, London, 1969; Praeger, New York, 1970).

A symposium of essays by six critics on Bresson's films up to *Mouchette*.

OSWALD STACK (ed.), *Pasolini on Pasolini* (Secker & Warburg, London, 1969; University of Indiana Press, Bloomington, 1970).

A very useful interview book in which Pasolini expounds his theories at length.

The script of Pasolini's *Oedipus Rex* is published by Lorrimer (London) and Simon & Schuster (New York).

ROY ARMES, *The Cinema of Alain Resnais* (Zwemmer, London; Barnes, New York; 1968).

A detailed critical analysis of all Resnais' films up to *La Guerre est finie.*

JOHN WARD, *Alain Resnais or the Theme of Time* (Secker & Warburg, London, 1968; Doubleday, New York, 1968).

Contains some striking insights, though it tends to distort some of Resnais' work to make it fit a preconceived theory.

Calder & Boyars (London) have published Marguerite Duras' script for *Hiroshima Mon Amour* (with *Une Aussi Longue Absence*) and Alain Robbe-Grillet's scripts, *Last Year at Marienbad* and *L'Immortelle.*

ALAIN ROBBE-GRILLET, *Snapshots* and *Towards a New Novel* (Calder & Boyars, London, 1965).

Though largely about literature, Robbe-Grillet's essays give some clear insights into the attraction of the cinema for novelists like himself.

RICHARD ROUD, *Straub* (Secker & Warburg, London; Viking Press, New York, 1972).

A sympathetic examination of Straub's work, supplemented by the script of his first feature.

Godard

RICHARD ROUD, *Jean-Luc Godard* (Secker & Warburg, London, 1967; Doubleday, New York, 1968).

The first full study in English; an informed if somewhat journalistic account.

IAN CAMERON (ed.), *The Films of Jean-Luc Godard* (Studio Vista, London, 1967; Praeger, New York, 1969).

Essays by various critics on each of Godard's features up to the date of publication.

TOBY MUSSMAN (ed.), *Jean-Luc Godard: A Critical Anthology* (Dutton, New York, 1968).

A wide-ranging collection of notes, reviews, interviews and essays by and about Godard.

TOM MILNE (ed.), *Godard on Godard* (Secker & Warburg, London, 1972).

A selection made from a decade or so of Godard's critical writings.

Lorrimer and Simon & Schuster have published a good selection of Godard's scripts: *Alphaville, Made in USA, Le Petit Soldat, Pierrot le fou* and *Weekend* (with *Wind from the East*). *Masculine-Feminine* has been published by Grove Press (New York).

The Underground

PARKER TYLER, *Underground Film: A Critical History* (Grove Press, New York, 1969; Secker & Warburg, London, 1971; Penguin Books, Harmondsworth, 1973).

A major study of the American underground, relating it to experiments in Europe and evaluating its beliefs and achievements.

GREGORY BATTOCK, *The New American Cinema: A Critical Anthology* (Dutton, New York, 1967).

A useful collection of articles and manifestoes, giving a good picture of the range of activities and interests flourishing under the label of the underground.

Index

A (Lenica, 1964), 194
Abraham Lincoln (Griffith, 1930), 102
Accatone (Pasolini, 1961), 212
Accident (Losey, 1966), 210
Adventures of Dollie, The (Griffith, 1908), 171
Age d'or, L' (Buñuel, 1930), 187, 188–9
Aldrich, Robert, 182
Alexander Nevski (Eisenstein, 1938), 178
Alexeieff, Alexandre, 193, 195
Alice in Wonderland (Disney, 1951), 195
Alphaville (Godard, 1965), 220
Amiche, Le (Antonioni, 1955), 199
Anderson, Bronco Billy, 93, 144
Andrews, Julie, 133
Angelina M. P. (Zampa, 1947), 68
Anger, Kenneth, 224–8
Animal Farm (Halas & Batchelor, 1954), 130
A Nous la Liberté (Clair, 1931), 56, 61
Anstey, Edgar, 44, 45
Antonioni, Michelangelo, 155, 177, 198–9, 200
Arbuckle, Roscoe, 107, 135
Artaud, Antonin, 187
Atalante, L' (Vigo, 1934), 56, 61
Auden, W. H., 46
Autry, Gene, 143, 144
Avventura, L' (Antonioni, 1960), 199

Baggott, King, 134
Bambi (Disney, 1942), 127, 129
Bande à part (Godard, 1964), 215, 218
Bandéra, La (Duvivier, 1935), 56
Bandit, The (Lattuada, 1946), 68
Bara, Theda, 135–6
Barbera, Joseph, 192
Bardot, Brigitte, 139
Baron Munchhausen (Zeman, 1959), 194
Bartosch, Bertold, 193
Bas-fonds, Les (Renoir, 1936), 58, 62
Bataille, Sylvia, 59
Batcheff, Pierre, 187
Batchelor, Joy, 130
Battleship Potemkin (Eisenstein, 1925), 40, 51, 175–6, 177, 203
Belle de jour (Buñuel, 1967), 190
Belle Equipe, La (Duvivier, 1936), 56
Bergman, Ingmar, 155, 161, 182–4
Bergman, Ingrid, 67, 139, 153
Bernhardt, Sarah, 98
Bête humaine, La (Renoir, 1938), 58, 59
Bezhin Meadow (Eisenstein, 1936), 178
Bicycle Thieves (De Sica, 1948), 67, 70
Bike Boy (Warhol, 1967), 224
Birds, The (Hitchcock, 1961), 156
Birth of a Nation, The (Griffith, 1915), 51, 100–101, 104, 118, 172

Bitzer, Billy, 99
Blackmail (Hitchcock, 1929), 156
Blackman, J. Stuart, 93
Blavette, 59
Blind Husbands (Stroheim, 1918), 51
Blinkety-Blank (McLaren, 1954), 193
Blow-Up (Antonioni, 1966), 199
Boat, The (Keaton, 1921), 111
Boetticher, Budd, 146, 147–8
Bogart, Humphrey, 123, 134, 140, 162
Borowczyk, Walerian, 194–5, 202
Boudu sauvé des eaux (Renoir, 1932), 58, 60
Boyd, William, 144
Brakage, Stan, 223
Brando, Marlon, 140, 227
Breathless (Godard, 1960), 217, 219
Bresson, Robert, 185, 199–200
Britten, Benjamin, 46
Broken Blossoms (Griffith, 1919), 103, 104
Brother Carl (Sontag, 1970), 210
Broughton, James, 224
Bunny, John, 93
Buñuel, Luis, 11, 186, 187–90, 202, 222
Burton, Richard, 138
By the Law (Kuleshov, 1926), 39

Cabinet of Dr Caligari, The (Wiene, 1919), 180–81, 182, 225
Cabiria (Pastrone, 1914), 100
Cagney, James, 123, 140
Canterbury Tales, The (Pasolini, 1972), 212
Carabiniers, Les (Godard, 1963), 219
Carné, Marcel, 56, 62, 196–7
Castellani, Renato, 68
Cathy Come Home (Loach, 1966), 79–81
Cavalcanti, Alberto, 44, 46
Cayrol, Jean, 206
Chabrol, Claude, 155, 162
Chair, The (Leacock, 1963), 73
Chaplin, Charles, 55, 93, 106, 108–11, 113, 114, 117, 127, 128, 134, 135, 173
Charlie Bubbles (Finney, 1968), 210

Cheyenne Autumn (Ford, 1964), 147
Chien andalou, Un (Buñuel, 1928), 11, 186, 187–8
Chienne, La (Renoir, 1931), 58
Chinoise, La (Godard, 1967), 220
Chotard et cie (Renoir, 1933), 58
Chronicle of Anna Magdalena Bach (Straub, 1967), 200–201
Chronicle of a Summer (Rouch, 1961), 75
Chumlum (Rice, 1964), 224
Cinderella (Disney, 1949), 129
Circus, The (Chaplin, 1928), 113
Citizen Kane (Welles, 1941), 181, 197–8
City Lights (Chaplin, 1931), 110
Claire, René, 56, 61, 173, 187
Coalface (Cavalcanti, 1935), 46
Cocteau, Jean, 186, 187, 222, 226
Cohl, Emile, 191, 192
Cohn, Harry, 117, 119, 120, 121
Colour Box (Lye, 1935), 192
Comanche Station (Boetticher, 1960), 148
Concerto for Sub-Machinegun (Vukotic, 1959), 194
Conjuring Away of a Lady at Robert Houdin Theatre, The (Méliès, 1896), 27
Connery, Sean, 133
Conquest of the Pole, The (Méliès, 1912), 27
Cooper, Gary, 139, 144, 146
Corman, Roger, 162
Coronation of Edward VII, The (Méliès, 1902), 26
Countess from Hong Kong, A (Chaplin, 1966), 110
Coward, Noel, 209
Crime de Monsieur Lange, Le (Renoir, 1935), 61, 62
Cukor, George, 123, 162
Culloden (Watkins, 1964), 77–8
Curtiz, Michael, 123

Dali, Salvador, 187, 188
Dame blanche, La (Stroheim project), 55
Dames du Bois de Boulogne, Les (Bresson, 1945), 200
Daniels, William, 137
Daves, Delmer, 149
David (Leacock, 1962), 73

Davies, Marion, 117
Davis, Bette, 123, 151
Dean, James, 140, 227
Decameron, The (Pasolini, 1971), 212
Delaney, Shelagh, 209–10
Delmont, Edouard, 59
De Mille, Cecil B., 89, 94, 123, 227
Deren, Maya, 224
De Santis, 67, 68
De Sica, Vittorio, 19, 67, 68, 70
Destroy She Says (Duras, 1969), 210–11
Deux ou trois choses que je sais d'elle (Godard, 1967), 217
Devil's Pass Key, The (Stroheim, 1919), 57
Diary of a Country Priest (Bresson, 1951), 200
Dickson, William, 91
Dietrich, Marlene, 123, 137, 139
Disney, Walt, 125–31, 191, 192, 193, 195
Dom (Borowczyk and Lenica, 1958), 195
Don't Look Back (Pennebaker, 1966), 74
Dovzhenko, Alexander, 34, 39
Drew, Robert, 71, 72, 73
Dreyer, Carl, 173, 185, 219
Dreyfus Affair, The (Méliès, 1899), 26
Drifters (Grierson, 1929), 44
Drôle de drame (Carné, 1937), 57
Drunkard's Reformation, The (Griffith, 1909), 99
Duchamp, Marcel, 187
Duet for Cannibals (Sontag, 1969), 210–11
Dulac, Germaine, 187
Dumbo (Disney, 1941), 129, 131
Dunn, Nell, 79
Duras, Marguerite, 205, 210–11
Duvivier, Julien, 56
Dwan, Allan, 162

Earth (Dovzhenko, 1930), 40
Eaux d'artifice (Anger, 1953), 225, 226
Eclipse, The (Antonioni, 1962), 177, 199
Eddie Sachs at Minneapolis (Leacock, 1961), 73

Eden et après, L' (Robbe-Brillet, 1970), 211
Edison, Thomas, 18, 90–96, 97, 115, 128, 134, 191
Eisenstein, Sergei, 9, 12, 34, 39, 40, 43, 51, 157, 174–8, 182, 185, 199, 203
Elephant Boy (Korda & Flaherty, 1937), 35
Eleventh (Vertov, 1928), 42
Elton, Arthur, 44, 45
Empire (Warhol, 1964), 224
Engel, Morris, 72
Enoch Arden (Griffith, 1911), 99
Enough to Eat (Anstey, 1936), 45
Enthusiasm (Vertov, 1930), 40, 42
Entr'acte (Clair, 1924), 187
Ersatz (Vukotic, 1961), 194
Exploits of Elaine, The (Gasnier, 1915), 186
Exterminating Angel, The (Buñuel, 1962), 189, 202

Face, The (Bergman, 1958), 183–4
Fairbanks, Douglas, 117, 140
Family Life (Loach, 1971), 80
Fantasia (Disney, 1941), 129
Fantoche (Cohl, 1908), 191
Faulkner, William, 122, 209
Fellini, Federico, 151
Femme douce, Une (Bresson, 1969), 200
Femme est une femme, Une (Godard, 1961), 162, 218
Femme mariée, Une (Godard, 1964), 219
Feyder, Jacques, 56
Filmstudie (Richter, 1926), 186
Fires Were Started (Jennings, 1943), 46
Fireworks (Anger, 1947), 225–6
First Days, The (Jennings, 1939), 46
Fitzgerald, F. Scott, 122
Flaherty, Robert, 18, 30–37, 38, 41, 43, 44, 45, 46, 47, 48, 71, 136
Flaming Creatures (Smith, 1963), 224
Fleisher, Max, 191
Fleming, Victor, 123
Flesh (Morrissey, 1968), 224
Flynn, Errol, 123, 140
Fonda, Henry, 139, 144, 145, **147**
Fonda, Jane, **73**

Fontaine, Joan, 158
Foolish Wives (Stroheim, 1920), 52
Ford, John, 36, 123, 143, 146, 147, 152
Foreman, Carl, 146
Fort Apache (Ford, 1948), 147
Fox, William, 94, 116, 117, 118, 134, 135
Franju, Georges, 48
Frenzy (Hitchcock, 1972), 154
Fresnay, Pierre, 60
Fuller, Sam, 162

Gabin, Jean, 56, 58, 59, 196
Gable, Clark, 122, 123–4, 139
Gai savoir, Le (Godard, 1968), 220
Gance, Abel, 173
Garbo, Greta, 122, 134, 137, 139
Garden of Allah, The (Boleslawsky, 1936), 160
Garland, Judy, 136
Garnett, Tony, 79, 81
Gaumont, Léon, 93
General, The (Keaton, 1926), 111–12, 113
General Line, The (Eisenstein, 1929), 176
Genuine (Wiene, 1920), 181
Germania anno zero (Rossellini, 1947), 67
Germi, Pietro, 69
Gertie the Dinosaur (McCay, 1909), 191
Gish, Lillian, 98, 102, 103, 138, 139
Go-Between, The (Losey, 1971), 210
Godard, Jean-Luc, 43, 161, 215–21, 222
Golden Coach, The (Renoir, 1952), 58
Gold Rush, The (Chaplin, 1925), 110, 113
Goldwyn, Sam, 52, 117, 118, 119, 120, 121, 159
Gone with the Wind (Cukor, Fleming & Wood, 1939), 120, 123–4, 223
Gospel According to Saint Matthew, The (Pasolini, 1964), 212, 213
Go West (Keaton, 1925), 111
Gowland, Gibson, 54

Grande Illusion, La (Renoir, 1937), 55, 58, 60, 61, 62
Grant, Cary, 139, 153, 158
Grapes of Wrath, The (Ford, 1940), 36, 123
Great Dictator, The (Chaplin, 1940), 110
Great Train Robbery, The (Porter, 1904), 96, 142
Greed (Stroheim, 1923), 51–5
Greene, Graham, 160–61
Grierson, John, 19, 34, 35, 36, 44, 45
Griffith, D. W., 18, 50, 51, 93, 95, 96, 97–104, 106, 108, 115, 117, 139, 171–2, 173, 174, 196, 202, 216
Grimault, Paul, 130
Gross, Anthony, 193
Guernica (Resnais, 1950), 204
Guerre est finie, La (Resnais, 1966), 207

Halas, John, 130
Hand, The (Trnka, 1964), 194
Hanna, William, 192
Hart, William S., 144
Hat, The (Hubley, 1964), 192
Hawkins, Jack, 209
Hawks, Howard, 149, 152, 161
Hearts of the World (Griffith, 1917), 15, 102
Henabery, Joseph, 101
Hepburn, Audrey, 139
Hepburn, Katherine, 139
High Noon (Zinnemann, 195), 146
Hiroshima Mon Amour (Resnais, 1959), 205, 210
His Trust (Griffith, 1911), 99
His Trust Fulfilled (Griffith, 1911), 99
Hitchcock, Alfred, 85, 141, 153–8, 161, 162, 182, 217
Hole, The (Hubley, 1962), 192
Homme qui ment, L' (Robbe-Grillet, 1968), 211
Hoppin, Hector, 193
Hôtel des Invalides (Franju, 1951), 48
Hôtel du Nord (Carné, 1938), 57
Housing in New Zealand (Furlong, 1948), 30
Housing Problems (Anstey & Elton, 1935), 46

Hubley, John, 192
Hughes, Howard, 117

I Confess (Hitchcock, 1952), 156
Idée, L² (Bartosch, 1934), 193
Immortelle, L' (Robbe-Grillet, 1963), 211
Inauguration of the Pleasure Dome (Anger, 1954), 225, 226
Industrial Britain (Flaherty, 1933), 34, 45
Intolerance (Griffith, 1916), 51, 101–2, 202
In Two Minds (Loach, 1966), 79
Invention of Destruction, The (Zeman, 1956), 194
Invocation of my Demon Brother (Anger, 1969), 226
Italian Straw Hat, An (Clair, 1927), 173
Ivan the Terrible (Eisenstein, 1945–6), 178
Iwerks, Ub, 127, 128

Jagger, Mick, 226
Jane (Leacock, 1963), 73
Janowitz, Hans, 180
Jazz Singer, The (Crosland, 1927), 117, 173
Jennings, Humphrey, 46–8
Jenny (Carné, 1936), 56
Je t'aime, je t'aime (Resnais, 1968), 207–8
Jeux des Anges (Borowczyk, 1964), 195
Joie de vivre (Hoppin & Gross, 1934), 193
Jour se lève, Le (Carné, 1939), 57, 196–7
Judith of Bethulia (Griffith, 1913), 100, 171
Jungle Book, The (Disney, 1967), 129

Karina, Anna, 218
Kaufman, Mikhail, 42
Keaton, Buster, 50, 108, 109, 110–13, 114, 115, 128, 150, 173
Kelly, Grace, 153
Kermesse héroique, La (Feyder, 1936), 56
Kes (Loach, 1970), 80
Kid, The (Chaplin, 1920), 113

King in New York, A (Chaplin, 1957), 110
King of Kings (De Mille, 1927), 227
Kino-Pravda (Vertov, 1922), 40, 43, 71
Kiss Me Deadly (Aldrich, 1955), 182
Kleine, George, 93
Kleptomaniac, The (Porter, 1905), 99
Korda, Alexander, 35
Krauss, Werner, 181
Kubrick, Stanley, 202
Kuleshov, Lev, 39
Kurosawa, Akira, 19, 64, 143
Kustom Kar Kommandos (Anger, 1965), 226

Labyrinth (Lenica, 1962), 194
Ladd, Alan, 144
Lady from Shanghai (Welles, 1947), 181
Lady Vanishes, The (Hitchcock, 1938), 153, 154
Laemmle, Carl, 94, 115–16, 118, 134, 135
Land, The (Flaherty, 1942), 36
Land of the Pharaohs (Hawks, 1955), 209
Land without Bread (Buñuel, 1932), 189
Lang, Fritz, 218
Langdon, Harry, 106, 108, 113
Last Laugh, The (Murnau, 1924), 173
Last Year at Marienbad (Resnais, 1961), 205–6, 207, 208, 211
Lattuada, Alberto, 68
Lawrence, Florence, 134
Leacock, Richard, 71–5, 77
Léger, Fernand, 187
Leigh, Vivien, 124
Leni, Paul, 181
Lenica, Jan, 194
Life of an American Fireman, The (Porter, 1903), 96
Linder, Max, 105, 135
Listen to Britain (Jennings, 1941), 46, 47
Little Annie Rooney (Beaudine, 1925), 135
Lloyd, Harold, 106, 108, 113
Loach, Kenneth, 77, 79–81

Lonedale Operator, The (Griffith, 1911), 99
Lonely Villa, The (Griffith, 1909), 99
Lonesome Cowboys (Warhol, 1968), 224
Long, Samuel, 93
Long Pants (Lloyd & Capra, 1927), 113
Lorenz, Pare, 36
Losey, Joseph, 210
Louisiana Story (Flaherty, 1948), 36, 71
Love in the City (Zavattini, 1953), 70
Lubin, Sigmund, 93
Lubitsch, Ernst, 123
Lucifer Rising (Anger, 1966), 226, 227
Lumière, Auguste, 22, 23
Lumière, Louis, 18, 22–9, 76, 86, 92, 93, 173, 191, 219, 223
Lye, Len, 192

Madame Bovary (Renoir, 1934), 58, 60
Made in USA (Godard, 1967), 219
Maeterlinck, Maurice, 120
Maggiorani, Lamberto, 70
Magnani, Anna, 68
Magnificent Seven, The (Sturges, 1960), 143
Mamma Roma (Pasolini, 1962), 212
Man Escaped, A (Bresson, 1956), 200
Mann, Anthony, 148
Man of Aran (Flaherty, 1934), 35, 45
Man Who Knew Too Much, The (Hitchcock, 1934), 153
Man with the Heads, The (Méliès, 1898), 27
Man with the India-Rubber Head, The (Méliès, 1902), 27
Man with the Movie Camera, The (Vertov, 1929), 42, 43
Marey, Etienne, 18, 91
Marion, Frank, 93
Markopoulos, Gregory, 223
Marseillaise, La (Renoir, 1938), 58, 60, 61
Marsh, Mae, 98, 103
Martin, Karl Heinz, 181
Marvin, Arthur, 99

Mayer, Carl, 180
Mayer, Louis B., 52, 117, 118, 119, 120, 121, 122, 123, 137
Maysles, Albert and David, 72, 73
McCay, Winsor, 191
McLaren, Norman, 193, 195
Medea (Pasolini, 1969), 212–13
Méliès, Georges, 22, 25–9, 85, 93, 96, 115, 191, 223
Melomaniac, The (Méliès, 1903), 27
Mépris, Le (Godard, 1963), 218
Mercer, David, 79
Merry-Go-Round (Stroheim, 1922), 52
Merry Widow, The (Stroheim, 1925,) 54, 55
Midsummer Night's Dream, A (Reinhardt, 1934), 225
Midsummer Night's Dream, A (Trnka, 1959), 194
Million, Le (Clair, 1931), 56
Mix, Tom, 140, 144
Moana (Flaherty, 1926), 34
Modern Times (Chaplin, 1936), 109, 110, 114
Moi un Noir (Rouch, 1958), 75
Monroe, Marilyn, 134, 138, 139
Monsieur Tête (Lenica, 1960), 194
Montand, Yves, 220
Monterey Pop (Pennebaker, 1968), 74
Morin, Edgar, 75
Morrissey, Paul, 224
Mother (Pudovkin, 1926), 40
Mozhukhin, Ivan, 39
Mr West in the Land of the Bolsheviks (Kuleshov, 1924), 39
Mr Wonderbird (Grimault, 1952), 130
Muriel (Resnais, 1963), 206–7
Murnau, Friedrich, 34, 173, 181
Muybridge, Eadweard, 18, 91
My Darling Clementine (Ford, 1946), 147
Mystère du Château de Dés, Le (Ray, 1929), 186

Nana (Renoir, 1926), 58
Nanook of the North (Flaherty, 1922), 33, 34, 36, 37, 38, 136
Napoleon (Gance, 1927), 173
Navigator, The (Keaton, 1924), 111, 113

Nazarin (Buñuel, 1958), 189
Nazimova, Alla, 139
Negri, Pola, 139
Nehru (Leacock, 1962), 73, 74
Night Mail (Wright & Watt, 1936), 46
Night on the Bare Mountain (Alexeieff, 1933), 193
Normand, Mabel, 107
North by Northwest (Hitchcock, 1959), 154
Nosferatu (Murnau, 1922), 181
Nuit et brouillard (Resnais, 1955), 204–5, 206, 219

October (Eisenstein, 1927), 176–7, 199
Oedipus Rex (Pasolini, 1967), 212–13
Olivier, Laurence, 136
Olvidados, Los (Buñuel, 1950), 189,
One Man Orchestra, The (Méliès, 1900), 27
One Plus One (Godard, 1968), 217, 218, 220
On purge bébé (Renoir, 1931), 58, 62
Orphans of the Storm (Griffith, 1922), 103
Orthon (Straub, 1969), 201
Osborne, John, 209
Ossessione (Visconti, 1942), 57
Ozu, Yashiro, 19, 64

Paisa (Rossellini, 1946), 66–7
Palance, Jack, 144
Parker, Claire, 193
Parrain, Brice, 218
Partie de campagne, Une (Renoir, 1936), 58, 59, 62
Pasolini, Pier Paolo, 9, 211, 212–14
Passion of Joan of Arc, The (Dreyer, 1928), 173, 219
Pathé, Charles, 93, 105
Paul, Robert W., 92
Peckinpah, Sam, 143, 148, 203
Pennebaker, Don, 72, 73
Pépé le Moko (Duvivier, 1936), 56
Persona (Bergman, 1966), 184
Petit Soldat, Le (Godard, 1960), 218
Petrified Forest, The (Mayo, 1936), 160

Pickford, Mary, 98, 103, 117, 134–5, 138
Pierrot le Fou (Godard, 1965), 218
Pinter, Harold, 210
Pintoff, Ernst, 192
Pippa Passes (Griffith, 1909), 99
Pitts, Zasu, 54
Plow that Broke the Plains, The (Lorenz, 1936), 36
Polanski, Roman, 190
Popeye (Fleisher, 1933), 192
Porter, Edwin S., 95–6, 97, 98, 99, 142
Port of Call (Bergman, 1948), 182
Precise Measurements for Engineers (Chambers, 1947), 30
Preminger, Otto, 162
Prévert, Jacques, 61, 62, 130, 196
Primary (Leacock, 1960), 73
Prokofiev, Sergei, 178
Psycho (Hitchcock, 1960), 155, 157, 158, 182
Puce Moment (Anger, 1948), 226
Pudovkin, Vsevolod, 34, 39
Punishment Park (Watkins, 1970), 78–9
Punition, La (Rouch, 1962), 75
Pyramide Humaine, La (Rouch, 1960), 75

Quai des brumes (Carné, 1938), 57
Queen Kelly (Stroheim, 1928), 54, 55
Que viva Mexico (Eisenstein project), 178
Quo vadis (Guazzoni, 1912), 100

Rabbit's Moon (Anger, 1950), 225, 226, 227
Ramona (Griffith, 1910), 99
Rank and File, The (Loach, 1971), 80
Raskolnikov (Wiene, 1923), 181
Rattigan, Terence, 209
Ray, Man, 186
Ray, Satyajit, 19, 64
Rear Window (Hitchcock, 1954), 158
Red Desert, The (Antonioni, 1964), 199
Reed, Carol, 160, 182
Règle du jeu, La (Renoir, 1939), 58, 59, 61, 62
Reinhardt, Max, 225

Reiniger, Lotte, 193
Renaissance (Borowczyk, 1964),
195, 202
Renoir, Jean, 19, 56–63
Renoir, Pierre, 59
Rescued from an Eagle's Nest
(Porter, 1907), 97
Resnais, Alain, 190, 204–8, 211,
219
Reynaud, Emile, 191, 192
Rhinoceros (Lenica, 1963), 194
Rice, Ron, 223, 224
Richter, Hans, 186
Ride Lonesome (Boetticher, 1959),
146, 148
Ride the High Country (Peckinpah,
1961), 148
Rio Grande (Ford, 1950), 147
Rite, The (Bergman, 1969), 182
River, The (Lorenz, 1937), 36
Robbe-Grillet, Alain, 9, 205, 208,
211–12, 213–14, 215
Rohmer, Eric, 155
Robinson, Edward G., 140
Robinson Crusoe (Buñuel, 1952),
189
Rogers, Roy, 143, 144
Rome Eleven O'Clock (De Santis,
1952), 68
Rome Open City (Rossellini, 1945),
64–6, 68, 69
Rooney, Mickey, 123, 136, 225
Rossellini, Roberto, 12, 19, 64–9,
213
Rotha, Paul, 9, 19, 36, 44, 45
Rouch, Jean, 74–5, 77

Saboteur (Hitchcock, 1942), 154
Safety Last (Lloyd, 1923), 113
Saint Joan (Preminger, 1957), 162
Sandford, Jeremy, 79
Sang des bêtes, Le (Franju, 1949),
48
Sang d'un poète, Le (Cocteau,
1930), 186
Sawdust and Tinsel (Bergman,
1953), 182
Scarlett Empress (Sternberg, 1934),
123
Schenk, Joseph, 117
Scorpio Rising (Anger, 1964), 225,
226, 227
Scott, Anthony, 223
Scott, Randolph, 144, 145, 148

Searchers, The (Ford, 1956), 147
Seberg, Jean, 162
Selznick, David O., 120, 123–4
Selznick, Lewis J., 116, 118, 120
Sennett, Mack, 105–8, 109, 110,
113, 173
Semprun, Jorge, 207
Servant, The (Losey, 1963), 210
Seven Chances (Keaton, 1925), 111
Seven Samurai (Kurosawa, 1954),
143
Shadow of a Doubt (Hitchcock,
1943), 156, 157
Shane (Stevens, 1953), 144, 146
Sherlock Junior (Keaton, 1924),
112–13
She Wore a Yellow Ribbon (Ford,
1949), 147
Shuker, Greg, 73
Sillitoe, Alan, 209
Simon, Michel, 59, 61
Sirk, Douglas, 152
Sixth of the World, A (Vertov,
1926), 42
Sleep (Warhol, 1963), 224
Smith, Albert E., 93
Smith, Jack, 224
Snow, Mike, 224
Snow White and the Seven Dwarfs
(Disney, 1937), 129, 131
Song of Ceylon (Wright, 1934), 45
Song of the Prairie (Trnka, 1949),
193
Sontag, Susan, 210–11
Sound of Music, The (Wise, 1964),
133, 223
Sous les toits de Paris (Clair,
1929), 56
Spaak, Charles, 62
Squaw Man, The (De Mille, 1913),
116
Stagecoach (Ford, 1939), 143, 147
Stage Fright (Hitchcock, 1950),
154
Steamboat Bill Jr (Keaton, 1928),
111, 113
Sterling, Ford, 107
Sternberg, Jacques, 207
Sternberg, Joseph von, 12, 123,
137, 138
Stevens, George, 144
Stewart, James, 147, 153, 158
Stiller, Mauritz, 137, 138
Storey, David, 209

Strangers on a Train (Hitchcock, 1951), 156

Straub, Jean-Marie, 200–201

Stride Soviet (Vertov, 1926), 42

Strike (Eisenstein, 1925), 174–5

Stroheim, Erich von, 18, 50–55, 56, 57, 60, 152, 173

Sunrise (Murnau, 1927), 173

Sunset Boulevard (Wilder, 1950), 55

Suspicion (Hitchcock, 1941), 156, 158

Sympathy for the Devil (Godard, 1968), 217

Tabu (Flaherty & Murnau, 1929), 34

Tall T, The (Boetticher, 1957), 148

Taylor, Elizabeth, 132, 138

Temple, Shirley, 123, 135, 136

Terra trema, La (Visconti, 1948), 67, 136

Thalberg, Irving, 52, 116, 120

Third Man, The (Reed, 1949), 160, 182

Thirty-Nine Steps, The (Hitchcock, 1935), 153, 154

Thomson, Virgil, 36

Three Songs of Lenin (Vertov, 1934), 40

Tillie's Punctured Romance (Sennett, 1914), 108

Toby (Leacock, 1955), 71

Toni (Renoir, 1934), 57–8, 59, 61

Touch of Evil (Welles, 1958), 181

Tout va bien (Godard, 1972), 220

Tracy, Spencer, 139

Trade Tattoo (Lye, 1937), 192–3

Traffic in Souls (Tucker, 1913), 116

Tragic Pursuit (De Santis, 1947), 68

Trans-Europe-Express (Robbe-Grillet, 1967), 211–12

Trip to the Moon, A (Méliès, 1902), 27

Tristana (Buñuel, 1970), 189

Trnka, Jiri, 193–4

Truffaut, François, 162

Turksib (Turin, 1929), 40

Turner, Florence, 93

Turpin, Ben, 107

Two Pennyworth of Hope (Castellani, 1951), 68

2001 (Kubrick, 1968), 202

Umberto D (De Sica, 1951), 68, 69

Under Capricorn (Hitchcock, 1949), 154, 158

Unicorn in the Garden (Hurtz, 1953), 192

Up the Junction (Loach, 1965), 79

Valentino, Rudolf, 134, 139

Vampires, Les (Feuillade, 1915–16), 186

Veidt, Conrad, 181

Vertigo (Hitchcock, 1958), 156, 158

Vertov, Dziga, 9, 18, 38–43, 71, 220

Vie est à nous, La (Renoir, 1936), 60, 61

Vigo, Jean, 56, 61, 187

Viridiana (Buñuel, 1961), 190

Vivre sa vie (Godard, 1962), 218, 219

Visconti, Luchino, 19, 57, 67, 68, 136, 151, 161

Vlady, Marina, 217

Von Morgens bis Mitternachts (Martin, 1920), 181

Voyage across the Impossible, The (Méliès, 1904), 27

Vukotic, Dusan, 194

Walking Down Broadway (Stroheim, 1932), 55

War Game, The (Watkins, 1965), 77

Warhol, Andy, 224

Warner, Jack, 117, 120, 121, 122

Watkins, Peter, 77–9

Watt, Harry, 44

Wavelength (Snow, 1967), 224

Waxworks (Leni, 1924), 181

Way Down East (Griffith, 1920), 103

Wayne, John, 132, 140, 144, 145, 147, 151, 216

Wedding March, The (Stroheim, 1927), 54

Weekend (Godard, 1967), 220

Welles, Orson, 19, 55, 152, 161, 181–2, 197–8

Wiene, Robert, 180–81

Wild Bunch, The (Peckinpah, 1969), 143, 148, 203

Wild One, The (Benedek, 1954), 227

Wild Strawberries (Bergman, 1957), 182

Wilder, Billy, 55

Woman to Woman (Cutts, 1923), 153

Wood, Sam, 123

Workers and Jobs (Elton, 1935), 46

Wright, Basil, 44, 45

Wrong Man, The (Hitchcock, 1957), 156

Wuthering Heights (Buñuel, 1953), 189

Wyler, William, 19

Zabriskie Point (Antonioni, 1969), 199

Zampa, Luigi, 68

Zanuck, Darryl F., 117, 120

Zanuck, Richard, 121

Zavattini, Cesare, 9, 19, 70

Zeman, Karel, 194

Zéro de Conduite (Vigo, 1933), 56, 61

Zinnemann, Fred, 146

Zukor, Adolph, 116, 118, 135

More about Penguins
and Pelicans

Penguinews, which appears every month, contains details of
all the new books issued by Penguins as they are published.
From time to time it is supplemented by *Penguins in Print*,
which is a complete list of all titles available. (There
are some five thousand of these.)

A specimen copy of *Penguinews* will be sent to you free
on request. For a year's issues (including the complete
lists) please send 50p if you live in the British Isles,
or 75p if you live elsewhere. Just write to Dept EP,
Penguin Books Ltd, Harmondsworth, Middlesex, enclosing a
cheque or postal order, and your name will be added to the
mailing list.

In the U.S.A.: For a complete list of books available from
Penguin in the United States write to Dept CS, Penguin Books
Inc., 7110 Ambassador Road, Baltimore, Maryland 21207.

In Canada: For a complete list of books available from
Penguin in Canada write to Penguin Books Canada Ltd,
41 Steelcase Road West, Markham, Ontario

Sex Psyche Etcetera in the Film

Parker Tyler

The film is still the Cinderella of the arts. Beside her 'the other arts take on the look of ugly stepsisters whose affability and condescension tend to caricature them' writes Tyler in this study of sex in the cinema. Yet the bane of Hollywood over fifty years, as he shows, has been the belief that the film's ideal function is the reporting of boundless 'facts' and spectacles. Too often the sex goddess of the silver screen rises more from foam-rubber than a sea of flesh. The success or failure of the great American epic depends entirely on whether it strikes popular sympathies in the right area.

Many are the directors and stars with a flair for experiment and plagiarism. Far above these stand the diverse geniuses of Chaplin, Eisenstein and Warhol, whose films Tyler regards as works of art in themselves. This book is a distinguished critic's evaluation of the film – past, present, and to come.

'Parker Tyler sees, hears and feels more than any of us' – Richard McLaughlin in the *New York Post*